EDUCATION OF HANDICAPPED CHILDREN

Education of Handicapped Children

Problems and Solutions

JANARDAN PRASAD
RAVI PRAKASH

KANISHKA PUBLISHERS, DISTRIBUTORS
New Delhi 110 002

KANISHKA PUBLISHERS, DISTRIBUTORS
4697/5-21A, Ansari Road, Daryaganj
New Delhi -110 002
Phones : 2327 0497, 2328 8285
Fax : 011-2328 8285
E-mail : kanishka_publishing@yahoo.co.in

Education of Handicapped Children:
Problems and Solutions

First Published-1996

Edition-2017

PRINTED IN INDIA

Published by Madan Sachdeva for Kanishka Publishers, Distributors, 4697/5-21A, Ansari Road, Daryaganj, New Delhi-110 002, Typeset by Sunshine Graphics, Delhi, and Printed at Rajdhani Printers, Delhi.

Preface

The utilitarians believed in the greatest good of the greatest number. But Gandhiji believed in the good of all; the Sarvodaya. Education is considered to be of immense help to not only to the socially disadvantaged children but to the handicapped children both physically and mentally.

Various methods and techniques have been evolved over the years in the developed countries of the West for providing suitable education to handicapped children. This education is in the form of skill development among the handicapped.

In view of the special needs of handicapped children, more sophisticated methods of imparting education are needed. This book discusses some of these methods of teaching, the need for special education for handicapped children, and the relevance of these techniques and methods in Indian situations.

The editors gratefully acknowledge the help taken from American sources in preparing this book which will prove of immense help to teachers of handicapped children and the social welfare agencies.

AUTHORS

Contents

1

Development and Education of Handicapped Children

LEARNING, as we have seen, is not confined to periods of formal training; it is implicit in every aspect of development. In the course of maturation new skills become attainable because of increasing size, stength and control over responses. The motor control of a child who can walk is much more highly integrated than that of a baby who can barely sit. Physical maturation by itself, however, is of little use if the potentially developing skills are not applied to a purpose. Without a purpose they remain rudimentary. The purpose needs to be the child's; it must lead him to a desired goal of his choice. Adults can play their part in making some goals attractive, but only goals within the child's range of experience have meaning. The significant experience of handicapped children may well be that which takes place in the presence of their parents or teachers. Nevertheless, there are long periods of the day when there is neither help nor supervision, and, if possible, these should also be times when the child can experiment and apply his skills at his own behest. He must be given the right conditions to do so.

Gathering experience involves the same stages of input, processing, output and feedback, as we have seen operate during formal learning. The same obstacles exist; learning and gathering experience are part of the same continuum. To gather experience means to gain information from the environment by observation, manipulation, experimentation. Past experience is a decisive factor, and information and meaning are closely bound up with each other. The available information changes and increases as skills develop, because more can be used by the child. The environment becomes enriched because the capacity of the child is extended. For normally developing children, progress perpetuates itself. The various obstacles to the development of skills of handicapped children delay such progress, so that the effective expansion of the environment is slowed down. The situation is parallel to the reduction of social demands on handicapped children discussed in the chapter on secondary handicaps.

It is therefore necessary to set up special conditions for these children for periods when they have matured beyond their existing skills, when their level of output is inadequate for their goals. Spastic infants are often ready to play with toys well before they have sufficient motor control to pick up things or hold them; a blind baby who gets pleasure from a rattle may not be able to retrieve it once it has fallen from his hand. If the positions of the toys are stabilized by hanging them from a rod attached over the cot, they will be kept to a constant region, and as a result the infant can learn to seek them within this region (and at the same time, he will extent his memory for direction in space).

Skills develop rapidly once walking is established, and even more rapidly when children go to school; the effects of the handicaps become correspondingly more specific. Data analysis, work analysis and problem analysis become increasingly useful for identifying needs which must be met in order to provide satisfactory conditions for learning, because the situations become more precise and less generalized. The overall consideration is that conditions should be planned so that the information needed by the child is readily available to him: that situations as well as problems are familiar and that they have been made familiar from classroom experience. The same-applies to skills. Until skills are fully established, they are of no use for general application. As long as a child still needs help when trying out or applying a skill, he is dependent on assistatnce, and cannot extend the application of the skill to new situations on his own. Partly established skills can therefore be disregarded when setting conditions for independent action.

The goals themselves must exist, or the provision of conditions can have no effect. A mentally handicapped infant who makes no attempts to seek toys is not stimulated to greater activity by surrounding him with even the most desirable toys. Inert infants need conditions which lead to active movements and responses. In many cases aims for the initial responses are sensory and perceptual rather than motor. The corresponding conditions are the use of different surfaces to lie on, changes in the direction in which the child's cot is facing and variation in the sound patterns around him. One simple device is to put different kinds of toys into different rooms; for instance, to keep soft toys in the bedroom, other toys in the living room and to let the child play with pots and pans in the kitchen. A simple arrangement of this kind can help a child to differentiate between the use of different rooms, and it enhances his observations and organization of space. Further examples of how the environment can be arranged to encoruage the child's experimentation and general development will be described in the rest of this chapter.

Conditions for developing motor and perceptual skills in mentally handicapped infants

Skills are made up of perceptual as well as motor components—input as well as output. For inert children the special conditions needed should ensure that movement and a change in position are accompanied by a change in sensation, and that these changes are repetitive and consistent. For instance, the surface on which the infant is lying can be covered with four different textures, like wool, plastic, cotton and carpeting, to give tactile experiences of different kinds.

Further clues can be added to reinforce the tactile discrimination: each area can be given its own characteristic smell by using scents applied to the surface. Each scent is first tried out by letting the child smell it and seeing if he reacts—either by approaching his nose to it or turning away. Only smells which cause him to turn his head one way or the other are used.

To give meaning to the different areas, each also has one or two toys attached to the surface: moving toys, sounding toys, soft toys and perhaps the sort which can be squeezed to give out a puff of air. The location of the toy is defined by the surface texture; its position on the surface can be indicated by a trail of scent leading to it. The biggest problem is to encourage movement; this can be overcome by having an uneven contour for the surfaces, making it uncomfortable to remain too long in any one position. The variables must be kept to simple proportions. If there are too many, they lose their purpose and the child is merely distracted—he can only acquire a limited amount of information with his limited capacity to do so. The sign of success is that an inert infant begins to make deliberate movements in this environment.

Arrangements of this kind are useful for mentally handicapped infants, as well as for the blind and the physically handicapped. They are for initial stages, when the aim is to elicit some deliberate, directed responses. Clearly they do not apply when infants are already moving around, exploring for themselves.

Conditions to promote exploration and independent action in infants who can crawl

Once infants have started to crawl and move around, the next phase of systematic exploration can be prepared by learning to follow set pathways. Mothers usually go quickly to their infants and young children when they cry or call for attention. At the appropriate stage of development this is inevitable because the infant cannot come to her. Older and more mobile infants run to their mother rather than waiting for her to come. If there are obstacles to movement due to a physical handicap, blindness or some forms of mental handicap, the mother will continue to go to her infant until he is much older because there are too many risks and problems attached to his attempts to make the journey. Unless conditions can be changed so that the infant can go to her safely, he cannot take the next step towards independence.

One device which may help is a special pathway (the Baby Safeway) made up of wooden barriers like a fence, which can be set up and taken down easily within the normal home. By this means it is possible to set up an extensive, safe area for play together with a passage leading from it to the kitchen. When the infant wants attention, his mother can therefore call him to come to her without fearing any risks. The infant is encouraged to act independently, and the significance of moving around in space is reinforced by reaching his mother as and when he chooses.

Such a pathway can be used extensively to enhance experience and extend the child's independence. The passage can be built to consist of a central area for play, like a play-pen, with a passage or compartments leading off to special areas provided with characteristic toys. The model is based on the same notion as the mattress with its different textures and toys, and serves the same purpose at a more advanced level of development. Toys are arranged according to their properties: movement (cars), sound (balls which rattle, etc.) dolls and so on, and these are grouped separately along their own section of the safeway. The passage therefore becomes a varied and interesting pathway, offering differentiated stimuli for play. The spatial differentiation also created by the different kinds of toys gives meaning to the succession of compartments and leads on to spatial learning. The relationship between lack of spatial orientation and later problems of concept formation is well established; appropriate early experience should therefore be provided.

There are other situations in which the safeway is useful. In a nursery or creche, infants are liable to be insecure and correspondingly demanding when left in large rooms with extensive floor space. A honeycomb network made up of a larger play area connected to other, smaller sections leading from it enables infants to establish their home base, from which to explore, and also creates more order for the care staff. This arrangement is as useful for normal infants in a creche as for handicapped children in nursery school.

Conditions for blind children

Blind children experience obstacles to input and feedback, and they depend on sound for information about events at a distance. Not all sounds are equally helpful. Only sound patterns which have acquired meaning and significance for the child can help him to orientate. Others serve as a background or as alerting signals. They indicate that conditions are generally static (a constant level of background noise) or that some change has taken place (an alteration in level or pattern of background noise) and that this change may require attention. The more auditory clues the child can identify, the better his orientation, and the more rapid his ability to deal with alerting signals by guessing at their meaning.

It was pointed out that sound patterns can be used to identify where people are, and this can be emphasized by using shoes which make a characteristic noise when walking: squeaking shoes, leather soles, rubber soles and metal tips all create their different patterns of sound. If the key persons make characteristic sounds as they walk, blind children can orientate to their movements. It is equally helpful for members of staff to sing or whistle as they move around (a certain amount of taste and tact helps to keep this to the right proportions). Such signals are especially helpful when people enter or leave a room. To enter or leave silently may be laudable for the normal classroom, but only creates uncertainty for blind children.

The sounds made by toys should be carefully considered when selecting toys for blind children. It is much more interesting for them to send a car across a room if they can hear its progress along the floor, than to have one which moves smoothly and softly.

In addition to clues provided by sound patterns, there are clues such as air currents near doors and windows, smells in different rooms, changes in temperature—for instance indoors and out, or when doors or windows are open—and all the tactile clues which can provide information about surface texture and contours of the floor, furniture, etc. Last, but as important as other clues, are those which tell a child what will happen next so that he can anticipate that there will be some change in his environment or prepare himself for a coming event. Systematic habits and arrangements are helpful and important, because once the system has been learned, the child is free to experiment within it; he can plan his own activities with assurance.

The physical layout should be constant so that tables and other furniture are kept in the same places. Additional clues can be provided by standing tables and chairs on a circumscribed floor cover (carpet or mat) with different binding for the long and short sides. The edges should be at a sufficient distance from chairs and tables to give proper warning that they are being approached. Similar clues can be given about the positions of wall cupboards, for instance by putting a strip of matting or carpeting in front of them. The child can be helped to orientate quickly to his surroundings if information is made available in this way.

For particular exercises and games inverted cones of the kind used for road works are useful to identify pathways to follow. Such indications can also be created by ropes, which can be stretched between chairs or tables to outline a pathway. If it is possible to have ceiling fittings in the classroom, ropes can be suspended and used for different purposes. Great variety of spatial subdivision can be created: the ropes can be hung at different heights from the floor, and by fastening sheets or blankets to them, compartments and labyrinths can be arranged to enhance directional clues for blind children. The advantage of such hanging barriers is that they can be put at the right height for a particular group of children, to allow them to walk erect, soft enough for safety when running, and therefore suitable for many exercises and dances. By using nets or a transparent mesh the teacher can observe the children more easily without losing the spatial clues for the children.

Conditions for deaf children

The learning and development of deaf children also meet obstacles to input and feedback, but these call for special conditions other than those needed by blind children. The major problems of deaf children are that communication is difficult and that they lack information about events outside their immediate field of vision. A child with normal hearing can orientate to many events without looking at them; deaf children can make guesses, and have to rely on memory for much that takes place in the wider surroundings. The easiest way to provide for better opportunities to inspect their surroundings is to mount strategically placed mirrors on the walls of classrooms, corridors and, if possible, around the playground. The mirros should be placed so that the whole of a room can be inspected from any position without having to look specially in a different direction.

One major difficulty is that one cannot attract the attention of a deaf child by calling him from a distance. As sounds cannot be used, visual attention can be attracted by means of a pen torch with a narrow but powerful beam. This does not solve all problems, but can go a long way toward helping the control of deaf children. The technique of use needs to be learned and the appropriate signals well practised so that the children come to attend to the signal efficiently.

Small pocket mirrors are also extremely useful and can be used by deaf children in much the same way as the driving mirror is used in a car. The earlier children can learn to use a special aid like a mirror, the more they will gain from them. It is particularly helpful at a later stage, for example when working in a factory, to have developed a habit of regular, brief inspections in a mirror for personal use.

Large inflatables are particularly stimulating for the free play of deaf children—although they are equally attractive to other handicapped and normal children. They consist of various big shapes like imaginatively designed air cushions, but on a generous scale. Theyare resilient when children jump on them, and because they are hollow the impact of a movement on one part of the inflatable is transmitted to other parts: when several children are playing on an inflatable, they can, to some extent, 'feel' what the others are doing; the contours of the inflatable change as the children move around, and this provides further clues about their activities for each other.

Special conditions for physically handicapped children

Physically handicapped children need aids to stability, mobility and communication. Where the handicap is gross, this can only be provided by specialists; details which go beyond the scope of the present discussion have been described elsewhere by Levitt (1975), K. Bobath (1966) and others. A physiotherapy department, hydrotherapy pool and heated swimming pool are necessary. Individually designed chairs which may have to be self-propelled, different kinds of walking and sitting aids all need to be worked out. Aids for writing may take the form of electric typewriters, perhaps fitted with specially adapted keyboards, and timing devices to allow for the kinds of inaccuracy expected from the child. A great deal of ingenuity has gone into the creation of such aids which can sometimes compensate for very incoordinated movements and make a relatively independent life possible for the child.

Specialist supervision is still necessary when physically handicapped children attend normal school. The width of doorways must be adequate for wheelchairs; lifts are needed if different floors have to be used. There should be no steps to the outside doors, and all corridors must be wide enough for wheelchairs,. Beyond such obvious requirements, the conditions to be met are intimately bound up with the teaching plans discussed further.

2

Teaching of Handicapped and Mentally Handicapped Children

TEACHING HANDICAPPED CHILDREN

THE general aim of teaching is to enable children to make the most effective use of their abilities at every stage of their development. They should learn to make extensive use of their skills and gain a wide range of experience as a basis for a clear understanding of the world in which they live. Teaching methods are adapted to the age and maturity of the children, and if they are handicapped, further adaptations need to be made in order to avoid obstacles to learning and to meet special needs as and when they arise. Well-adapted teaching plans should allow the damaging effects of a handicap to be kept to a minimum, but remain sufficiently flexible to deal with problems which were not managed successfully at an earlier age.

Two types of plans are needed. first, plans for future development and, second, more specific plans which are brought to bear on situations when a child cannot progress because there is an obstacle to learning. General plans for the earliest stages of learning are discussed in this chapter; others, which are specifically designed for a particular handicap, are considered separately in the following chapters.

Plans for the earliest stages of development

Parents who are distressed by the knowledge that their child is handicapped need practical advice: what to do for their child and how to do it. Advice should be available as soon as the diagnosis is made, and in some cases, for example Down's babies, the diagnosis is made at birth. There are two guiding principles which can always be followed when deciding how best to advise the parents what to do next with their infant. One is that the active interest and participation of the infant is engaged in an event which has meaning for him; the other guideline is provided by the next stages of development which would be expected under normal circumstances. The parents need to know that development is an active process, and that the aim of special treatment for their infant is to let him anticipate events. In the course of time, further aims will be introduced so that he will become increasingly active, participating more and more in events which concern him, and then develop his own plans, for instance when he is playing.

During the first weeks of life there are opportunities to train the baby to anticipate feeding. Before inserting the nipple or the teat of his bottle into his mouth, the corners of the mouth and lips can be gently stimulated to elicit lip movements. The nipple is then inserted when the lips are moving in response to the stimulation. The focus at this early stage is on selected responses which the baby makes in particular situations. By constant repetition, so that the same set of responses are always elicited before the next, meaningful stimulus or satisfaction is offered, the baby comes to anticipate the event, in this case, being fed; he takes his first step toward organization of his environment.

Another early form of training to anticipate can become part of a routine followed when picking up the baby—in order to nurse him. The routine can be started at about the third week; before that, it has little effect. When coming to pick up the baby, the parent first goes to stand by the side of the cot, and attempts to attract the baby's attention, by calling, whistling or perhaps by waving his hand slowly in front of his face. When the baby makes a chance move of his head, or of his eyes towards the parent, the arms are lowered with hands within the baby's range of vision, and kept there until the baby makes a chance movement with his arms. At that moment he is picked up and nursed. This routine should be followed consistently, and culminates when the baby responds regularly to both manoeuvres: being called when the parent comes to the cot and extending his arms in order to be lifted.

The parents need to understand that though these early forms of approach are important, they will not succeed until the routine has been followed for some time. The routine should continue, however, even when it seems to have no effect. The whole point of the measures being discussed is that they should prepare the baby for the next phase of development. if he responds immediately, this does not mean that the attempt is made at the right time; on the contrary, it shows that it should have started much earlier, and that the baby is already prepared for further progress. This point must be repeated often, so that the parents are not disappointed by the initial failure of the baby to respond.

The manner in which many early influences are brought to a baby follows a pattern described by Piaget (1950) as a 'circular response.' In essence, this happens when a baby produces some chance effect by his own movement, observes the effect, and then seeks to produce it again. It is a process in which a particular effect is differentiated from its general background, and when a movement is identified by its purpose.

Another way of describing the same course of events is that the effect reinforces the movement which was the cause. When this happens, the infant learns from his own actions and about effects of his own actions on his environment. Handicaps commonly delay the time when circular reactions begin, either because input and processing are not differentiated, so that he fails to notice the effect, or because there is no differentiation of output and feedback so that he does not identify his action. Special conditions can therefore be set up to increase opportunities for circular reactions to take place.

A common way in which babies are kept interested is to give them something moving to look at: a mobile is hung over the cot, and when it moves, the baby follows the movement with his eyes because of the changing visual pattern in front of him. If he does not follow the movement, there is no selective input from the mobile and the point of the exercise is lost. The effect should then be enhanced, by having one or two parts of the mobile hung low enough to brush his face as it passes, for instance a feather or coloured ribbon. Each time the feather or the ribbon passes over his face, there is an additional chance that he will be alerted by its touch as well as by the visual change to entice his responses. Suitable adaptations of a mobile or a hanging display within the baby's reach can also form part of the transition from active observation to active intervention, when the baby starts to reach for the mobile, or when he grabs it and puts it in his mouth.

Reaching for an object is a more differentiated response for a baby than putting his arms up to be lifted. Like other reactions it is delayed in handicapped babies. Large, brightly coloured plastic balls, or perhaps balloons, can be offered when the baby is lying on his back. The initial response tends to be reaching by all four limbs, and so the legs should be free from clothing in order to increase stimulation (input) from the feet. When reaching becomes more differentiated, there are opportunities for promoting directional responses, by offering a toy first centrally so that it can be taken by both hands, and then giving it from different directions so that the movement becomes further adapted to the conditions in which it is made.

Another early stimulation is to give the baby opportunities to see himself in a mirror. He can be dressed and bathed so that he can look in a mirror at that time. The intention is to let him have the earliest opportunities to recognize himself, and so to distinguish himself from other people. Until he does so, giving and taking have no special meaning, and social interactions remain at a rudimentary level. Later, when he can raise his head while lying on his front, and perhaps can turn from front to back so that he can play on the floor, a mirror should be fixed at floor level to one of the walls so that he can see himself when he is playing. Not only is he stimulated in his play by his reflection, he is also given a powerful motive to crawl and to move towards his reflection.

Around the time that a baby begins to respond to his image in a mirror, he also responds to the sound of his own voice, if this has been recorded and is played back to him. Like the other experiences described in this section, early attempts to record his voice should be made so that he is able to listen to the record. If it is difficult to obtain a record of the baby's voice (and it can be very frustrating to do so), then the voice of another baby at a slightly more advanced stage of development can serve the same purpose. At first the baby will tend to react by becoming alert, and just listening, but after a numebr of repetitions, he will start to join in. Babbling is an important precursor of speech and also gives opportunities to copy and imitate sounds; imitation is a major part of learning at a later stage.

Rocking, 'dancing' and playing rhythmically to music is another way in which sound and movement become associated, especially when the sound comes from the mother's voice. Rocking a baby and singing to him is, of course, a universal practice, and it also leads on the various ritual games with songs like 'this little pig went to market' or 'round and round the garden.' in which the baby is introduced to representative actions even if these are in the form of a game.

Many handicapped babies are very late to start crawling, and some never make the attempt. There are many reasons for this, but a common one is that the limbs are too weak. Strengthening the arms is relatively easy because the baby can grasp, and while he is holding on to something he can be enticed to pull against resistance or to pull himself up from lying down to sitting up. Strengthening the legs is more difficult, but one way to try is to hold the baby upright, with his bare feet in contact with the parent's thighs or knees. Gentle bouncing movements may then gradually develop increasing push from his legs against the parent, and after a while he may straighten his legs. It is important that the feet retain their contact with the base, otherwise the baby will just flex his legs and draw them up without making the effort to push for himself. This is a very tiring process, especially for mothers, and if possible some extra, hanging device can be fitted to help. One way to do so is to screw a pair of hooks into the lintel of a door and to suspend the baby in a harness, attached to the sort of long, covered springs used for a car roof rack. Springs of this kind have enough give, but are also strong enough to support the baby. If the mother sits under such an arrangement, she can leave most of the work to the springs, and merely add the final touches without becoming exhausted.

Whent he baby is able to hold up his head while lying prone, he can be taught to turn over from back to front. He needs to learn to flex his legs and move them in the right way, while the impetus to turn is generally provided by holding a favourite toy, rattle or whatever he finds stimulating, in such a way that he can only reach it by moving his arms into the turn, and then following suit with his legs. To help him, by giving a little push or by placing his knee in the right position, is not to prevent him from learning as it merely puts him in the right position to make the movement. If attempts to get the baby to imitate movements, gestures and sounds have been successful, lying on the floor near the baby and moving arm and then leg for him to copy sometimes has the desired effect and the baby turns over by himself. When babies are able to turn over, they tend to use the movement for getting around the room. A mirror at floor level really comes into its own at that stage, and there are added reasons for crawling, when the rudiments of the move are acquired.

To try to teach a baby to crawl is a laborious process and many parents give up in the attempt. It involves a complex set of manoeuvres and should not be attempted before the baby has learned to turn over by his own efforts. The parent kneels over the baby, who is lying prone on the floor, and brigns her knees up to contact the baby's bare feet. She supports the baby with her hands under his shoulders, and brings her elbows together, pushing the baby's knees straight. When the baby has pushed forward, she raises his shoulders again to free his arms and to put them in a position to support himself; this can be done with the mother's fingers. She then shuffles her knees forward to make contact with his feet.

Efforts of this kind make considerable demands on the parents, but they should only be attempted if the baby does not protest. If he cries or gives other signs of distress, further work must be delayed until a later date, when he is more accepting. It goes without saying that the effort to crawl is given meaning by having toys lying ahead of the baby, which are reached when he moves forward.

By this time, babies are usually playing actively with toys, alert to their image in a mirror, and welcome nursery rhymes, finger games and generally being fussed. The time has come to introduce more far-reaching notions about distance, object constancy and simple sequenes. Bath time, dressing and undressing have not been mentioned so far, but they offer important opportunities for play and for the baby to learn from his play.

Whenever possible, the baby should be prepared for his bath in the bathroom, and the bath water should be run in while he is being got ready. The association between the sound of the running water and being undressed in the bathroom allows him to anticipate his bath. In the bath he should have floating toys to begin with and later, when he can sit up (usually at the stage when he can roll around on the floor, but before he can crawl), he should have containers which he can fill and empty in his bath; a toy teapot or watering can is particualrly useful as the stream of water coming out of the spout can be sent in different directions. A baby who is worried by being in a bath is usually helped by putting a bath mat in it for him to sit on.

Pouring water out of containers and filing them up again is one link in a chain of experiences which later on continues when the infant empties and then fills boxes. Emptying boxes usually presents few problems for the baby; filling them is quite another matter. Attempts to do so often need much encoruagement and may not be successful before the infant reaches the stage of development when he can feed himself; by then he can also imitate movements and sounds, and enjoys peek-a-boo and simple forms of hide-and-seek. Reference to the way in which different interests and skills develop together was already made and the various activities which have just been mentioned illustrate what happens; they also show relationships between earlier and later stages of development: pouring water from can and emptying a box, putting a spoon into his mouth and putting toys into a box, hiding and reappearing in peek-a-boo and putting a toy into a box and taking it out again, and being able to copy actions and learning to put a toy into a box.

Dressing and undressing can be managed from an early age to help the baby anticipate what will happen next, by stimulating him to 'help' put his arm into a sleeve or to raise his legs before taking off his pants. The arm can be stimulated to straighten at the elbow by gently massaging the shoulder blade and pushing a little from the upper arm. If this is done consistently from around the time he is shown his image in a mirror, the baby will begin to anticipate being dressed, by making appropriate movements, around the time when he starts to recognize and respond to his own image. At a later stage, he can learn to anticipate that he is going out for a walk by putting his outdoor coat next to him where he can get hold of it for two or three minutes before it is put on.

Using a spoon to feed himself, instead of relying on his hands, is often delayed and resisted by many babies. It is a complicated operation, and spoon feeding starts because the baby needs more than just milk, and not because his skills have developed sufficiently to use a spoon. Any attempt to teach him how to use a spoon at a time when he is hungry and therefore anxious to get the food is doomed to failure. The baby can be given the chance to use a spoon at times when he is not hungry, preferably when both he and his mother have had a good rest. The best moment to let him try to use a spoon is when he has had his afternoon sleep, and when he has been cleaned and changed. Needless to say, both baby and mother should be dressed for the occasion, and it helps to have a bag full of plastic spoons ready for use.

Peek-a-boo and generally hiding and reappearing are games which play a major role in development. They give the baby experiences which prepare him for the later development of notions of constancy, and from the time when a baby can get around by rolling or crawling, hiding and being found becomes a favourite game. The next stage of development is reached when the baby begins to look for hidden objects, when a toy, for instance, is covered with a cloth and he pulls away the cloth to get at the toy. Notions about constancy develop as and when an infant learns that objects do not cease to exist when they are out of sight, and until they have developed, a child cannot go on to learn about sequence and order, let alone concepts which involve arrangements in space or ideas about numbers.

Hiding and being found leads on to games in which the child runs away in order to be chased and caught. The functions of the parent, who does the chasing, and of the child, who is being caught, are complementary. The child's anticipations and his attention span are extended by the game; it gives practical experience of an alternating sequence of escape and being caught, and the child has to adapt and adjust to his surroundings while making his escapes.

When an infant responds to his mother's request, by gesture, to give her a toy, he begins to learn about reversals, and a great deal of his later development depends upon his understanding of what these involve. A simple example fo a reversal is that if a quantity of beads is poured from one container to another, then the number of beads does not alter during the transfer, so that the original amount is still there when the beads are poured back into the first container. Children only learn to understand what happens in a reversal relatively late in their development after they have gained from many other experiences about exchanges. Giving and taking belong to the early experiences in a chain of developments which will enable the child to understand complex notions when he gets older.

Learning to imitate movements, gestures and sound is another important part of early development. Some of the first imitations begin when the mother imitates her baby's voice and when the baby makes further noises to encourage her to go on. Their interactions follow a familiar pattern: the baby does something, the parent copies it and the baby repeats his action, and so on. The baby begins to organize his behaviour and learns to anticipate events when he takes part in a chain of interactions with his parents. It is particularly important for handicapped babies to be encouraged to take part in chains of interactions with the parents because many new actions will be learned by imitation. A baby who has started to imitate movements, for instance, can be taught to wave his arm as a sign of greeting, and he can be encouraged to give and take when he plays with his parents.

At an early stage of development, when a baby has learned to sit unsupported, he might also be able to manage half a turn from his back to lie on his side without being able to get on to his front. If he has begun to imitate movements, he might be able to learn to move his arm and then his leg by copying corresponding movements made by his parents. The development of many other actions can be speeded on by imitation.

Crawling: objects at a distance, and exploring and experimenting

When a baby can crawl and get around a room by himself, he becomes interested in objects at a distance and in finding out about them. His interest can be stimulated by typing tapes with suitable grips to some of his toys, and palcing the toys out of reach but putting the grips close to his hands. When he learns to pull on a grip and finds that this brings a particular toy close to him, he learns to take notice of the direction in which the tape is lying by following it to the toy. A further development is to introudce play with hidden objects by covering the toy with a beaker or a cloth but leaving the free end of the tape uncovered. Pleasure in hiding and finding starts with peek-a-boo and assumes increasingly complex forms at successive stages of development. Older children play hide-and-seek, and the aim of many other games is to discover how to put some component parts together.

Many new experiences can be introduced when a baby has learnt to crawl. Playing with moving toys like cars or balls can take place without help because the baby can reach the toy unaided after it has rolled away. His interests can be stimulated by giving him a board placed as an incline down which he can roll his cars and, at a later stage, 'garages' for aiming where the cars should go. Other games which develop at about that stage involve filling and emptying boxes, playing with bricks, using a posting box and trying simple inset puzzles. A little later, the infant will become interested in putting together the parts of a Russian doll, nests of boxes and other simple shapes. All the experiences he gains from playing in these different ways lead on to a next stage when the infant begins to use words to communicate his needs.

An infant who can crawl can be encouraged to come to his mother when she calls instead of waiting for her to come to him. She can stimulate him to attend to her voice by calling out suggestions to him, and by singing and engaging his attention when she is in the kitchen and he is playing in the sitting room. Social contacts and the awareness of other people are stimulated by simple games in which the infant and his parents take it in turn to do something: rolling a ball to each other, fetching things, finding them and giving them to the parent. Infants can usually carry out verbal instructions, especially when they are asked to bring a familiar household article, well before they use the words for their own purposes.

Infants whose language development is particularly delayed should be stimulated to use pointing and gestures. The gestures must be understood by all members of the family so that the infant is not frustrated when he uses them; it helps if all the family can learn to make certain gestures when they talk to each other.

Plans for later stages of development and for older children

It does not often happen that one can work from birth with a handicapped baby and his fmaily. Children usually start to get special help around the age of school entry, when secondary handicaps have already been added to the primary handicap, and when there is some fragmentation of learning and experience. In order to be able to plan how best to help the child, he is first assessed by a suitable psychometric test; a training programme based on the assessment can then be set up. The content of the programme can be derived from the answers to three questions about the child's present developmental stage:

1. What are children usually able to do before they reach this stage?
2. What other skills are usually developed at this stage?
3. What skills are attained at the next stage of development?

The answer to the first question shows how past experience and learning might have been fragmented; the answer to the second question shows what special help might be needed to overcome obstacles to learning; the third answer can be used to define the aims which should be attained by the child.

In the normal course of development, an infant who is beginning the feed himself usually babbles much more than he did; when he starts to walk he mâkes use of words to express his needs, and when he widens his social contacts, for instance by going to play-school he develops new syntactic elements in his speech and uses phrases or sentences to express himself. The language development of a handicapped child is often more delayed than the development of his general motor skills.The result is that all sorts of social applications of his skills are either delayed or lost altogether, because many social interactions cannot develop until the child has an adequate command of language.

The training programme for a handicapped child should be designed to avoid the delay of developement of one set of experiences due to the child's failrue to develop all the skills he would need for active participation. Physically handicapped children need to be carried from one place to another if they cannot walk; if the handicap interferes with articulation so that the child does not or cannot ask questions, he should be given the kinds of answers offered to children who ask how or why something happens. Mentally handicapped children need to be encouraged or persuaded to take part in activities, if they can only learn about the purpose when they have experienced what happens. A child who does not understand what is going on often shows by his bearing that he is frightened: he cannot predict the course of events. Many children become frightened when they cannot decide what to do when they are faced by a new demand. For instance, a child might refuse to enter a swimming pool, but owe his fear to the confusion of the place, without being at all frightened of the water. If he can be taken to the pool another time, when there are only a few people in it, he might enjoy bathing so much that he will go in the next time in spite of the noise and confusion.

The child's behaviour in company must be osberved in order to assess how he differs from other children at and around his own stage of development: his social interactions within his family and with other children, his social experiences outside the family, and his skills, and his ability to use them in different situations. Some handicapped children are helped excessively at home but have very few opportunities for playing with other children before entering school. Until they are used to mixing with other children, their apparent ability at school tends to be much lower than at home in a familiar environment. Other handicapped children might be used to the company of their peers without having learned how to play with them. In order to benefit from being with other children, a child needs to be given an active part in their games.

During pre-school life much of the educational planning which concerns handicapped children sets out to provide them with a wide range of experiences, in order to avoid the fragmentation which can be so damaging at later stages of development. The answer to the third question, about the next stage of progress, can be used to guide the parent or teacher when deciding what new skills should be taught to the child, while the answers to the second question tell why he sometimes seems to be unable to use a skill which he can apply successfully on other occasions.

The next stage of progress might be reached when a child starts to play together with other children and does not just play alongside them; or when he starts to replace single words and simple phrases by complex forms of language; or when he can draw pictures instead of merely scribbling with a pencil. All his present attainments should continue to develop and become more highly organized and integrated with his general behaviour. The demands which he must be able to meet so that his actions can become more highly organized show what should be taught.

The plan for the exercises which will be used should proceed from gross motor activities to fine motor skills. A child who is playing alongside of other children might be brought into a co-operative game of a simple kind, in which two or more children can take interchangeable roles: one child leads and pulls along one or two other children who hold on to a skipping rope tied around the waist of the first child; or one of the children could sit in a box which is pulled or pushed by the others. In other suitable games the children play complementary roles, as 'mothers and fathers' or 'hospital' or 'school'. Fine motor skills can then be introduced into such games by dressing up or making up for the game; when this happens, the content of the game also tends to become more complex.

Children need to develop adequate motives in order to go on to more complex levels of activities. A theory about motives for learning was proposed in chapter 11: that higher orders of roganization become desirable when children find that their present mode of response cannot achieve goals created by their new experiences. A major aim for the teaching plan is to ensure at an early stage that children can experience the effects of actions which they can only attain under special conditions at first, but which they will be able to manage independently at thier next stage of development. Handicapped children, for instance, may need more than just the company of other children in order to learn to play together; they need help and encouragement so that they can take part in games which are suitable for their existing skills and abilities. The role of the teacher is to ensure that appropriate games are called into being and to encourage them to continue.

Complex skills and early experience

Many of the early experiences which are later integrated into a complex skill, take place at a stage of development when that skill is not more than a thought for the future. The outcome of successful planning should be that the early experiences are fully and firmly established. Years of planning ahead are needed to prevent experiences and learning from being fragmented or from coming to a half because there are obstacles which the child cannot overcome. Some of the early experiences prepare the infant for dealing with information and help himto organize his responses; others are more specific and help him to deal with particular kinds of information: about people, about objects and about actions. He learns to relate experiences to each other. At first sight it might seem far-fetched to start preparing an infant for a skill, like writing, which he might never achieve as a child; it is far more regrettable at a later stage of development to find that handicapped children cannot make satisfactory progress because their early experiences had been neglected.

Writing draws on many early experiences. The general basis for writing is to be able to plan and perform sets of movements according to recognizable patterns, as in shaping letters. The patterns need to be kept separate, but joined to other patterns to form a sequence, as in putting letters together for a word, or words for a sentence. The point of writing is to record information. The ability to copy movements and to learn to perfrom differentiated movements in response to different, symbolic cues is important for general development and learning; early writing practice consists of copying. The child needs to be able to recognize when his copy is satisfactory and to identify and correct his mistakes. Other, more specific experiences are derived from fine motor skills like manipulating small objects and placing them accurately in the right position, as well as painting and drawing pictures.

Experiences which are important for the later development of complex skills are gained at all stages of childhood. General progress from gross motr experiences to fine motor skills runs along the following lines:

1. Differentiated movements of the body and limbs for reaching, holding, pointing, etc.
2. Movements to place or to relate objects to each other.
3. Responses to set arrangements of objects such as toys or furniture.
4. Anticipating events and responding selectively to people, objects and actions.
5. Co-ordinating the relationships between different experiences.
6. Integrated movements of the body and limbs, when playing, moving to music or doing gymnastic exercises.
7. Skilled use of the hands when drawing and painting or engaged in constructional games.
8. Specific practice of the application of the skill.

The time taken to pass on from one stage of development to the next depends on the general progress of the child. The later stages would be unthinkable for any infants or young children, let alone for those who are handicapped. If there is a block, so that progress seems to come to a halt, recapitulation of earlier stages will show what the child can do and when he lacks the necessary skill to proceed.

If the long-term effects of early experiences are kept in mind, it is usually possible to find productive ways of stimulating and encouraging children to be active. What they experience depends on their present levels of skills and attainments, and if they need help, the aim should be to enable them to build on their experience, to pass on to higher levels of organization, and to gain greater mastery over their environment.

TEACHING OF MENTALLY HANDICAPPED CHILDREN

Teaching plans for the earliest stages of development were set out in the previous chapter. The plans set out in this chapter are for older children of school age. They show how plans were worked out for children at different stages of development and of different levels of ability, beginning with the least able group. In each case, group work rather than individual work has been selected because this is the more common working situation. All but the first group of boys were attending schools where they followed a general curriculum of education; the exercises to be described were directed towards specific problems caused by obstacles to learning or due to the fragmentation of earlier experience.

Plans for teaching severely mentally handicapped and psychotic adolescents the elements of communication

Twelve such boys, aged between 12 and 16 years, made up the 'group'; they were part of a larger group of twenty-six, who were on a ward for the most severely disturbed, mentally handicapped adolescents in the hospital. None of them used words for communication, though most of them said words at times, but generally without meaning. All had had a variety of different kinds of teaching but none of them could be accommodated in school any longer because of their bizarre and unpredictable behaviour: climbing on cupboards, jumping into the room, unexpected aggression to each other or to members of the staff. Such behaviour only occurred at times, and all could be approached on an individual basis when they could take part in such routine tasks as sorting or building with bricks for short periods. Signs that they could respond to training were that simple behaviour modification had recently begun to have some effect on familiar routines like dressing and on their conduct at meal times.

Everyone of the boys in this group was not only mentally handicapped but also psychotic. This meant that their development had been restricted by the mental handicap and that all their experience and learning was fragmented because of the psychosis. Social interactions were only significant when they met an immediate need and did not lead to any further development. The behaviour of the boys was paradoxical because their complex manoeuvres showed that their sensori-motor skills were highly developed, and yet they were totally devoid of social context. All the boys were incontinent, but some of them had begun recently to respond to a token reward system for controlling bladder and bowel elimination. The ability to control their basic functions was there, but in the absence of social awareness, they had developed no motives for exercising any control.

When planning a teaching programme for communication, the answers to the three questions about general development, run along the following lines:

1. What are children usually able to do before they begin to communicate? The answer depends on the level of communication which should be trained. In this case, the aim is that the boys should respond appropriately to requests from members of the staff, and to show by their behaviour that they can anticipate what is going to happen next, and to adapt their actions accordingly.

   In normal development, the early signs that a baby can communicate at this level are that he makes differentiated movements to indicate his needs instead of generally crying and kicking, and that he can anticipate a simple game with his mother, like 'round and round the garden.' by putting out his hand for her to tickle. Responses he makes before reaching this stage are to show signs of pleasure in being nursed or fussed, opening his mouth in readiness for a spoon when he is fed, holding up his head when lying prone, searching for a toy when he has dropped it, and responding generally to his mother's voice by becoming alert when she calls him and by calming down if she sings to him when he is upset.

The teenage boys we are considering cannot be compared directly with normally developing infants, especially with respect to their highly developed motor skills. The lack of social development of the handicapped boys makes a comparison with the behaviour of the infant much more realistic. According to their moods, they showed signs of pleasure or displeasure when approached by a member of staff; they were more advanced at meal times, being able to take their food independently, use spoons or knives and forks, and, of-course, move in a highly co-ordinated fashion; but their responses to the voice were spasmodic and at times non-existent.

2. What sorts of skills are usually attained at this stage? At the stage of development we are considering, babies are very keen to be occupied, perhaps because so many activities are possible when the mother plays with her baby, but impossible when he is left on his own. Babies at this stage of development use their voice and make more and more different sounds, especially when encouraged to do so. They are stimulated to repeat movements or sounds when these are copied by adults: they imitate.

   When the behaviour of the boys in hospital in parallel situations is considered, there are striking contrasts which show what differences there are between their behaviour and that of the normally developing infant. Instead of seeking company because it is stimulating, they flee from company, intent on their movements without developing any other aims or purpose. They seem to listen to the sounds they make, but without appearing to be interested in repeating the same pattern of sounds; for a baby the attempt to repeat a sound appears to be the stimulus which encourages further vocalization. The boys certainly imitate at times, but they do so without purpose and the imitation is simply incorporated into their general movements.

3. What kinds of skills are attained at the next stage of development? In the normal course of development, an infant who finds pleasure in enticing his parent to play

with him develops set anticipations about the parent's next move which run parallel to his own increasingly differentiated responses. Instead of being satisfied with any mode of play, he develops expectations of particular modes of play. The signs are that he shows that he is dissatisfied if his expectations are not met when the parent uses an appropriate, rather than a particular, response. At the same time, the baby attends with greater interest to the details of effects from his actions. He is no longer satisfied when he repeats a movement and there is some effect; he becomes selective and is only satisfied when the effect is the one he had planned.

The boys in hospital show an interesting parallel to this kind of development. Though their inclination was to flee from social constraints, they were not able to avoid all social influences on their development. The result is that certain routines were learnt. The apparent similarity between their behaviour and that of normally developing infants is that both are disturbed by change in an expected routine. There is a difference between them, however, because the infant learns to adapt change, while the reaction of the boys is to flee from the situation and to avoid it without learning anything new. Instead of extending their responses, they resort to flight and lose the potential benefits of the experience for learning.

A teaching plan for communication should take note of all these points, but they do not all have to be met in one attempt. Success depends on the effect of each step which is attempted, so that every step can be co-ordinated with others. Progressive steps are therefore taken one by one, rather than as a whole.

The general plan was that the boys should develop ways of communicating with other people. From the answer to the first question, about behaviour at the time communication begins to develop, it was known that the boys could be approached in order to work with them if this could be attempted on an individual basis, and that they would show whether or not they welcomed the approach. From the answer to the second question, about other elements of behaviour which develop around the time that communication begins, the boys could be expected to try to escape from the teaching session, but that they would be likely to imitate movements and that they would attend to sound patterns in the form of music. They were not expected to integrate their movements with the music unless there were special conditions which made this possible. The answer to the third question, which concerns the next stage of development when communication has begun, confirmed the expectation that the boys' initial reactions would be to try to flee from the session, and that the first hurdles to be overcome were their avoidance of contact and their flight from social pressures to adapt their behaviour to social demands.

This meant that the room used for the training sessions had to have locked doors, and that the form of training had to be very simple and repetitive. Every move had to be planned in advance so that the socially disorganized behaviour of the boys would be met by organized demands, to allow them to take part and to develop set anticipations about the teaching sessions.

The model for the exercieses

The model used for teaching communication was based on the elements of a conversation: information is exchanged in an orderly manner between two or more people. Each participant must be aware of the information which is offered and interpret it so that he can make a suitable response which can be recognized by his partner. Conversation makes use of sounds which can be interpreted: it involves a language. The conversational exchange takes place between specified partners who remain together long enough to communicate effectively with each other.

All the boys who took part in the teaching sessions were able to articulate words which they spoke on some occasions, but generally without purpose. This was consistent with their advanced level of sensori-motor development, and showed that the development of speech had not been prevented by input or output obstacles to learning. Processing and feedback, especially social feedback, were the obstacles which had prevented their development of language. Their general failure to develop social aims and their lack of social skills showed that they did not process the corresponding information. As they did not use social skills they had no opportuities to develop the appropriate feedback system. Their lack of concern for other people showed this because they all sought to make contact with others at times, but did not modify their behaviour as a result of such contacts.

The conditions which had to be met by the plan for the sessions were that they should be made up of simple, repetitive acts, and that each part of the session should be restricted to a time scale and level of complexity which could be managed by the boys. As there was no obstacle to output, the actual movements which were to be performed presented no problems. The aim was to keep going a simple, repetitive pattern of movements in time to a rhythm, and to set out the exercise in a way in which it could be understood by the boys and could provide them with immediate and continuous feedback. This was provided by the boy's partner (a nurse, doctor, teacher or social worker) who guided the movements. Because the movements were guided during the initial stages, obstacles to processing were avoided or kept to a minimum. The partner directed the boy's attention to the input from the steady rhythm of the music, and he also took over the role of processing by selecting the output, in this case, the movements to be performed.

The skill of the partner was to be sensitive to any new responses from the boys, and to direct their attention to the musical rhythm to time their movements. In time, the early cues provided by the partner could be faded out until the point was reached when the boys kept time to the rhythm without extra help; the boys also learned to select the successive patterns of movements which were used during the sessions.

These conditions could only be met by working on a one-to-one basis in the initial stages, and this could only be achieved once a week for periods of up to ninety minutes.

The stimuli took the form of selected pieces of music; both the music and the responses to be made were simple and repetitive, to give opportunities for repetition and practice. Variations consisted in performing similar kinds of movements with different parts of the body, and this took place in two stages—sitting down for the first set of responses and then repeating the same movements standing up:

1. Stretching and then bringing the arms together.
2. Rocking the trunk from side to side.
3. Stamping alternately with the legs.

Between the sitting and standing stages, there was a quiet period spent sitting and listening to a calm and quiet piece of music.

The plan for the session was that each boy had his partner and they both carried out the movements together. During the first stage the boys sat in a circle, while the partner stood or knelt in front of him holding his hands to do the arm movements, guiding his trunk or keeping his legs stamping. During the quiet period each pair sat together, while the third stage tended to develop into a series of dance forms. Each of the seven episodes lasted about three minutes.

The musical pieces were carefully selected so that they had three different, strong and contrasting rhythms to act as 'instructions' for partiuclar ways of moving while the fourth piece for the quiet interlude was flowing and tranquil. Contrast between the movement pieces was further emphasized by having a vocal, an orchestral and a solo instrumental piece with two-step, waltz and march timing, respectively. An efficient, professional approach was essential. Any hitch, such as a wire breaking, someone coming into the room, in fact any interruption, spoilt some of the initial sessions and required much extra work to get the session going again.

The only motive we could hope for at the start was that the boys' curiosity might be aroused by the strange events which were taking place. The usual reactions of pleasure from individual attention could not be expected from boys who usually fled from such attentions.

The first sign of response was the attentive attitude of the boys to the music during the tranquil period, while their partners were struck by the way they came to know the boys as individuals when they were working together, and how their personalities became apparent in ways which had barely been suspected before. A two-way communication developed between the boy and his partner. Signs of progress were specific as well as general. Specific signs were the increasing ability of the boys to maintain the set movements and their spontaneous change from one episode to the next. General signs were that they came to anticipate the sessions, helped to put out the chairs, sat down ready for the start and also selected their own partners for themselves.

When the responses of the boys had made enough progress, it was possible to make further plans for the sessions. An early change was that instead of stooping or kneeling in front of the boy for the first stage of the session, the partner was able to sit down facing the boy because so much less effort was needed to keep the movements going. A later development was to pass from one-to-one pairing to a one-to-two grouping, in which one assistant worked with two boys.

Exercises using speech

Another set of exercises for the same group of boys was simply to walk arm in arm with a boy, and to speak to him while doing so. The aim was to draw his attention to speech without worrying about his ability to respond to the words; if he did follow the meaning, so much the better but whether or not he did follow the meaning was of secondary importance for the exercise. Speaking to a non-responding partner for any length of time is difficult and so set phrases were used: 'Gerry, this is a table; this is a window; let us go to the door.' Planning to use such simple phrases was necessary in order to keep up a continuous patter of talk. Contrary to expectations, the boys did not try to escape from their partners though they often chose where they wanted to go for themselves.

The next stage was to introduce an exchange of partners to make it clear that the boys were being addressed as individuals. Any one pair would walk up to another one, make formal introductions such as 'Gerry, this is Andrew; Andrew, meet Gerry,' and then 'Andrew would you come with me?,' exchange partners, and continue. The aim was to present a model of interchange at the level of a gross motor exercise which involved each individual participating in the exchange: a concrete experience of what happens in a conversation.

As in the case of the music and movement sessions, the next stage of progress was to pass from a one-to-one arrangement to a threesome: an assistant walking with a boy on either arm. The same exchanges took place and speech was directed alternately to each of the two boys.

To make the 'walk' more structured, tables were set out in the room, so that two pairs could always approach each other around a table from opposite sides, meet, exchange partners, and pass on to another table, much as in a very simplified minutes.

Question and answer in gross motor form

A gross motor exercise which embodies the elements of question and answer ran along the following lines. A circle of pairs of chairs was set up so that each boy could sit next to his partner. One pair got up, hands joined, and walked over to a pair on the other side of the circle. The first pair made an arch by raising their arms, waited for the other pair to pass beneath, and then took their places. The second pair then went through the same ritual with another pair, and the process continued. Questioning was symbolized by soliciting, standing with raised arms; answering was made by passing under the arch as suggested by the 'question.'

Other elements of a conversation in gross motor forms

The larger the group, the more important it is for the members to be able to wait and observe, as well as to take their turns in a conversation or in any other social interaction. One exercise in which taking turns alternates with observing and waiting involved music and movement. All but one pair stood holding hands in a circle, while the remaining pair was at the centre. When the music began, the lone pair moved around the circle, weaving in and out between the other parts, who raised their arms to let them pass. When the first pair had completed a round, the others took it in turn to follow in the same way. The members of the group making the circle therefore had to attend and anticipate when to raise their arms, and for the rest of the time they had to wait until it was their turn to move around. All had a chance to be active and passive participants.

Many developments were tried and others could be envisaged. They generally took the form of group dances which were adapted to the current abilities of the boys.

General effects

Boys who are left to their own devices for much of the day, and who normally do not take much notice of each other, react strongly to the social stimulation which has been described. They are always much more active after the end of a teaching session, and this can result in total chaos. Steps should be taken to ensure that the end of the session passes on to some familiar routine like taking a light meal or snack, but seated in orderly fashion according to their usual practice. It is essential to bridge the period of high involvement to the return of normal conditions, just as it is important to start in an orderly manner and to pass from one activity to the next without pauses and their associated disruptions.

Plans for less severely mentally handicapped children

The next examples are chosen from work at a school for severely handicapped children, but where the level of abilities of the pupils were of a completely different order from that of the boys in the hospital who were described in the previous section. The children at the school were all taking part in a regular teaching programme. They were all mastering the mechanics of the three Rs, though the gap between the mechanics of writing numbers and understanding the meaning of what they were doing still caused them considerable difficulties. All the children were socially competent, played well together and knew how to conduct themselves in public. The children who took part in the following exercises were between 12 and 14 years old; there were sixteen boys and girls, two teachers to help during the sessions, another who played the piano, and one to guide the activities.

As the exercises were concerned with numeracy, the three questions and answers to them are as follows:

1. What are children usually able to do by the time they can start to use numbers? As the children in this group had mastered the rudiments of mechanical uses of numbers and of very simple addition, the question refers to the understanding and practical use of numbers rather than to merely writing them down or counting.

   In order to be able to use numbers and to understand their significance, children must have fully established ideas about sequences: they must be able to put all kinds of items into series, by size, weight, shape or colour; they must be able to separate objects into their own classes according to various criteria, and to categorize the members of a class of objects by their special properties. Before a child can use numbers effectively, he must be able to deal with sequences of actions as well as understanding how to classify objects. Until both kinds of sequences can be managed, number work stays at a mechanical level, and at best there are specific, well-practised situations in which the child seems to use numbers with understanding.

The children who took part in the exercise at the school showed how confused they were about sequences of movement and how difficult they found any task which involved instructions about some way of moving, for instance marching, as well as an instruction about where to start or finish, or how to group themselves while they were marching.

2. What other kinds of skills or competences do children usually acquire when they begin to use numbers with understanding? One sure indication is that the child begins to use concepts of time in a confident way; this is usually the stage when he learns how to tell the time on a clock, and knows how to apply the names of days of the week and of months of the year. Some children, who have been suitably drilled by their parents or teachers, become mechanically fluent users of such phrases long before they have any useful understanding of their significance.

   The children at the school were quite unable to manage any of these notions without a great deal of prompting, and even then it was doubtful if a successful answer had any real meaning for the child.

3. What kinds of skills does the child attain at his next stage, when he has mastered the elements of numeracy? A child who has a clear understanding of numbers can manage a whole host of social situations which are impossible while number work continues to pose problems for him. Instead of relying on a set order of events without the ability to adapt when a course of actions is changed, he can fit in with a change in plans (even if he does not like doing so) and he

can also anticipate events for extended periods of time. The ability to use numbers competently opens up a higher level of orientation within his environment for a child.

The group of children who did the exercises which will be described could not manage any of the spontaneous social adjustments which are needed to act independently of parental or other support. They played actively in the playground at school, where there was always help available from the teachers when a situation threatened to go wrong; but their play took the form of well-practised and familiar games, and the children all knew each other, so that they could adapt to situations as they arose, as well as to the other children who took part in the activities.

The answers to the three questions about developmental progress with respect to numeracy all combined to direct attention towards movement exercises and to organize the movements by using musical rhythms for timing them. The answer to the first question showed that concepts of time were still to be established, while notions about ordering, classifying and categorizing had been practised extensively in the classroom. The answer to the second question confirmed that notions about time were not being used by the children who were not yet sufficiently advanced in numeracy to be able to do so. The answer to the third question indicated the general experiences which will become possible at the next stage, when the children will attain a higher level of independence. Preparing them for that stage in good time, by setting up specific situations, is important, and the children should learn to shop or to take a particular bus route unaided, but those experiences are beyond the scope of the present discussion.

The model for the exercises

All the following exercises were modelled on the same plan, which was that the children performed one or more circuits around the outside of a ring of chairs, but that they should keep to particular rules which were specially formulated for each of the exercises; the rhythm they followed in going round the circle was set by the music played on the piano. The rules laid down for the exercises were formulated so that following them meant using numbers.

The aim for the exercises was to give the children experiences of applying number work in the form of gross motor activities. They were known from their class work to be able to classify and sort various kinds of objects and to be able to count and to use simple rules of addition. In line with the notion that the relevant gross motor experience underlies the development of fine skills and later symbolization and abstraction, it was important to find out how far they could go in applying principles of numeracy to gross motor activities. The successive exercises which will be described were graded so that they called for increasingly complex levels of organization of responses from the children, and they very soon showed how far the children could go. The children found it increasingly difficult to follow instructions when they had to attend to more details, and even more difficult when the number of conditions to be kept in mind were increased.

It was important to identify what obstacles to learning had to be overcome in order to make further progress. Input was adequate as they were able to keep time to a simple rhythm when they walked around the circle. Output was intact, as they could perform the separate elements of each movement required by the exercises. Processing what to do and how to do it was the obstacle which the children could not overcome when they reached the limit of their ability, either because there were too many details which required attention or because they could not attend to all the conditions. Their response as a group deteriorated when they ceased to use feedback from the actions of their colleagues to guide their own activities. The result was general confusion. What the children needed in order to develop their use of numbers was further experience of processing numbers and using the appropriate feedback in gross motor activities.

The conditions which the children had to meet in order to succeed with the exercises were to make the right movements in time to the music and to attend to the pathway set by the circle of chairs while maintaining a set relationship to their partners, and, as a relatively long-term aim, to reach the end point at the right time. The use of numbers was how many movements to make to each beat of the music, how many children made up a group which moved along together, and how many chairs to pass beyond the chair from which they started, when they came to the end of the exercise. A more difficult use of numbers was introduced when the precise character of their movements followed a particular pattern: to hop and to skip alternately. Children who are confused when they try to put these conditions into operation are confused by all kinds of number work which depend on symbolic processes, like addition or subtraction, of a corresponding but higher level of organization.

The first exercise was as follows. Chairs were arranged in a circle, one for each child, who stood behind the chair at the start of the exercise. Each child had his special, tall hat, which he placed on his chair before beginning to go around the circle of chairs. A march was played on the piano and everyone marched around the outside of the circle of chairs until three circuits had been completed. The march stopped abruptly when the leading child reached the chair beyond the one from which he had started. Each child then took his hat, put it on, and waited to continue the exercise. So far, so good: the exercise was understood by all of the children, and though there was some occasional confusion, it was overcome by practice. The most difficult element of the response was to stop at the right time and at the right chair.

For the next exercise the chairs were arranged in pairs and the children had to march in pairs, with one behind putting his hands on the shoulders of the one in front. The inevitable problems arose, but interruptions were temporary and did not bring the exercise to a halt. One child wanted to overtake the others; another refused to put her hands on her partner's shoulders; another child opted out. Every pair experienced some difficulties in adapting their movements to one another, in keeping to the convention (arms on shoulders) and moving at the same pace: processing and feedback caused problems. With encouragement from the teachers, the set order was resumed when input from the music was reinforced by personal exhortation from the teacher. Without such help the group would have drifted apart.

The same problems were met again, rather more intensively, when this exercise was tried with groups of three children: the same problems, the same solutions.

The next stage was to introduce a new condition: a simple dance step while going round the circle, hopping and skipping in time to the music. This created major obstacles. It was no longer possible to pick out the individuals who did not keep to the rules. Every child made mistakes and did so at a rate which made individual corrections impossible. There was a general obstacle to processing. All the children found it disproportionately more difficult to keep going the alternating motor sequence of hopping and skipping than to keep to the previous rules about their grouping or finding the right chair at the end of the rounds. Groups of chairs and groups of children are cardinal groups which can be seen and which remain constant throughout the exercise; alternating movements make up an ordinal series, and if one of the movements goes wrong, the next movement is likely to fail. A motor sequence calls for continuous adjustments and adaptations so that the movements remain co-ordinated with each other.

The exercise was beyond the capacity of the childern, and practising it without modification would have been merely frustrating. The elements which made up the complex whole had to be learnt one at a time: the children had to learn to hop and skip in succession, without reference to music, groupings or direction, before imposing the other conditions. The point is laboured in order to emphasize that there are complex experiences which mentally handicapped children can only gain by learning them one stage at a time. The exercise which has just been described and the difficulties faced by the children when they first tried to do it show that they could not have extended their motor experiences with respect to numeracy unaided. There might be many opportunities to developn experiences about the relationships between numbers and actions in free play, but children can only benefit from the experience when they can manage to cope with the conditions for learning by their own efforts. The wider understanding of number concepts depends on learning from many complex experiences. Mentally handicapped children can often be taught how to integrate the various stages of a complex of actions, and thereby to extend and develop their conceptual understanding. They can only develop their understanding, however, when systematic teaching has enabled them to gain a wide range of experiences. Without this, they are left with a secondary handicap, and their learning is fragmented and without significance.

Plans for moderately handicapped children

Parents and teachers are sometimes uncertain whether a particular child should start school in a normal infant class, or whether he should have some kind of special education. Children in this category often seem to be able to function at the normal level for their age on some occasions, but fail to do so at other times. They are often children who communicate little or who are easily distracted and perhaps also clumsy. There might occasionally be signs that such a child can manage a problem which calls for a superior level of ability. It is difficult to predict the future development of a child of 5 even by very careful psychometric assessments because there are so many factors which need to be weighed. A child's progress at school does not depend only on his academic potential; it is closely bound up with his personality and also very much influenced by his home background. A child whose correct placement is in doubt is usually admitted to an assessment class.

Some of the answers to the first question, about what children are usually able to do before they start school, are formulated in the referral to the assessment class: there might be problems about playing with other children, or behaviour problems and difficulties of adaptation to rules and social conventions, or the child might have learning problems due to his inadequate sensori-motor development or his lack of social skills. The work in an assessment is planned in a way which enables the teacher to recognize gaps in the experiences of the children and to show how their learning is fragmented.

The answers to the second question, about the skills and competences children usually acquire when they enter school, are provided by the curriculum and by the teaching plans of the normal infant class. The third, question, about the skills the child will need to manage at his next stage of development can be taken from the work of the second-year classes, and the two answers together set out the aims set for the children in the assessment class.

An assessment class needs to be sufficiently small to allow for detailed individual observations of the children and to enable the teacher to work with small groups of children or with individuals.

The following discussion is concerned with problems of communication and with teaching plans for non-communicating children. The aim is to show both how the plans are designed and what to look for when a plan is formulated.

Teaching plans for children with communication problems

Communication problems in infancy are sufficiently common to warrant a diagnostic label: the non-communicating child. The age when the problem is recognized varies almost as much as the nature of the underlying causes. Sometimes there are associated sensory or motor handicaps, but these tend to be slight and cannot 'explain' the lack of communication: many children who have far more serious handicaps manage to communicte perfectly well (but then their problems are recognized and allowances are made for them). There are usually emotional problems and these often involve other members of the family; they may be easy to identify but it can be very difficult to treat them. Non-communicating children need to be taught in an undemanding setting in which they can develop at their own pace, without any pressure to conform to a 'normal' pattern. They need to be in small groups with opportunities for individual attention.

Because communication is the area in which development is especially delayed, there is a corresponding lack of development of social feedback—the inevitable result of lack of contact with other people. The insecure and uncertain manner in which non-communicating children respond to new situations and their tendency to withdraw rather than to risk failure reflect their general confusion. They miss vital opportunities for developing their use and understanding of symbols by failing to use speech and by not asking question. Non-communicating children often find it difficult to change from one acitvity to another; at least they resist doing so and are reluctant to follow instructions. Clues which might seem to be obvious are missed, perhaps because they have failed to use information which is usually picked up as part of normal social intercourse. When a non-communicating child begins to read and write, he is often more confused than other children by the orientation of letters, especially by 'd', 'b', 'q' and 'p', though other letters or numbers are also formed the wrong way or put in the wrong order. Such problems are usually associated with confusion about other sequences or new arrangements of any kind. Failure to communicate deprives these children of help which other children gain unwittingly when parents and others respond to their questions or correct their mistakes: lack of interaction becomes a general, secondary obstacle to learning.

Non-communicating children withdraw from contact, stand or sit still, in fact 'freeze' when approached by an unfamiliar person. A direct approach merely reinforces this reaciton and does not help. Approach should come from the child, and so the teacher needs to attract the child to him by actions rather than by a direct invitation; the teacher might play with favourite soldiers, cars, a castle or a dolls' house, so that the child can watch and join in when he knows the way in which the teacher's activities are developing; when the child finds that his predictions about her actions are right, he can involved himself directly.

Once the child has become involved in a game, his level of development can be gauged: his skills, his use of inforamtion and any emotional overtones in his play. It is characteristic for such children to fit into an ongoing pattern of events, but to resist responding to a direct personal, verbal approach. The difference between the two situations is that, for instance, once a game has started, it follows a foreseeable plan and allows the child to anticipate how and when to make his contribution; a general request like 'come and play with me' is open-ended and does not tell the child what 'play' will involve. There could be risks of failure, misunderstanding or punishments; verbal encouragement cannot removed this kind of uncertainty, but active demonstration shows what is meant, so that fear can be set aside.

Problems caused by the need to make a choice or to take decisions can be kept to a minimum by using well-established skills and thoroughly familiar situations. A child who is confused when he tries to draw (visual representation) or when he is writing (symbolic representation) is helped more by gross motor exercises which give him experience of visual or symbolic representations than by just practising drawing or writing: for instance, arranging forms in the school hall so that they make up a complicated pathway with points of choice and alternative routes gives the children experience of choosing to go right or left, turning back or going forward, and pursuing one child or avoiding another. Gross motor experiences which develop symbolic representations can be created in music and movement, exercises, miming, gymnastics and 'role taking' in various games. In each case the situations are arranged so that choices and decisions are taken about the same kinds of problem posed by the fine motor skill—drawing or writing—but that the responses are apart of a gross motor exercise. Needless to say, the children continue to practise drawing and writing at other times; the gross motor exercises are designed to help with problems which hindered the development of a fine motor skill, and the progressive improvement of that skill shows when the gap in experience has been bridged.

3

Teaching of Physically Handicapped Children

THE particular handicap of the children whose learning problems will be discussed in this chapter is that they lack control over their movements. These are jerky and uneven, and when a movement approaches completion, it becomes shaky; there is an intention tremor. Children who lack control over their movements cannot articulate words clearly, and it may be hard to understand their speech. Their muscle tone is usually spastic, though there are some children who are athetoid and their muscle tone is flaccid. All grades of severity of motor incoordination exist, and different parts of the body can be more or less affected by the disorder, or they may be spared altogether. The incoordination is due to brain damage and it cannot be abolished, but the amount of control a child has over his movements varies according to circumstances: motor control is best when the child is at ease, and worst when he is excited, anxious or under stress.

Movements always become more incoordinated when a response needs to be changed or adapted. The change might be to move in a different direction or to move at a different rate; it could be to change from using one hand to using the other; it could also be to change from one stage of a complex action and going on to the next stage. Changes which belong to a planned sequence of actions cause less disruption of movement than changes caused by trying to respond to an unforeseen event or trying to correct a mistake. A general change in the environment can be as disruptive as a change in the pattern of moving: the effect of a stranger coming into the room, or the impact of changing a familiar routine, is familiar to all teachers. The movements of physically handicapped children always become more incoordinated when something unexpected happens.

Lack of co-ordination is not the only abnormal feature of the responses of physically handicapped children who may be unable to select the right response to a particular demand. When copying the drawing of an angle, for instance, a physically handicapped child can perceive that one of the lines is horizontal and that the other one is oblique, but when he draws his copy, the oblique line goes in the wrong direction:

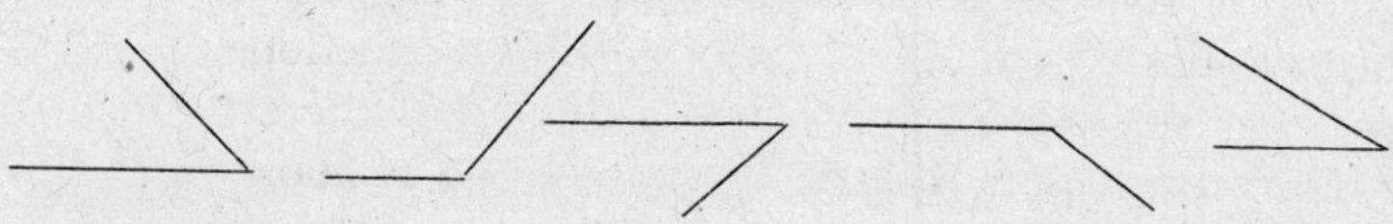

original copy or copy or copy or copy

When a child has just made a wrong copy of an angle he can be asked if his copy is the same as the original, and he will assert that the two are the same. If, however, he is shown that angle again, together with a right and a wrong copy, he will be in no doubt which is the right copy: he can identify the right product without being able to produce it by himself. Physically handicapped children are often confused by problems which refer to spatial orientation.

Children whose movements are incoordinated often become confused when they try to follow instructions which call for a series of responses. Their confusion increases when the successive stages of a task depend on each other for their outcome. The instructions are understood, and the child can repeat them and say what they mean, but if there are obstacles to output and feedback, they must be overcome in order to enable him to carry out a complex instruction. All the children who are taking part in a music and movement exercise may well be able to understand the instruction 'get up and start walking around the circle when the music starts,' without making any moves to get up at the right time. Detailed observation of their behaviour shows that it does change when the music begins: the children stop chattering to each other and some of them make rhythmic movements with their bodies and arms, but they do not get up until they are reminded to do so. If the obstacle to learning is caused by a handicap, so that the children cannot act on the instruction, then they learn gradually to associate one step of the action with the next if they are taught by repeating the experience, but they do not learn to deal with complex instructions.

A similar problem exists when a physically handicapped child is given the instruction to 'run your finger along the four sides of that door,' and his response is to make a curved upward sweep with his arm and then a general downward sweep which ignores all the corners and might not touch any of the sides. His failure to interpret the instructions accurately is often put down to laziness or lack of interest, but concentrated attempts to attend properly and to look at what he is doing merely result in frustrations for the child and his teacher. Another common experience occurs with children doing number work who have reached a stage when they understand what is meant by units, tens and hundreds and when they have mastered the elements of simple addition and subtraction. Combining these skills in order to add 8 to 65 shows the confusion which is created when they try to apply theory to practice. Under normal circumstances, children learn to overcome their own problems by constant repetition of the task, but physically handicapped children, whose learning problems are caused by the handicap, need more than simple repetition in order to learn.

Physically handicapped children find it difficult to deal with all kinds of changes as well as lacking control over their movements. Lack of motor control is due to some form of brain damage, and it is tempting to attribute the other learning problems of these children to the same cause. There could, however, be other reasons which are due to the special conditions of the early development of spastic babies and children, and which will become more apparent when their early development is compared with that of other children who are also physically handicapped but who do not lack control over their movements.

Effects of physical handicaps on early development and learning

There are many physical handicaps which can interfere with development during childhood, but not all of them disrupt the learning process. Children can be deprived of many experiences by a handicap, and their development may be hedged in by special conditions, and yet their learning processes continue to develop without becoming fragmented and secondarily handicapped. They may feel frustrated by their handicap and perhaps develop all sorts of emotional complications which call for treatment in their own right, but their learning processes remain intact. There are metabolic disorders which stunt growth and weaken children, and there are deformities of bones and muscles which stop children from taking part in games or learning skills which need strength and effort to succeed; but provided the child is able to control his own actions, he can draw on his experiences, and his learning does not become fragmented.

Handicaps which interfere with the control of voluntary movements impose special conditions on early development and on early learning experiences, which do not apply to other handicaps. A spastic baby, or one whose movements are lacking in co-ordination for some other reason, may well respond as actively to stimulation as any other baby, but if his responses are bizarre and disrupted by muscle spasms, he cannot repeat his movements at will. A baby who cannot repeat his movements cannot meet the conditions needed to learn from the circular reactions to which Piaget ascribes the very earliest learning experiences of a body: all his early experiences become uncertain when the baby cannot adapt to the usual pattern of early learning.

The elements of a circular reaction are that the baby makes a movement which has a recognizable effect on the environment, and this stimulates him to make further movements to repeat the effect. In order to do so, he must be able to identify that particular effect (or he could not try to recreate it) and he must have enough control over his movements to be able to repeat them. He begins to learn when his movements change from being chance actions and become deliberate attempts to produce a particular effect. The motor incoordination which is the handicap of the children we are considering is described as an intention tremor, because movements become progressively more uncontrolled as they approach completion. The motor disorder of a spastic child therefore becomes particularly disabling at that stage of a circular reaction when movements change from being random acts and become intentional: motor incoordination interferes specifically with learning from circular reactions, and no other physical handicap interferes with the process of learning in this way.

The movements of a baby who is spastic are interrupted when groups of muscles become tense and contract together in a spasm, instead of tensing and relaxing in a co-ordinated manner. Spasms differ from voluntary movements because they are incidental and unintended, and occur as unwanted interruptions of the voluntary movement. When the change in the environment which stimulates a circular reaction is brought about by a spasm, the baby would need to induce the same spasm again to repeat the effect, or he would need to produce the effect in some other way. In either case, he cannot maintain the circular reaction: the spasm is not under voluntary control and so it cannot be repeated in its original form, while if he resorts to a different movement to get the effect, he loses the essential experience of a circular reaction, which is to get the same effect by making the same movement.

Other physical handicaps may make certain movements difficult or they may prevent a baby from creating particular effects, for instance if the limbs are stunted or if some of his muscles are undeveloped or paralysed; but when he does create an effect, he can repeat the same movement again and learn from the experience. The effect of the handicap might be that the experiences of the afflicted children are less rich and that they learn less than they might under normal circumstances, but their learning processes are not threatened because their movements are co-ordinated.

Early training programmes for physically handicapped children

Early exercises for physically handicapped babies are developed along the lines set out in chapter 12, but with special emphasis on the conditions of learning which should enable the child to perform actions and achieve effects by his own efforts. As always, the training programme should ensure that the child gains the experiences he needs in order to learn, and also that he develops his skills and applies them to new situations so that he can make further progress. Some of the exercises have been mentioned already, but as the contexts were different, it is not helpful to the following discussion to refer back every time.

The first-learning experience of mentally handicapped babies was learning to anticipate being fed by stimulating the lips to move before inserting the teat, and this is also the first response which can be used for training a physically handicapped baby. A physically handicapped baby needs to be given orderly experiences and he needs to be trained to anticipate orderly events. This can be done at an early stage by repetitive patterns of touching him lightly with a cloth, for instance to touch the right hand, the right shoulder and the right side of his mouth in succession. He learns where and when he will feel the next touch and experiences an orderly sequence of events. Gentle, rhythmic stroking or massage and steady rocking in the mother's arms are other orderly experiences, and it is no accident that they are ways of calming any baby when he is upset.

Before a physically handicapped baby can be trained to make a welcoming gesture when his parent comes to stand by the side of his cot, he should be given exercises which stimulate him to follow moving objects with his eyes and to turn his head towards a sound, so that he will turn towards his mother when she calls to him, and watch her hands when they move in his direction. His responses can be reinforced by touching the side of his face from the direction of the sound or by stroking his forehead in the direction of a movement which he should watch, and he might be given extra help by letting him smell something he likes from the side to which he should turn.

One of the first differentiated movements which can be trained even in cases of severe physical handicap is to bring the hand up to the mouth. This is done in the same way as described for blind and deaf children. A baby who has had experiences of being touched on his hand, his shoulder and his mouth, and who has learned to turn his head towards a sound, can be induced to suck a cloth if he has also learned to make anticipatory lip movements before the teat is put in his mouth. These actions can then be combined into a relatively complex series which starts by inducing him to turn towards a sound, touching his hand with the cloth and then getting him to suck at the cloth at one end, while keeping the other end on his hand. Babies very often grasp the end of a cloth at the same time as closing their lips on the other end and sucking it.

Turning the head in response to visual and auditory stimuli is an early differentiated action which enables the baby to take in information from particular sources; it is the first directional response from which others can follow. A baby who cannot turn his head or follow a movement with his eyes is unlikely to be able to be stimulated by looking into a mirror, and the development of his sense of identity, as distinct from other people, will be correspondingly delayed. Physically handicapped babies need help to develop differentiated responses, rather than to be stimulated to respond, which is what mentally handicapped babies need. It is not possible to abolish the motor incoordination, but physically handicapped babies can be given experiences about systematic, consecutive events from an early age. Stroking one arm and touching the hand, followed by doing the same to the other arm and hand, helps him to identify the arms and the hands, even if there is little that he can yet do with them. Touching can be coupled with passive movements to give a combined experience in which the touch acts as the signal that a part of his body will be moved. By combining simple experiences which the baby can learn to anticipate, he can be given the experiences of circular reactions which he cannot attain by his own movements, and his learning can develop in spite of the handicap.

Bath time is a particularly important period for the play and development of physically handicapped babies. A warm bath is relaxing and a spastic baby can achieve a greater degree of control over his movements while he is in his bath than at almost any other time. They toys with which he can play in his bath are very important; they should give him opportunities to pour from cups and cans, to push them arond as they float, submerge them and let them jump up agian. A baby can gain a great deal from the examples of playing in his bath given to him by his mother, and at the same time, he learns to imitate her.

Physically handicapped babies usually do not develop the skill to sit unsupported until late infancy, or they may not be able to sit at all without help, and it is most important for learning and development that, from the age of about four months on, a baby spend part of his time sitting up. Provided that his posture is right, that the periods of sitting are not too long and that there are times in between when he lies prone, there should be no danger of developing postural deformities. The advice of a physiotherapist should be sought if there is uncertainty with respect to sitting. While the baby is sitting, he should play, facing a mirror, and his toys need to be arranged so that they do not fall out of reach by suspending some of them and by typing others to his chair. If the hanging toys are of suitable size and weight, the baby can set up circular reactions with them and gain experience about his own movements.

Physically handicapped babies are slow to start babbling and to make differentiated sounds. For many babies, copying sounds belongs to the first experiences of imitation, which is such a significant stimulus for early learning. A taped recording of a normally developing baby's babbling can be played back regularly to a physically handicapped baby to help him gain from the recorded patterns of sounds. The development of all the differentiated movements which are usually brought into play by imitating, copying and by giving and taking is delayed by a physical handicap. Instead of waiting until the baby can respond accurately enough to take a full part in such play, it should be adapted so that the baby's role is to show that the can anticipate what will happen next by making a generalized response, instead of having to make a specific response in order to maintain the game. When there is a physical handicap, the emphasis of early teaching plans should be on developing the baby's anticipation of details in the sequences of actions and involving him actively in the progress of actions so that he learns to observe in a differentiated manner.

It is sometimes difficult to strike the right balance between training the movements of a physically handicapped infant and giving him the experience of events which will stimulate his learning and general development. If it is accepted that a child's motives for replacing simple responses by complex action at a higher level of organization are that he cannot gain the effects of new experiences without doing so, then the development of his ability to observe should follow a similar pattern. If he can be engaged to take an active part in the evnets which surround him, then he is also faced with a need to organize his observations in order to follow what is going on. Training him to observe is at least as important as training his movements.

The process of training the movements of a physically handicapped child is very like the plan outlined for the training of mentally handicapped children in chapter 2, but the details of each complex movement need to be analysed so that they can be practised in stages. Physically handicapped children should be taught to plan their actions so that they can prepare to go on from one stage of a complex task to the next.

The three questions about the general development of other children at the same stage of development as the handicapped child serve two purposes: one is to ensure that the child has been actively engaged in a wide range of experiences, as described earlier in this chapter; the other is to plan in good time to practise the elements of complex actions which will be needed at the next stage of development, as set out in this chapter.

Successive stages of experiences for physically handicapped children

The successive stages of experience needed for all-round development are the same for all children, and for physically handicapped children this means planning along the following lines.

Differentiated movements of the whole body

For physically handicapped babies there are some movements which are mainly passive, such as straightening paralysed limbs, correcting the posture of the trunk, and some movements for the head and neck, and these need expert guidance from a physiotherapist. Other movements can be set going by eliciting a reflex response, like the movements of the limbs when the head is turned to one side or the other. Movements of this kind can be performed with the baby lying down, held on the lap or in a bath. Because of the handicap it is necessary to aid and assist when the physical problem of movement is too great. In doing so, attention to the state of tension or relaxation is important, and it may help to give anticipatory clues, for example by stroking the side to which the baby will turn before helping him to do so.

Differentiated responses of the limbs

To enable the child to reach, hold or grasp at something, active stabilizing of the rest of the body may be required at the same time. Movements of this kind are best carried out on the lap. All the early movements of a baby are generalized: he does not grasp just with his hands but with his arms, legs and, often, mouth at the same time. To wait for the differentiated movements to develop, when other, incidental movements have been eliminated, would waste much valuable time, so the infant should be provided with the experience of whatever action is involved, even when his response is a total body response; he will develop the refinements later. Success at an early stage is when the baby shows pleasure in the event and in the outcome; this shows that he is actively involved in the process.

Movements to place or relate objects to each other

By the time physically handicapped children have developed to a stage of trying to place their toys in particular positions and to use them in constructive fashion, they can be helped by setting the toys out for their use; it is likely that the mother will need to help by retrieving toys and replacing them for use. Toys can be attached to wooden bars or to sticks so that they can slide; or they can be suspended within reach of the baby so that he can move them about without losing them.

When a physically handicapped infant begins to shuffle around (physically handicapped infants tend to shuffle on their bottom, rather than crawl, and at a later stage this is a real impediment to learning to walk), set arrangements in space on the floor are useful. The basic pattern for this was described. By keeping to a regular pattern of setting out his toys, the infant learns where to find them. At this stage he should have a long mirror at floor level so that he can see himself when he is playing.

Responses to set patterns of objects

This is an extension of the previous phase. Physically handicapped infants play a passive role in many daily events, like feeding, washing and dressing. Anticipatory clues should be introduced into every situation of this kind to encourage the active participation of the baby.

Inferring and demonstrating relationships and anticipating events

The restricted abilities of physically handicapped children usually mean that they have few contacts with other children, though the need for special help, such as physiotherapy, gives them opportunities to meet different adults. Learning to play with other children is vitally important for the child's development, and the time spent aiding and assisting him to make such play possible is time well spent. It is important at all times to support his active participation and involvement in taking decisions, particularly at times when he is being given help. If his decision can be foreseen to lead to a mistake, it should still be endorsed so that he can learn and recognize how the mistake came about; there is always a risk of fragmented learning.

Co-ordinating relationships

This is encouraged by planning for all routine engagements in which the child takes part: going for a walk, shopping, meeting friends, as well as by active participation in household routines. Every kind of preparation for familiar events helps the child to learn to plan his own actions.

Skilled use of the whole body in social interactions

Music and movement are as helpful for the development of physically handicapped children as for others. Learning to organize movements in time to a rhythm and to anticipate other movements accurately is part of generally, learning to organize and control movements. The actual movements can be simple, but cuing their timing by musicial rhythms is a preparation for planned and systematic movements in future.

Skilled uses of the limbs and fine manual skills

The ability to master fine movements of the hands may still be at a rudimentary level at stages of development which usually take for granted that fine finger skills can be applied. Free play with sand and water, moulding with dough or plasticine and collage work are useful experiences for physically handicapped children to work with their hands, without having to adapt their movements to details which they cannot manage. Such play gives handicapped children motor experiences which other children gain from more demanding forms of playing; the significant aspect is that the child will play actively and without assistance.

Specific practice for a particular skill

This is important for all children. For physically handicapped children aids like electric typewriters may be necessary to learn to write; indeed, in very severe cases, a typewriter may be the only way in which the child can communicate with words. Close co- operation between home and school is essential, and, whenever possible, children should be provided with the same tools at home and at school so that what they learn at school can also be done, free from supervision, when they are at home.

Practical illustrations of teaching plans for physically handicapped children

The following two examples illustrate the application of teaching plans for different degrees of incoordination. In the most severe cases, every response creates as many problems for the observer as for the child. The observer has to make sense of the mixture of distorted movements and their core of intention; the child becomes frustrated because his attempts become more incoordinated as he approaches his goal. In extreme cases, the effort to sit still is as exhausting as any attempt to move.

The first illustration refers to an extreme instance of this kind. He was an adolescent boy, intelligent, able to understand speech perfectly and to think in terms of abstractions, but with a very serious motor handicap: he could not even sit in a wheelchair without being strapped in because any attempted movement had such repercussions that he was flung out of the chair if he was not firmly restrained. Motor skills were minimal and he had to be wheeled around in his chair by others. Only an expert could understand his speech and this required much time and patience.

The first aim was to create some kind of experience of active but orderly motor responses so that he could at least sit in his chair. He was a young man of unusual ability, who could use a specially adapted electric typewriter, and because he could reason well, the object of the exercises could be easily explained to him. The aim was to teach him to perform rhythmic movements and to keep on with the movements while listening to instructions about plans to change the movements so that he could plan ahead to make the change. His biggest problem was the inability to sit in a chair without restraints, and this was largely due to the violent movements he made whenever he observed some change in his surroundings. If he could learn to observe, without responding by moving when a change took place, he might be able to stay in the chair without restraint.

A simple pattern of movements which he could perform was to pat his knee with his hand. The exercise started when he and the instructor were sitting facing each other alone in the room. After an initial pause, he was given the following instruction, which is quoted in full because listening to the instruction was as important for the exercise as acting on it. 'I want you to sit still and listen to my instructions. Do not move until I ask you to do so. I shall give you plenty of warning, so remain sitting still for the present. I am going to ask you to pat your knee with your right hand and to keep to a rhythm. Don't start until I ask you to do so. The rhythm is the same as the rhythm of my hand when I begin to tap my knee. I shall begin to tap my knee in a moment but I want you to sit still. After you have started to pat your knee, I shall give you further instructions. Each time, I want you to continue without changing what you are doing, until I have told you what to do and how to do it. Start patting your knee when I nod my head downwards.'

The instructions had to be careful and long in order to give the boy enough time to settle down for the beginning of the exercise. Whenever it seemed as though the instructions interrupted the pattern of his movements (so that he lost the rhythm or went into spasm), a long further introduction was necessary to allow him to regain his steady state. At first he went into spasm in response to every change, so that the tone of voice of the instruction had to remain even, and the words had to be spoken in a slow, steady manner which was more like hypnosis than a conversation.

The first change in the pattern of his movements was to tap the other knee with his left hand, then one foot at a time. The introduction of every change followed the manner of the introductory instruction. Each new action was brought into the ongoing rhythm, one at a time, and then so that two or more movements were made in succession. When he was able to make four movement responses rhythmically in sequence, the individual movements were made more complex. First, he had to raise his hand higher when patting his knee; this meant using a slower rhythm; then he had to make an additional arm movement by extending the elbow after patting his knee, and, after that, to move his hand over to the other shoulder before bringing the hand back down again.

Throughout the period of instruction, alll external distractions had to be excluded. The whole process required the full concentration of pupil and instructor, but it worked. He was able to sit in his wheelchair at ease and went on to learn other rhythmic movements, and at other times he was able to plan successful actions.

Physical handicap and developmental delay

Fortunately such extreme forms of motor handicap are rare. The following example concerns a boy who had a milder degree of spasticity but who had considerable learning problems. He was the only child of devoted parents who ignored the early signs of developmental retardation. They put down his slow development to his physical handicap and resisted the idea of special education. He remained in the infant class of his school for three years and then saw the move to a special school as a sign of failure. He became emotionally disturbed, sometimes he refused to go to school, and when he was taken, he fought, kicked and screamed.

He was 12 years old when the following teaching plans were set up. He was making little progress at school, could not read or write, and he was confused by numbers, notions about time and serial arrangements. At home, on the other hand, he had developed acceptable social behaviour and always seemed more able than at school, where his learning seemed to be generally fragmented.

At the developmental level seen at school he would have been expected to paly with older children, engage in simple pre-reading and pre-writing exercises, and take part in introductory games in order to develop number concepts. The next stage of progress would have been expected to come when he became proficient with these early skills. The obstacles to learning were that he was short-sighted (input), all his reactions were very slow (processing), his movements were somewhat incoordinated (output), and he relied on his parents to tell him if his actions were right or wrong (feedback).

The initial plan was to set out gross motor exercises modelled on the fine motor exercises he could not manage at school, and they were presented to him in a way which enabled him to work out his own plan of response without having to rely on his parents to tell him what to do or when to do it.

Serial actions and motor control

The starting point was to adapt his actions to certain simple conditions: to walk along a special path. Bricks were set out at close enough intervals so that he could step from one to the next, and another kind of pathway was made by putting up planks to connect one brick to the next; in both situations he had to adapt his walk to the pathway and balance on the bricks or on the planks. There were three variations of this exercise:

1. The pathway can simply lead from a starting point to an end point—like drawing a line. The start and the finish should be specially defined, for example by having an extra brick on either side of the plank or on each side of a pathway of bricks at the first and last brick.

2. A pathway is made up of a series of bricks placed in groups of three to six bricks close in line with a wider space which separates the groups from each other, or a similar pathway is made up of series of planks of different lengths—like lines of writing with words and spaces between the words.
3. Pathways are devised involving points of choice where two paths diverge in different directions to bring in more complex adaptations to get the right path for the right end point and to remain upright and balanced when changing direction.

After he was familiar with the initial exercises, more complex actions were introduced: while walking along the pathway he carried a stick to push a ball along the side of the path. The combined action makes more demands on co-ordination and balance, and creates problems about feedback: whether to attend to placing the feet or to look where the ball is rolling.

This exercise becomes considerably more difficult when two sticks are used to push along two balls, one on each side of the planks. The additional problem, apart from having to attend to all three components of the exercise, is to keep the two balls rolling forward at the same rate. The exercise can also be changed to put greater emphasis on planning: guiding a ball along a route which weaves from side to side between successive bricks. In these cases, problems caused by incoordinated movements were overcome by planning actions in advance.

The next aim was to apply skills he was practising to other uses like learning to ride a bicycle. This combines the same kinds of co-ordination and attention to balance and forward movement, but follows a more rapid time scale and requires more precise, fine adjustments.

Various exercises and games in which he had to aim cars or roll a ball along a pathway, as set out in chapter 2, were used to teach him to aim for a particular goal and adapt the force of his impulse to the object he was using.

Pieces of Lego were used for exercises which required fine motor skills. At first he had to learn to copy a three-dimensional model accurately and then to plan a number of constructions from a limited number of pieces, for instance a house, a farm and a block of flats. The copy depends on accurate observation and application; the combined plan involves choices and decisions and judgements about the end result. From these exercises, he went on to make up models from two-dimensional plans.

His spatial memory was trained by an exercise in which he was given a model which was placed behind a screen, so that he could only explore by touch, using tactile clues to build his copy. In order to succeed, he had to use his memory of the tactile sensation to arrange the pieces for his copy and to judge if his copy was right. At the end he could confirm that his copy was right, but he was not allowed to look at the original and the copy together until he had stated whether the copy was right or wrong. Another exercise showed that he was confused when he had to use a combination of clues to make a judgement: the model he had to copy was made up of pieces of different colours and sizes. This exercise posed problems which are more closely related to number work, and it depends on cardination and ordination: selecting pieces of the right size and colour and placing them at the right place in relation to the other pieces.

Along with all the other exercises, he was given increasing responsibilities for household tasks, fetching and carrying, shopping and remembering what to get and where to get it. An exercise which took place within the house was a more general form of the Lego building behind the screen. His mother placed an arrangement of common household articles on a table in one room, and the boy's task was to copy the same arrangement on the kitchen table. While he was doing so, he was practising his use of spatial memory, and he had to interpret his mother's description of her arrangement and formulate his own questions whenever he was uncertain about her instruction: it was quicker to call out his question than to go to her room and look for himself.

A fine motor exercise which combined the training of spatial memory with practice at drawing was as follows: his father drew an object or a 'shape' on a blank page. The boy traced over the drawing until he thought he could remember it, and the drawing was then turned over while the boy took another blank sheet and tried to repeat the drawing from memory. If he thought he had made a mistake, the copy was removed and put to one side while he took the original and went over it again until he felt ready for the next attempt from memory. The process was repeated until he said confidently that the copy was right, but he was only allowed to make a direct comparison between the originals and his copies at the end of the exercise.

Writing exercises were presented in the following separate stages:

1. A short passage was read with him.
2. The passage was set out for him in large letters and he was asked to cancel each word:
   ~~THE~~ ~~CAT~~ ~~WAS~~ ~~IN~~ ~~THE~~ ~~ROOM~~.
3. The same words were repeated and this time he had to underline them:
   THE CAT WAS IN THE ROOM.
4. The next stage was to cancel each letter and then to cancel the word.
   ~~THE~~ ~~CAT~~ ~~WAS~~ ~~IN~~ ~~THE~~ ~~ROOM~~.
5. Only then was he asked to copy each letter under the written example:
   THE CAT WAS IN THE ROOM.
   THE CAT WAS IN THE ROOM.

Every one of the exercises just described was at the limit of his ability when he first tried it. The next step was to learn to type, which he did with such pleasure that it became the reward for doing other work. Handwritten exercises were left until he had mastered spelling on the typewriter and he could arrange the letters in the right order.

The aim of the teaching programme was to get him to plan his actions; the form taken by the exercises was designed to fill in gaps in his learning and experience. Fortunately he had parents who were keen to work with him and who did so without inducing stress at the same time.

4

Teaching of Socially Handicapped Children

CHILDREN become socially handicapped when they consistently ignore the impact of their behaviour on other people and when their development is insensitive to social influences and unaffected by their social experiences. Social handicaps are caused by the circumstances and conditions in which a child grows up; they are not due to psychiatric disorders which damage the emotional development of neurotic or psychotic children, and they are not due to the child's inability to learn. The child is handicapped when he cannot deal with conditions or manage situations which call for a flexible approach and a readiness to adapt his responses to those of other children. When there are no other children about, his activities can develop successfully, at such times there is no handicap because there is no need for social integration. The impact of a social handicap is twofold: it prevents the social development of the handicapped child, and his behaviour interferes with the development of other children; when there is a socially handicapped child in a class at school, his behaviour can make it impossible for the others to learn.

Social development fails when the circumstances in which a child grows up leave him confused about the significance of his social interactions. The result of his confusion is that he cannot learn to anticipate how his social encounters will develop or plan to meet events as they arise. The cause of the confusion can be either neglect and lack of guidance or exposure to inconsistent and conflicting forms of management.

Neglected children

Children who are neglected in their early years develop their own standards for their behaviour, and the younger they are, the more immature their standards will be. When a mother imposes controls on the behaviour of a child, she can draw on years of experience to guide her decisions, while a child who is left to take decisions for himself is continually, faced with new situations in which he cannot refer back to any relevant experiences for guidance, so that he is driven to develop his own special guidelines for his behaviour. Personal motives for emotional satisfaction, gain or pleasure become the dominant factors which guide the development of neglected children, to the detriment of their social interactions and social integration. Some children are sufficiently outgoing to assert themselves socially in spite of unfavourable circumstances by their dominating and aggressive behaviour; other children fail because they are too weak or too fearful to assert themselves, and they withdraw from the company of others and flee into the world of their own fantasies.

When children who have been neglected at home come to school, their circumstances change, and understanding teachers sometimes achieve miracles of success when they teach socially handicapped infants how to plan their activities and how to anticipate and predict the social consequences of their behaviour. Children who have been neglected are often keen to learn when they are given the opportunity to do so; they are usually shy at first, but they learn to seek the attention of their teacher. They tend to pick up information in a haphazard way and their experiences and learning are fragmented. They need to learn to conform to rules, to take their turns in group activities and to observe how situations develop before rushing in with an unplaned response. Often such children need speech therapy in order to widen their vocabulary, to clarify their articulation and to improve their ability to express themselves. Fine finger skills usually need to be practised, and they need all kinds of experiences of ordering objects and planning the successive stages of complex activities. They also need to learn to judge the outcome of their actions independently. Above all, they need help to learn how to play with other children.

Children who have been exposed to conflicting experiences

When children are confused about social interactions because they have been exposed to conflicting kinds of management, they cannot anticipate how adults who are responsible for their care will respond to their behaviour. This happens when a child goes in and out of care through no fault of his own, and it also happens when children are passed around from one babysitter or childminder to another while the parents work or are otherwise engaged. If the child is sometimes expected to be obedient, to conform to a routine and to accept strict controls, while at other times, in different situations, he is left to his own devices so long as he does not disturb his parents, he is likely to be confused by both experiences. Some children learn to adapt to conflicting experinces by keeping them apart and by developing specific responses for each situation; if they can do this, they do not become socially handicapped. Other children become confused and cannot adapt because the demands made upon them are inconsistent in each case, so that there is no way in which they can develop any appropriate set of responses. If children are socially handicapped because they are confused about conflicting adult controls, they learn to ignore adult interventions and avoid them when they can do so.

It is difficult to help a child at school if he is socially handicapped because he is confused by the implications of adult controls. A child who has learned to avoid adults and who ignores their admonitions does not learnt o modify his behaviour when attempts are made to help him to conform. What tends to happen is that children who are handicapped because they are confused by controls instigate disturbances by goading other children to be mischievous while the teacher's attention is elsewhere, and then sit back and wait for the effects. It is sometimes difficult to be sure that the effects were due to interference of the handicapped child because of the skilful way in which such a child can engineer what happens. Actions of this kind are very difficult to change because so many other children become involved, and the teacher's first need is to re-establish order in the class, before he can deal with the cause of the disturbance; and when he can do so, it is usually too late to be able to do anything about it. The handicapped child stoutly denies his actions and refuses to relate his actions to their consequences.

The havoc which a socially handicapped child can cause in a classroom or on a playground is paralleled by the way he tends to break toys and destroy his own property and that of other children. Like his other disruptive actions, he usually breaks things when the teacher cannot take preventive action, and often does so in a way that puts the blame on another child. Socially handicapped children who are disturbed in this way are often excluded from class, perhaps to be looked after by the headteacher; unfortuantely, instead of learning to get on with their peers, they have to be kept away from them.

In order to counteract the effects of confusing and conflicting early experiences, the child needs to be placed in a stable household, perhaps with foster parents, where he can establish consistent expectations and develop a trusting relationship with adults. School certainly plays an important part in teaching and helping socially handicapped children, but the child needs to be sufficiently confident in the teacher before he can benefit from the experience. When he is ready to respond, he needs to learn the same skills which were set out for neglected children: learning to keep to rules at games, to take turns in an activity, to observe and fit in with the activities of other children, as well as making up for delays in the development of skills and consolidating fragmented experiences and learning.

Conflicting experiences can also be caused by inconsistencies of management at home which do not involve changing patterns of care. Parents who fight and quarrel with each other can damage the development of their children as seriously by their behaviour to each other as by abandoning them to various conflicting regimes of care. Children tend to respond to violence between their parents by developing a mixture of clinging and defiant behaviour. At times they seem to be equally indifferent to threats, cajolery or bribery; at other times they are demanding and will push their demands to their limits irrespective of their parents' anger or the punishments they receive.

The classroom behaviour of children whose social handicaps are due to parental violence is usually attention seeking and lacking in confidence. These children usually have a low opinion of their own abilities and destroy their work rather than face criticism. They can be greatly helped by an understanding teacher who can achieve a careful balance between support and attention and who can give the child opportunities for achieving success without apparent help. As before, planned activities, skills and communication should be given special attention, and the children should learn to accept frustrations without opting out of a situation.

Delinquent children

Children whose social handicaps are due to their membership of a delinquent family are only mentioned in passing, because they are not handicapped in the same way as other socially handicapped children. They are often well adjusted to their family and social group and have no learning handicap, though they may miss out at school if they are often truant. Delinquent children pose porblems because of their delinquent acts when they steal or cause damage to property; they may be sent to special residential schools by the courts, but the special management they receive is dictated by lack of adaptation to conventions, not lack of adaptation to people. They commit their misdemeanours when there are no adequate controls, and they act on the spur of the moment. For both these reasons, delinquency is not often changed by teaching, and it is often resistant to all other kinds of treatment.

Fragmented learning

Many children who are socially handicapped at the time they come to school benefit so much from their teaching that they can learn to overcome their handicap and continue successfully in the normal school system. Nevertheless there are some children who fail to respond sufficiently and whose handicaps become more troublesome and difficult to control as they grow older. They fail to acquire basic skills and are effectively unable to read or to write. Reading problems are often more obvious than writing problems because the latter are more easily disguised if a child can caopy from a sampale. Writing problems can pass unnoticed until the child tries to spell and write unaided. Good remedial education can overcome some of these problems, but it must cover wider aspects of experience than simple practice at the three Rs. Spatial orientation, seriation, cardination, left-right confusion and poor phonetics all pose problems which can be quite as serious as they are for other handicapped children. In addition there are all the problems of learning to keep to rules and conventions, and learning to adapt to the needs of other children.

It is often impossible to deal with all these problems in a normal classroom merely because there are too many children vying for the attention of the teacher. Thirty or more little children can be taught together if each one of them only requires occasional and brief attention to keep their efforts in the right direction. A socially handicapped child demands such consistent attention from the teacher that he must be neglected in order to do justice to the needs of the others. Obstacles mount throughout primary education because consistent attention to one child can only be achieved in small classes, and if there are several handicapped children in one class, the teacher's task becomes impossible

Children who remain socially handicapped when they come to the end of primary school education and who cannot meet the conditions needed to be successful at a comprehensive school are best educated at a special boarding school for maladjusted or disturbed children. The following account concerns children in this category, and so the three questions which refer to the abilities and the development of other children at about the age of eleven can be answered along these lines.

Existing skills

It is particularly difficult to gauge what the children were able to do before coming to special school because of their fragmented learning and their variable performance. Skills which seem easy in a quiet room, with the individual attention of the teacher, may be non-existent when there are distractions and other children about. The best level of performance is the best guide to the child's abilities becuase theoretically the best level should always be the aim if the conditions of learning can be geared to the needs of the child.

Skills which other children have at the same stage of development

The answer to the question about abilities which are usually attained at the stage of development reached by the child is particularly important when arranging teaching plans for socially handicapped children. Social skills, such as adapting to the needs of other children, understanding rules and the ability to conform to them, concentration span and perseverence at a task, and tolerance for frustrations, are always inadequately developed by sociallly handicapped children. They are ill-informed about current affairs, social systems such as the postal system, government or commerce; and their conduct in simple everyday situations like shopping, eating in a restaurant or looking for a book in a library can sometimes show bizarre confusions.

Skills to be expected at the next stage of development

Skills which can be expected at the next stage of development show what a wide range of work and experience needs to be offered in order to consolidate the existing, fragmented experience of the children into a useful whole. Socially handicapped children often show surprisingly strong motives for learning when they can be brought into a situation in which their needs can be met. They have failed so often and have had so many interruptions of schooling, for whatever reason, that the simple continuity of attendance and the concentrated attention available in a small class lead to rapid progress in the early stages of school attendance. Many problems which were caused by misunderstandings are overcome just because their work is not interrupted and because there are no major distractions. The aims for teaching, however, go beyond the straightforward academic curriculum and include the development of social skills; in fact, they should be particularly concerned with social skills. Examples will be brought in to indicate how motives for developing social co-operation can be incorporated in classroom teaching, as well as in the general life within the school.

Obstacles to learning

Obstacles to social input are due to lack of awareness of others and of their needs and wishes. Obstacles to processing are recognized in the limited attention span and the confusion of the children about order and relationships; they only have rudimentary notions about causality. They are able to discuss the importance of social issues but cannot act on their insights in practice. The only standard which can be applied is how the daily conduct of the child reflects his awareness of social relationships, and even then it remains an open question whether he will apply the same standards of social conduct when he is at home, away from the influences of the school. At such times he might revert to his initial, disordered state; indeed, this is what would be expected for quite a long time. Obstacles to processing also occur at school whenever a child has a temper tantrum, when processing seems to fail altogether and no amount of influence has any constructive effect because all the responses of the child become chaotic.

Output obstacles take many forms. The most striking is the general lack of fine motor skills of socially handicapped children. Gross motor skills may be clumsy when accurate, planned movements are required as in gymnastics, but they are often well developed and co-ordinated in games like football.

Feedback, especially social feeback, is blocked by major obstacles. The children have become confused by inconcistent management and neglect, and they need constant attention from the staff; someone in authority is needed to confirm the outcome of their actions because they are too unaware to judge for themselves. The teaching plans should therefore train the children to observe and evaluate what they do; they should practise making choices and taking decisions about social and academic issues. The result should be that the children become sensitive to social influences and that their actions pursue social aims.

The general plan

The general teaching plan started from gross motor experience and led on to use fine motor skills and symbolic expression. Although 11-year-old boys make use of motor skills and communicate, the application of their skills to social purposes showed how fragmented their experiences of social interactions had been. The children were badly equipped to adapt to the needs of others and so their social skills needed to be built up at every stage of development as part of their learning process at school, whether this applied to gymnastics and sport, handicraft and art or academic exercises and communication.

The following practical illustrations are taken from teaching plans developed at a boarding school for socially handicapped (maladjusted) boys. The basic conditions were met by having small classes and good staffing ratios. Teaching plans were set out to provide remedial work and to ensure that all the children became literate. The content of the teaching plans was based on the normal school curriculum, but teaching methods and classroom practice were designed to develop the social experiences and skills of the children.

General guidelines for the staff had to be simple and few in number in order to be used consistently by everyone. Three general principles can be managed in the classroom as well as at other times, for instance when engaged in household activities, without creating an artificial atmosphere in the school or interfering with the freedom of action of the staff.

1. As a general principle, individual attention was avoided whenever possible: if one of the boys needed special instruction or help, at least one of the other boys would be called to

take part so that both could be taught together and then given work which entailed co-operating with each other on a joint task.

2. Before starting any but the simplest activities, a set task was separated into an initial stage for gathering all the tools and materials which would be required, followed by doing the actual work at a second stage. This seemed to be an obvious arrangement for creating habits of systematic work and avoiding *ad hoc* arrangements which interrupt the continuity of a plan of action.
3. When a member of staff had to tell a boy to stop doing something irritating, he tried to plan ahead so that he could give an instruction about what to do next, instead of just bringing the boy's actions to a halt. The instruction could be as simple as 'open the window' or 'shut the door' or 'bring me that book', because its purpose was merely to redirect the boy's activities. Children who are left unattended when they have just interrupted what they were doing are liable to go on to do something irritating, because without guidance their immediate reaction is to join in and interfere with some other ongoing activity.

The boys who took part in the following exercises were aged between 10 and 14 years. The exercises are not to be taken as an alternative to the normal curriculum, but as additional activities to help promote the overall aim, which was to integrate the children socially as a group.

Gross motor exercises for mutual co-operation

A variety of games was devised, based on a familiar fairground game: drawing a metal ring along a complicated track made from a twisted wire which is connected to an electric circuit so that whenever the ring touches the wire, a bell rings.

In this case, the ring was held by two pieces of string and two boys played, holding one string each. Their problem was to adjust the movement and tension of the string in such a way that the ring passed along the right course without touching the wire.

Another exercise was to move a football from one chalk mark on the classroom floor to another by balancing it on two lengths of string. Each string was fastened to the same point of table leg at one end, while the two free ends were each held by a boy. The two partners had to adapt the height and tension of the strings to move the ball balanced between them.

In order to be successful in either of these exercises, the boys had to adjust their movements very carefully to each other. The exercises were intended to be entertaining and perhaps to lead on to further attempts in free play. This did not materialize. Both elements—mutual observation and mutual adaptation—were particularly difficult for the boys, and the intense concentration needed was a further problem. It was only possible to manage the situation as part of classroom instruction.

Movement as a form of communication

A model for social communication by menas of movements is to have a group of five to six children, with one acting as soloist. A general theme is taken, for instance that the solo actor tries to entice the group to follow him or to help him to do something. He has to make his meaning clear to the others by mime, facial expression and gesture, and the others make their replies in a similar way. All acts are presented in the form of alternating responses: mimed questions and answers. The pattern is that of a dialogue which evolves its own 'movement language.' The rate at which the questions and answers succeed each other is prompted by an accompanying rhythm of drum beats:

Socially handicapped children usually have poor language development, in the sense that their linguistic skills are simple, even if they often talk a great deal. By giving them the opportunity to communicate with movements, they learn to concentrate on expression and on the non-verbal accompaniments of speech. Much of the pleasure of such sessions is due to the discovery that one can communicate successfully without speech. When the children develop expressive gestures, their speech also becomes easier to understand because it is accompanied by expressive movements.

Gross motor-responses and spoken instructions

The primary aim of this exercise was to practise motor responses to spoken instructions, and therefore to listen carefully and respond accurately. A second aim was to practise formulating precise instructions, while a third was to practise ignoring distractions.

Two pairs of boys worked at the same time; one member of each pair gave instructions to his partner who had to carry out the required action. The apparatus consisted of two barriers, shoulder height: two boards were placed upright and parallel with each other. One of the boys in each pair had a stick, to one end of which a string with a stone hanging from it was tied, rather like a fishing line. The stick was held across the top edge of the board so that the strings were between the boards and could not be seen by the boys who held them. Two undulating chalk lines were drawn between the boards on the floor.

The other two partners stood at the ends of the passage formed by the boards so that they could see whether the stones at the ends of the lines were on or off the chalk lines.

The task of the observers was to call out instructions to their partners, telling them what to do with the stick in order to keep the stone moving along the line. They were not allowed to give any additional help by demonstrating with their arms, which had to be held, hands clasped, behind their backs.

The notion was that the boy giving the instruction had to choose a form of words which gave a clear and usable message so that his partner could act on them successfully: a problem of encoding. The problem for the boy receiving the instruction was to interpret it and also to ignore conflicting messages used by the other pair.

The exercise was simple in principle, but it stretched the abilities of the boys to their limits. It required great concentration, and they had to overcome repeated frustrations when the responses failed to match the instructions. In practice, the demands did not exceed their limits of tolerance because the pairs developed their own standards as they went on. The game was too difficult, however, to be taken over into free play.

Motor responses and verbal content

A different problem is posed when movements have to be adapted to the content and general meaning of speech, instead of being direct responses to simple instructions. In this exercise, the boys had to mime the appropriate actions for a play-reading. The first stage was to record a play read during a morning class. The recording was made available during the evening, when roles were redistributed so that each boy was miming a part recorded by one of the others. The play had been read and rehearsed a number of times in the morning so that they were all familiar with the content. The evening situation was new, nevertheless, and in each case the reaction of the actor was to stop and listen to his part while the others called out to tell him what to do and when to do it.

As an exercise in communication, this experiment touched on one of the basic problems of all the children: that attention to a clue interferes with the response. The form of the exercise—miming to the recorded play—allowed for repetition and practice so that the clues and the responses could become integrated into a successful production.

Relevance to classroom teaching

The aim of these and of many other exercises was to give specific opportunities for practising solutions to social problems which cause obstacles to learning. General situations which create particular difficulties for socially handicapped children were rearranged into a form in which obstacles could be overcome successfully. To be effective learning experiences, however, the exercises needed to lead on to further work in the classroom so that the children could experience their subsequent improvement.

The pattern of the exercises was that the boys should develop motor sequences which could only attain their goal when two or more partners worked together. They used verbal and gestural communication, and therefore generalization should be towards better verbal communication, mutual adaptation and awareness of each other. General interactions such as discussions, free play and social contacts might become more successful. In order to lead on to class work and especially to written class work, other exercises using written records were introduced.

Inferential thought and written statements

The intention was to bring pairs of boys together in a situation where both had to work out successive stages of a common train of thought. The model used was question and answer, and the form of the exercise gave each partner a problem to solve with respect to a shared experience.

Eight boys had been on an outing to a nearby town. As usual on such occasions, they had visited a church, played in a public park, had tea at a restaurant. No suggestions were made that this outing would be used subsequently for classroom work, but it often happened that this was the case.

The following day, a set of ten questions was posed in a special way. The questions were recorded on a tape, and by arranging that the tape recorder played back to four sets of earphones, four boys could listen to them in relative isolation. Their task was to write down the appropriate answers without using the words of the questions. 'How long did we spend in the church?", for instance, might be answered by 'about one hour'.

Each of the boys listening to the earphones was paired with another who only saw the written answer. It was his task to guess the question which led to the answer, and then to write it down. In most cases, the question was guessed in principle, and in some cases, the actual words were discovered.

The success of their efforts created interest in the situation, and further work developed along the same lines. Part of the success was due to the spoken record of the questions, which created fewer problems for understanding than written questions; it was also useful to have the earphones, which cut out a certain amount of distraction.

The next stage was to show that the ease or difficulty of inferring the questions depended on the kind of question and also on the boys' familiarity with the material from which the questions were drawn. A question which relates to factual answers is relatively easy to solve, while questions to do with value judgements are difficult, as shown by the next exercise.

A passage from a newspaper was given to each of the boys, and they were asked to read it carefully in order to construct their own sets of ten questions about the passage. The same form of answering and guessing was then attempted by the same pairs of boys.

It was clear from the results that the questions posed to them by the teacher (in the first tape recording) had been much more readily inferred than any of those prepared by the boys. The questions had to be simple, clear and factual to be discovered from the answers. Those questions which the boys had devised for themselves and which were correctly inferred were of a similar kind. 'Who drove the car?' 'When did the accident happen?' or 'How many people were killed?' were found successfully. Other questions which could be answered by 'yes' or 'no' were useless for the exercise. Questions like 'Did the other people get away?', as well as value judgements like 'Whose fault was it?', had a marginal success which depended on the answer given.

An exercise in sequential thought

One problem shared by all children is that their attention span is short, and this makes long-term planning difficult. The following exercise was used to illustrate what happens when only part of an overall plan of work is known. It took the form of an account of another outing, packed with information and extending over a whole day. The boys had been to London, so there was a lot of material to draw on.

The pattern of the exercise was that two boys came into the room alone with the teacher. The teacher told the first of them that he wanted him to dictate what he had done on the excursion into a dictaphone. The other boy was given no instructions, except that he should wait. When the first boy had reached a point which might serve as the end of a paragraph, he left the room and another boy came in and was told to wait. The second boy was then given the same instructions as the first, and the process went on until all the boys had done their dictation.

When the dictation was written up and the resulting account read out to the whole class, it was obviously disjointed, repetitive, contradictory and limited to a few events which kept reappearing while other events were omitted altogether. Continuity within the successive paragraphs was reasonable, but otherwise the whole form was fragmented.

The exercises fulfilled the requirement that they should lead on directly to further work in class, and that they should give the boys opportunities to inspect their own work in a critical manner. The general point of the exercises is to show a way in which specific learning problems can be tackled, as well as to show that they can be incorporated in class work and that teaching plans for socially handicapped children can be set out along the same lines as teaching plans for other handicapped children. The content is specific for each kind of handicap, but the same principles of planning apply in each case.

5

Visually Handicapped Children in Schools

SOME IMPLICATIONS OF VISUAL HANDICAP IN SCHOOL LEARNING

A positive philosophy for the visually handicapped pupil and one to encourage his effort will be that most of the educational goals set for the fully sighted will not be unattainable for him on account of his lack of vision or because of its impairment. But the pupil who has little or no sight is likely to have heavy demands made upon him in reaching comparable measurable standards of school success, although this may culminate in the passing of externally set and evaluated examinations, in some cases up to university entrance level. Examination successes at all levels are likely to rank high as criteria of effective education in the view of many parents, since they are quotable and comparable tokens of achievement shared with their child's fully sighted friends, brothers and sisters; they may also open up opportunities for further education or widen career choices.

But, of course, measurable academic successes are not sole, or in some cases even prime, educational goals, and realistic appraisal of the means by which the visually handicapped pupil can be provided with the means of achieving his optimum potential require careful consideration. The question of stress in the case of the blind and also the partially sighted pupil discussed by Williams (1973) and also by Kell (1973). A diminished or non-existent visual input combined in some instances, as in braille reading, with a slower working rate may indicate that either an extended period of education or small group and sometimes individual tutelage are desirable if pupils with severe visual handicaps are eventually to attain the educational levels of which they are capable. Difficulties in the presentation of materials can be minimized if these are thought out in terms of the pupil's visual competence as well as in respect of his other assets or deficits. The question of relevance of content in the curriculum is a complex one since some contexts may have a different frame of reference for visually handicapped pupils than for the fully sighted in cases where they may or may not have a reservoir of visual memories upon which to draw.

Whether he is in a special school, a unit, or in an ordinary class, the visually handicapped child will be within a group of pupils with a range of visual competence including varying limitations of visual experience. His teacher must be aware of this in planning and presenting work and will need to contrive circumstances accordingly.

Presentation of learning material

Pupils who see poorly or who do not see at all are in particular need of definition of purpose and clarity of instruction from their teachers. Impaired vision or total lack of vision carry the possibility of increasing the difficulty for the pupil of knowing what is expected of him. Gesture and other forms of non-verbal communication can be indistinct or lost to such pupils, whereas the fully sighted have the opportunity of noting almost incidentally many visual signals which reinforce or amplify verbal explanations or descriptions. In addition, the pupil with a visual handicap may not be able to see or may only see imperfectly the way in which other children are tackling the learning tasks expected from them. Child-centred discovery activities are likely to require more guidance for the visually handicapped than for the fully sighted child. It cannot safely be assumed that verbal references to objects or actions familiar to the fully sighted will be clear to the blind or visually defective, although their manipulation of language may mask deficiencies of experience. Clouds and distant mountains familiar in actuality, or at least in illustration or television representation to the seeing child, can be bafflingly difficult to describe in meaningful terms to those who have never seen them clearly—or perhaps at all. Even detail taken for granted by fully sighted such as the composition of a wall from separate bricks held together with cement, was not understood by a visually impaired 14 year old who had a good level of general intelligence and application likely to bring him examination successes. Thus it is evident that the teacher will need to develop considerable skill in helping the visually handicapped child to relate references to known and experienced contexts as well as to help him to increase his understanding of the environment. Solely verbal descriptions may not be enough to clarify a reference but care must be exercised in presenting diagrammatic material, whether in embossed form for tactile discrimination or in clearly presented visual form. Over-laboured presentations can sometimes confuse rather than clarify an issue.

In presenting diagrammatic material, its relevance in conveying information to the visually handicapped is of prime importance. This very obvious teaching point can, surprisingly, be underestimated, especially in two-dimensional work, since the eye loves detail which confuses the finger.

Since the visually handicapped pupil's means of recording or receiving information can be time-consuming it is vital that he has sufficient time to complete his tasks so that he does not build up a frustrating accumulation of unfinished assignments. The pupil who is unfortunate enough to suffer from a deteriorating visual condition is in particular need of the adaptation of circumstances and presentation of material, perhaps on a temporary basis, so that he is still in a situation of being able to complete tasks successfully; the use of the tape-recorder is particularly valuable at such a juncture. The adventitiously blind pupil also will need to be presented with learning situations in which he can succeed, and in this case too, auditorily presented material is particularly valuable during the period when the fluent reading of braille has not yet been achieved.

Special techniques

Both the teacher in the special school, and the peripatetic teacher or adviser giving support in a unit or mainstream school require a secure mastery of the techniques and adaptations needed in presenting materials and information for visually handicapped pupils, and also a knowledge of how these can be effectively employed in helping the pupil's learning. The presentation of adapted materials in itself represents only part of the solution to some of the learning problems. Skill and guidance in their use will also often be needed to obtain the greatest use in furthering the pupil's understanding and competence in handling and comprehending adapted material. The ability of the teacher to do this will call upon a blend of training, insight, and experience in meeting the needs of visually handicapped children.

There is a good deal of commerically available material that is well suited to the needs of visually handicapped pupils such as Colour Factor mathematical apparatus, but for a child who sees little or nothing this may be used in a manner slightly different from the way in which it is handled by fully sighted children. There is some expertly designed specialized apparatus available such as the miniature light probe which emits a sound varying in levels according to the density of the object at which it is beamed. Simpler adaptations such as the special geometry set or the adapted Japanese abacus (Cranmer) are listed in the catalogue of apparatus and games obtainable from the Royal National Institute for the Blind. Highly sophisticated adapted apparatus even includes a 'talking calculator.' In curriculum areas with some practical bias, such as the sciences, home economics, and craftwork, apparatus and equipment can also be drawn from both commerical and specialized sources provided that it is carefully considered in terms of its use by those who are visually impaired. The general movement in education which emphasizes the child's learning through activity has resulted in the production of much colourful, three-dimensional material such as scales, varied shapes and containers which are well suited for the child with little vision, provided that he has the materials presented at a stage appropriate for his learning.

Tactile material

For the pupil who is a braille user, a first essential is that the braille material with which he is presented, whether teacher-made or produced by volunteer transcribers, should be totally accurate and set out with a layout designed for finger reading and not for visual appeal. In the case of braille, an extra dot slipped in by mistake, a dot missing, or a contraction wrongly used, can alter the entire meaning of a word of phrase to a much greater extent than a spelling mistake in print. A knowledge of the different types of equipment and methods of embossing braille is useful to the teacher since although the upward braille writer is standard equipment in the UK, the small hand-frame and stylus still has some value as a quiet, unobtrusive and portable means of taking notes that can supplement the use of the portable tape-recorder.

The Thermo form machine which, by a thermo-vacuum process, enables embossed copies of raised maps and diagrams to be produced on plastic sheets speedily and in any quantity, has greatly facilitated the provision of appropriate diagrammatic work for children using their touch modality to interpret information. Devising and reproducing material can be so fascinating that it can tempt the teacher into being almost over- ingenious so that the resultant work is overcrowded with a diversity of texture and detail.

Adaptations for pupils with some vision

The visually handicapped pupil in an ordinary class can benefit from having 'desk copies' of tactile or clearly printed diagrammatic material available at the same time as blackboard or visual aids are being used in the classroom. Co-operation between the regular teacher and specialists in visiual handicap is needed here so that the visually handicapped pupil is not unnecessarily in a 'remedial' situation by going over work previously undertaken by his classmates, but rather he should be using his adapted materials simultaneously with the sighted children in the group.

Whilst the value of low-vision aids has gained significance for some pupils with poor sight, and may be a factor in determining whether a pupil needs to learn braille or not, other means of helping to clarify visually presented material to pupils who have some vision should not be neglected and these may often involve a combination of appropriate illumination, working position, and the use of closed circuit television and tape-recorded material. Attention to techniques in visual search and scanning may also be needed for some pupils.

Classroom organization

Some aspects of classroom organization can help to lessen the likelihood of stressful situations or confusion for pupils with problems in seeing. For these children it is helpful that there should be clear indications in advance when a lesson or an activity is about to come to an end, so that each pupil can gather up his own belongings and return them to their appropriate places. The development of orderly habits with regard to the storage and retrieval of equipment and working materials helps in the subsequent location and retrieval of these for future use, minimizing confused searching and waste of time. So far as possible the visually handicapped pupil should be increasingly responsible for fetching and retrieving his own books and work; desks, shelves, and cupboards labelled in braille and clear print and the opportunity to explore and locate landmarks in a classroom will facilitate this. If furniture or storage places are altered, he should forwarded of this. Undue passivity and dependence on others may result if either a teacher or better sighted pupils invariably undertake the collection and distribution of materials whilst the less well seeing child simply receives it. It can be difficult for the blind or poorly seeing child to know when and how to ask for help when it is needed and to reject it without offence when it is not. The classroom situation can provide a good basis for such crucial social training.

Teaching points

In the midst of all the technical advances it may be all too easy to neglect the teacher's own contribution. The teacher's voice, use of vocabulary, and manipulation of language would seem particularly valuable in motivating the child who sees little or nothing. Clear enunciation, as well as an audible and interesting voice are considerable assets since boredom can be a hazard to the child for whom visual stimuli are reduced or absent. It can be salutary for the teacher to tape-record and then listen to a lesson and note any cliche-ridden approaches, inaudible or inexplicit directions or over-long descriptions which occur.

The pupil who is visually handicapped will need to learn some skills systematically that the fully sighted can usually pick up incidentally such as orientation, mobility, and travel skills. Some of the methods he must use for his day-to-day classwork will be very time-consuming; some concepts taken for granted by the fully sighted may present difficulties for him. He may be in a class where the tecaher is anxious to help him but because of unfamiliarity with the problems of visual handicap or lack of specialized training or even information does not know how to set about this in a constructive way.

In the ensuing passages attention is drawn to some of the specific areas in which the visually handicapped pupil is likely to need specialized adaptations and an understanding of his needs. In whatever educational setting he is working, it is important that these special needs should be both well understood and realistically met.

DISCOVERY THROUGH TOUCH

The most evident, and perhaps to some people the most interesting aspect of learning by touch, is the tactile reading of braille but this highly specialized and refined use of the sense is only one of the ways in which information can be transmitted by the fingertips. Nor are the fingertips the only transmitters of messages about the characteristics of materials and objects to be explored. The connection between movement and the interpretation of information through touch must be appreciated so that learning situations can be presented in which the child has ample opportunity to move his fingers over learning material that has been organized in terms of touch discrimination. The ability to discriminate fine tactile detail in two-dimensional form and to interpret embossed symbols represents a culmination of skills which need to be preceded by activities of a more generalized nature. These will embody larger movements in the exploration of a variety of three-dimension objects whose form and texture can be examined in kinaesthetic terms. The environment holds a wealth of different surfaces—the rough bark of trees, the grainy texture of wood, the cold smoothness of plastic, and the warm tackiness of new bread. But usually it is through sight that the attention is drawn to these interesting things; comparisons of the qualities that objects present to the touch, their roughness, coolness, weight, or viscosity will not take place automatically in the case of the child who does not see. The pupil's curiosity may need to be aroused by verbal intervention, sound cues that attract attention and action learning involving the handling and manipulation of materials. Discussion can ensue with regard to the attributes of the object or surfaces being explored, the size, shape, texture, weight, and flexibility compared with that encountered in previous tactile discoveries. The identification of critical features, including texture patterns, direction of raised lines and shapes, and easily discriminated symbols can follow. In due course classification should follow as a result of a consideration of the function or representation embodied in the object which can be compared with previous experiences in tactile recognition. Only after sufficent opportunity has been given for activities in relating tactile exploration of varied three-dimensional forms can the presentation of two-dimensional surface representation be meaningful.

Tactile activities in play

Early activities in the pre-school and ealry school years can provide excellent opportunities for tactile discovery through play. The hands need to be used in different ways, in strong movements of pulling and pushing which help to give strength and flexibility as well as in the later finer movements involved in surface discrimination by the fingertips.

It is not unusual to find that congenitally blind children in particular have considerable difficulty in handling and manipulating materials that seem easy to deal with by the fully sighted. Cutting out cardboard or stiff paper with scissors, for instance, can provide difficulty, so can holding and using cutlery at mealtimes. The figners may not have been used in different ways in manipulation and so seem weak and flabby. Clay or plasticine pushed about with the hands into balls or sausages, the use of finger puppets, the use of commercially available manipulative toys, building blocks and nesting cubes can all be helpful. More structured activities include shape matching with wooden or plastic geometric forms, and texture matching with pieces of fabric with interesting surfaces to feel which can be glued to cards. However, as with attempts in other areas to stimulate attention to learning through using the senses, a rigid overprogrammed approach is undesirable. The activities should help to carry foward the process of thinking and should have an enriching and interesting content that motivates towards increasing the enjoyment of tactile discovery. Handicrafts and the construction of simple models by the pupils themselves can encourage the handling and utilization of materials of varied textures and consistencies in a creative way.

Drawings and diagrams in tactile form

More specifically, and at a later stage in schooling, Pickles (1966) advocates both the value and viability of drawing for the blind, even for totally and congenitally blind pupils. He claims that after such a child has learnt to recognize objects by exploring their shapes and dimensions through touch he should be given the means of making his own diagrams. Since this process is time consuming and offer's difficulties in execution, its value can be questioned but Pickles believes that it is an activity helpful both to those relying on touch alone, as well as for those using touch and vision in their understanding of embossed diagrams. The ability to use touch in this way is a skill which cuts across the curricula areas of the secondary school, for example underlying work in maths, science, and geography. The child with too little vision for making use of illustrations and visually presented diagrams is especially in need of training in understanding diagrammatic work in embossed relationships and connections, such as in the layout of a piece of laboratory apparatus. Furthermore in justifying his emphasis on undertaking surface representation for diagrammatic work, Pickles claims that executing diagrams can be one way of learning to understand their implications. With a rubber mat providing a resilient base, a sheet of aluminium foil can be sued to take a negative (downward indented) line made by a ball-point pen. The Sewell apparatus (RNIB) embodies a thin film of transparent plastic sheeting stretched over a rubber-surfaced board, and again, a special ball-point pen, an ordinary biro, or a spur wheel which cuts small dot-like indentations can be used for lines. Manilla paper as used for braille writing can take imprints from a spur wheel also, and the specialized geometry set available from the RNIB enables the user to make raised geometric figures on paper. Vincent (1970) has constructed a special drawing board which enables the student to prepare perspective drawing, but it is important that the pupil's understanding of what he is attempting to do is not superseded by devices that help him to produce work only understandable in sighted terms.

Surface representation

The teacher considering the question of producing surface representational diagrams is likely to turn again, to Pickles' work in *Teaching Maths and Science to the Blind* (1970). Here there are detailed step-by-step suggestions as to how to build up a master copy using string or wire for outlines and textured materials such as scrim or fine wire mesh to provide distinguishable surfaces on a firm base. The master copy thus constructed can be used in the Thermoform machine which by thermo-vacuum suction can produce copies of the diagram imprinted on thin sheets of opaque plastic. The resulting copies take the imprint of the matrix copy clearly, but there can be some lessening of the differences in texture constructed in the original diagram. In investigating the effectiveness of work produced in this way, blind pupils at Worcester College for the Blind found a rough line more distinguishable than a smooth one, a line with a triangular crest gave optimum discriminability and a diagram of about 14 cm square gave the most comfortable size for exploration by the fingers when the base of the hand was placed at the bottom of it. Moreover, a large diagram 1 m square in which arms, hands, and fingers had to be stretched out to encompass the entire width, gave some general impression of relationships, for example in the relative position of countries of continents to each other.

Enthusiasm to make the map or diagram as informative as possible can lead to overcrowding of symbols, whilist the addition of braille words in the body of the diagram causes confusion. A tactile diagram needs to have enough information to encourage exploration and interest but not so many raised lines, braille labels, and varied textures that clarity is lost. A series of maps or diagrams each displaying a particular aspect of what is to be presented provides a more comprehensible illustration. For example, several basic raised outline maps of a country can be made with additions on one version to indicate climate, on another indications of vegetation, on another population or geological features. To crowd all this information on to one map by using different raised symbols is likely to be confusing.

The information received from such presentations needs to be discussed so that misapprehensions can be cleared up, and the pupils will also need training in interpreting the symbols used. The teacher will need to draw attention verbally to the information represented and even to ensure that the map or diagram is being used the right way up. Cutting along the top of it with pinking shears gives a quick way of checking.

Histograms and graphs

Whittaker (1967) gives interesting examples of ways in which tactile representation can be used in histograms. Basic work here involves the use of small toy cars and tiny dolls which can be used first on a one-to-one basis to represent a number of children in a group or, for example, the number of cars owned by parents in a class.

Increasing complexity is introduced as one object is used to represent several, one-car for every ten, and then tactile symbols can replace miniature objects in indicating comparisons. Tactile representations of this kind follow on the use of Dienes Multibase or Colour Factor mathematical materials which should have helped the pupils to understand the relationships of numbers.

Three-dimensional models

The value of both two-dimensional diagrammatic work and of three-dimensional models in the teaching of visually handicapped pupils is likely to be the cause of continuing discussion and examination since its effectiveness is hard to gauge. Beautifully constructed scale models of buildings or of animals may have a primarily visual appeal. Characteristic qualities of texture, temperature, or even the smell of the original, are not present in a model, but many things are impossible to bring into a classroom. Whilst first-hand experiences offer a vital form of exploraion even these are not always possible. The sighted child is likely to have seen seas, mountains, and wild animals at least on television or in Illustrations. So far as possible the blind child needs real experiences too, but as a supplement to these and to clarify the relationships of parts to a whole, to understand function and construction both three-dimensional and two-dimensional tactile presentation is a useful if imperfect supplement to other way of presenting information.

Tactile exploration for the child with some vision

For the child with some vision learning through touch should not be neglected. This is not simply because he may have a deteriorating visual condition which could at some time result in having to learn braille, or eventually resulting in a work situation where lighting is not ideal for using vision and thus the use of touch rather than sight is needed. Early attention through interpreting through touch may indeed help to ease difficulties in such situations should they occur later, but in any case through this sense of touch the visually handicapped child has a means of gaining fuller information and of finding out characteristics and qualities in objects so that he gains a more complete appreciation of his environment. If he uses his hearing and his haptic sense sensitively it does not follow that he will use his defective visual sense less. His teachers and parents need not fear that using his unimpaired senses will make him behave like a totally blind person. Increased awareness of touch may in fact help him to receive fuller information and a greater realization of the qualities of the obejcts in the world about him.

LISTENING SKILLS

Why develop listening skills?

There is no conclusive evidence to show that a child who lacks visual intactness will automatically compensate for this deficit by listening with such skill and concentration that he is able to interpret envrionmental sounds with accuracy, and gain information which will help him in his cognitive development simply through being presented with material in auditory form. And yet investigations show that at school, if he is using braille he is like to read at a much slower rate than a sighted child using print (Williams, 1971) and if he is partially sighted he may need to rely on auditory material as an important supplement to his print reading. The need to use broadcast and taped material effectively will be particularly important to the pupil with deteriorating vision or sudden sight loss since learning braille will take some time, while gaining information from print may be increasingly difficult or impossible for him.

Teachers of visually handicapped children tend to have anecdotal evidence of their pupil's ability to recognize people by the sound of their footsteps and to gauge their moods with accuracy from tones of voice as well as by the words used in situations of personal interaction. It would be interesting to have more hard evidence with regard to the characteristics of children with this capacity for interpreting sound and to see if it relates to pre-school activities in which parents have related sounds to objects and actions rather than giving too much unrelated sound stimulation, for example by leaving the young visually handicapped child in a room with the television on or with the wireless playing.

Listening responses in the pre-school child

Barraga (1974) suggests ways in which the young visually handicapped child may be helped to give attention to auditory stimuli by being motivated to respond to specific sounds in the environment. But she draws attention to the connection between responses to sound and the development of purposeful movement, for instance in the example of the child turning his head towards his mother when she speaks, or the toddler reaching out or walking towards a squeaking toy. In such cases, a perception of position and distance is being developed as a result of sound, but even more important is the relationship of auditory information to language and conceptual development. In emphasizing this connection Barraga discounts the value of training schemes which call for the repetition of meaningless sounds and words since she considers that they may simply reinforce the tendency for severely visually handicapped children to imitate words and phrases without any attention to their content.

Auditory activities in school

However, in the case of children who have not had help before they come to school in learning to relate sounds to actions, events, and people in an increasingly meaningful way, a structured programme may be helpful in motivating them to give attention to sound cues through a series of games and activities. The programme outlined by Bishop (1971) suggests such an approach to help the young visually handicapped child to enhance his ability to succeed in simple sound identification and thence to develop a greater ability in his powers of listening with discrimination. Beginning with simple examples such as the sound of a spoon in a cup or of a book being closed, the suggested schemes continue with taped recordings of a telephone ringing or a clock ticking followed by identification of the voices of different speakers; exercises in tonal and volume discrimination include recognition of the differences between near and far, high and low, loud and soft sounds. Traditional stories can provide excellent material for recognizing the different sound in voices of individual characters as in *The Three*

Bears and *The Three Trees*. Sound and rhythm replication can be practised in 'Do As I Do' games. Discrimination between words that sound similar but not identical can be the means of leading into a phonic programme, but the aim should be to progress as quickly as possible into work that involves the comprehension of auditory material rather than simply presenting sound for identification, location and discrimination of tone and volume.

Tape-recorded material

Good quality taped material is easily available but the teacher needs to consider this carefully and to clarify the purpose for which it is being used. It is essential to listen to the tape beforehand to ensure that the content is not beyond the experiential level of the visually handicapped pupils using it. Appropriate introductory work and questions and acitivites designed to follow up the taped material will reinforce the content. Pupils may find it difficult to deal with the taped material if it contains a density of facts or complex references, but narrative and dramatic material and poetry are well suited to this means of presentation.

Some attempts have been made to analyse the different levels of attention involved in listening, particularly to taped material, by blind people. In the Upsala Pedagogiska Project. Trowald (1975) investingated listening strategies for blind secondary school pupils, concluding that there are three activity levels in listening, and suggesting that an understanding of these can be of value in helping visually handicapped pupils to increase their capacity to gain information from material presented in auditory form. He describes hearing as a relatively low-level activity, in some ways equivalent to seeing whilst he considers listening to involve a greater degree of mental activity comparable to observing; he uses the term 'auding' to describe a higher level of mental processing of recorded sound which includes listening with analytical ability and critical reasoning and thus there is some resemblance to the thinking process involved in attentive reading.

In view of the necessity for the visually handicapped pupil to use auditory material as a means of learning, the techniques which Trowald puts forwad for increasing efficiency in this work warrant careful attention by the teacher of such pupils. As reference work and textbook information play an increasing part in the secondary school and further education curriculum, the visually handicapped pupil will need to use taped material more and more as a central means of input if he is blind and using braille texts which may sometimes be difficult to obtain or can be slow to read; they will offer a supplementary means of obtaining information if he is partially sighted.

Techniques for improving listening efficiency

Trowald (1975) recommends that rather than having periods of unbroken listening to recorded material the pupil should, instead, stop the tape at intervals and construct questions about the content of the material he is using. One tape recorder can be used for playing the recorded material whilst another is used for taping questions. Suggested answers can be recorded on a second track on the tape on the latter machine. A complex process such as this presupposes that the pupil has been taught how to handle the machine skilfully. The use of a tape recorder with a variable speed control gives the listener the opportunity to increase the speed, and in some ways this replicates the process of skimming in reading. In fact, this researcher observed that the blind pupils in his study preferred to listen to taped material at 50 per cent higher speed than normal speaking; while the speed preferred by fully sighted children was 20 per cent faster than normal speaking; in both cases the preferred speed varied with the difficulty of the text. The blind pupils showed less fatigue and maintained their level of comprehension, whilst the comprehnsion of the sighted children diminished towards the end of the tape.

Visually handicapped pupils will need to develop efficient study techniques through listening in order to gain specific information and to acquire the ability to practise selective listening. Concentration against a background of distracting sound and eventually the highly developed skill of evaluative listening can be achieved. Sound advertisements and propaganda broadcasts provide material for discussion and for developing discrimination between claims opinions, and facts.

The language laboratory provides a learning situation and a group activity useful for more than learning foreign languages. It can be successfully used for auditory taped work of the kind described above and for the pupils to read and play back their own creative oral expression. Tape recorders with one or more plug-in earpieces can be used in part of a classroom for project work; this has been a successful method used in mathematics for working out problems orally, and because of the facility for recording it gives more opportunity for self-criticism in oral work than ephemeral discussion. The portable tape-recorder can be used as a 'sound diagram' giving directions for following a specified route in mobility.

The student in further education will be particularly dependent on listening and using taped material in his work but he will have been greatly helped if, during his school days, he has received training and practice in making maximum use of his powers of attentive and discriminating listening.

READING AND WRITING IN BRAILLE

Development of tactile codes for reading

Early attempts to present letters or words in a tactile way so that they could be interpreted by the blind present a wealth of ingenious forms evidencing varying degrees of effectiveness. These ranged from different shaped knots in string, to modified capital letters embossed and large enough to be discriminated by the fingers. The two embossed codes which have stood the test of time are known as Moon and Braille. The former which bears some approximation to a raised form of large-print letters is not used in schools, but since 1872 braille has been the established code in educational as well as in most other areas where symbolic communication is used by and for the blind. This code was adapted by Louis Braille from an eight-dot form to a six-dot form; the original was a means of secret communication used in the French army and described by its inventor, Charles Barbier, as *ecriture nocturnal.*

Its disadvantages in the modern educational setting are that it is bulky and in its contracted form it has arbitrary rules not in line with current vocabulary usage. But is has advantages also which have stood the test of time in over a century of international usage.

Indeed, the eventual mastery of braille reading is a complex skill which includes the memorizing of a code based on the permutation of six raised dots which form the braille cell. Despite disadvantages this six-dot form of communication is remarkable since both a mathematics and music code have been developed from it as well as the two basic forms generally used for reading. The first of these, 'Grade I' or uncontracted braille, consists of a braille symbol for each letter of the alphabet. The form of braille normally used for reading, however, is referred to as 'Grade II' and when used in this way the dots are employed in different combinations which can be used for syllables of words or indeed in some cases for whole words. These representations are referred to as 'braille contractions' and their usage is governed by a series of quite complex, and indeed at times, apparently arbitrary rules.

Pre-reading activities

What constitutes 'reading readiness' for the child who will need to use braille as his medium of literacy? As for the sighted child, a vital consideration will be his level of language development and the need not only to be able to read and write but to have something to read and write about. But there are a number of additional factors to consider in the case of the child using braille. He will need his own kind of pre-reading programme giving attention to communication through language and first-hand experience in exploring objects. Whereas most sighted children will have newspapers, magazines, books, posters and slogans at least within their visual environment if still beyond their full comprehension, this will not be the case for the child who is blind. The blind child's association of words with actions, objects and events, may need particular attention before he is ready to link the symbols of braille characters with spoken words. The pupil who is to become a proficient braille reader needs to develop skill in the tactile discrimination of small forms as well as to have developed a sufficient use of language to appreciate meaningful content presented in the code. Powers of both short- and long-term memory will be needed in order to retain the impression of the configuration of the symbols and to remember when and in what circumstances the contracted form of the code may be sued. Thus it will be readily understood that a heavy cognitive load, together with the need for fine tactile discrimination, is imposed on children who must use this form of symbolic communication as their means of literacy. In addition as Lorimer (1975) has indicated, the pad of the pupil's finger usually deals with only one braille cell at a time and the ability to perceive the symbols for the word as a whole thus increasing speed and encouraging contextural guessing is not possible for a finger-reader in the same way as for the sighted reader who has many more cues available simultaneously.

Lowenfeld's comprehesnive study, published in book form (1969) as *Blind Children Learn to Read*, enumerates the type of prereading skills that he has found helpful in developing the necessary requisites for reading braille by the young child. These include matching and sorting objects of different shapes and discriminating textures. The left-to-right movement of the hands can be encouraged with games and puzzles involving following a raised line with the fingers.

Teaching of braille reading to schoolchildren

In view of such problems for the pupil learning braille it is not surprising that a number of studies have been undertaken in which the characteristics of effective and accurate braille readers have been observed, and the problems of those finding the task difficult or impossible have been investigated.

In the UK a survey on braille attainment undertaken by Williams (1971) and incorporated as a substantial item in the report of the Vernon Committee (1972) focused attention on the most evident causes of lack of success in the teaching of braille reading. It was emphasized strongly in this study that the outstanding difficulty for pupils in school was their reading rate. The level of comprehension did not differ significantly from that of sighted children of comparable age on the Ballard Silent Reading Test, but 40 per cent of the blind children in a sample of 488 subjects between the ages of 10 and 16 were unsuccessful in completing the reading test, and the average rate for silent reading was between 80 to 100 words per minute, about half that for sighted pupils. Williams gave detailed cossideration tc the sources of failure amongst the children tested, and concluded that both absence from school at critical learning periods and late admission to a school for the blind had been contributory causes in a substantial number of cases. Factors relating to the way in which braille was regarded also had a bearing on failure, especailly in cases of low motivation on the part of the pupil, lack of sufficient practice in reading, the absence of a consistent policy of teaching braille throughout the school, and an insufficiently positive attitude towards braille reading on the part of the teacher. Low mental ability was an important contributory factor in the difficulties of some 25 per cent of the pupils considered whilst a few had the additional problem of slight spasticity in the hand. Indeed a careful observation of the hand movements of the readers in this study was one of the most fascinating aspects of it, since the researcher carefully noted whether her subjects used one or both hands in reading, which fingers were used predominantly, whether the pressure exerted was light or heavy, and whether up or down movements of a searching nature were used. The fast readers had a number of characteristics in common which should receive attention in the teaching of braille reading. The movement of the hands was light and skimming, 72 per cent of the fast readers used both hands for reading and there was a tendency for them to have other fingers besides the predominating one on the line of symbols. The slow readers evidenced less skilful, searching movements and in a number of cases were children who had not concentrated fully on either print or braille but were somewhat divided in their attention between these two forms of presentation. Williams's findings with regard to hand movements are in accord with those of Lowenfeld (1969) and also with a more recent study in the Netherlands by Mommers (1975) who also noted that the quicker, more successful pupils reading braille did not rub the dots in scrubbing movements, were less likely to lose their places on the line, had good posture, with only slight pressure on the fingers as they passed over the dots with a flowing movement. He also confirmed the connection between a good level of intelligence and successful reading, but found no significant affect on technical reading competence as a result of the degree of blindness.

Reading speeds and comprehension in children using braille

A major investigation into the competence of pupils using braille in schools in the UK, undertaken by Lorimer (1975) considered both comprehension and speed and resulted in conclusions highly relevant to the curriculum of blind pupils. Williams's 1971 study had given rise to concern with regard to the attainment of braille reading among pupils and Lorimer considered that although teachers usually had small groups of pupils and thus had a considerable knowledge of their pupils' individual progress, nevertheless it was desirable that there should be a means of objective measurement of their attainment in braille reading. Two useful tests were already in use throughout schools for the blind. The Tooze Speed Test (1962) for pupils between 7 and 13 years which gave 120 words of three letters to be scanned for speed, and the Lorimer Recognition Test (1962) offering 174 braille contractions to be used for word recognition for the same age-group. Lorimer finally chose the Neale (1958) Analysis of Reading which presents graded reading for the 6- to 12-year-old group of sighted children. This test has the advantage of parallel forms to permit re-testing, and indicates age norms for accuracy, reading rate, and comprehension. In using a braille version of this test throughout schools for the blind in Great Britain, Lorimer confirmed earlier findings that it was in the rate of reading that braille users were at a considerable disadvantage compared with those using print. Although there was some retardation in comprehension with the braille user the gap between the blind and sighted narrowed in the upper age group. The blind were also slower than the sighted in word recognition skills. Lorimer confirmed the fact that the size of the fingertip as a conductor of information limits speed in reading, so that in the case of his subjects it was observed that even better touch readers were achieving about 55 per cent of the reading speed of average sighted readers. An important aspect of this research lies in the recommendation for dealing with some of the difficulties inherent in a braille teaching scheme. For instance, the researcher recommends a consistent teaching policy throughout the school with remedial programmes for those pupils who need this, including stress on a good knowledge of the code. This could be improved, he states, by systematic character recognition training and speed training in the secondary as well as in the primary school. He also recommends specific reading courses for those requiring academic or commercial approaches to their work and regular objective appraisal of the progress of all pupils.

Grade I and Grade II braille

Since the braille code can be used in the two forms, Grade I uncontracted and Grade II contracted, there have been different approaches over the years with regard to presenting the material to beginners. The two divergent policies with regard to the introduction of braille are described by Hechle (1974).

The teachers who have favoured using Grade I at the beginning of reading schemes leaving Grade II until the uncontracted form has been mastered, might well claim that this method gives the child the opportunity of reading experience without having to cope with the complexities of contractions at an early stage and gives encouragement for the fingers to move along the line. Precedence is given in this teaching approach to the phonic element and to word-building practice in reading. On the other hand, a child who learns words in their contracted form from the start learns them in the form in which he will subsequently always encounter them without re-learning.

Specialized braille reading schemes for children

Finding appropriate material in braille, well suited in content for beginners, has posed a problem. Books that look easy in print can contain a surprising number of quite difficult contractions when transcribed into Grade II braille. Teaching approaches have been reflected in the choice of reading schemes for transcribing from print. Attempts have been made to introduce contractions gradually or to use a number of reading schemes in which graded books for the sighted were transcribed for the blind. However, teachers in schools for the blind in the UK were convinced that a specialized reading scheme was needed which would take cognizance of the particular difficulties of the braille code especially with regard to its contractions. They wanted readable material that the pupils would enjoy as well as being relevant to the vocabulary of young blind children. Tobin (1972b) undertook a study of the written and spoken vocabulary used by 132 young blind children.

Vocabulary of young blind children

It was felt that a braille reading scheme for beginners must give real attention to the vocabulary that children knew and used. The limiting effect of word lists as a basis for reading is well understood but it is stressed by Tobin that in the case of blind children who need to learn a reading code by using fingertips which take up information at a slower rate than the eye, it is especially important that difficulties be reduced to a minimum and an added burden of new topics and unfamiliar words might militate against the ease of reading experience. Tobin's study includes a searching review of previous work on the language development of blind children highlighting the noticeable verbalism sometimes encountered. He also notes that some research, including that of Hayes (1941) indicated overall 'an inferiority in the understanding of words.'

Consideration is also given to the findings of Maxfeld (1936) that blind children asked more questions, gave fewer commands and in her opinion indicated a need for security which, in some respects, could be satisfied through verbal communication. Tobin's study which took cognizance of previous studies of the vocabulary of sighted children (Burroughs, 1957) showed the extent to which the vocabularies of the sighted and the blind overlap. However, he justifiably draws attention to the fact that the repetition of frequently used words from a list results in a tedious context and suggests that the word lists compiled should rather be used as building blocks with additional pre-reading activities. An interesting analysis is given of the differences between words used by the blind and those encountered in lists of words used by the sighted children of equivalent ages. Colour words were used relatively infrequently by blind 5- and 6- year- olds but increased during the 7- to 8-year-old group who had been exposed to more diverse verbal references by teachers, classmates, and older children.

'The Family Books'

In 1971 a Reading Committee set up by the College of Teachers of the Blind, composed of teachers from schools for the blind developed a specialized reading scheme in braille, bearing in mind the findings of Tobin's Vocabularly Study and also the problems arising from the contracted form of braille. After different approaches with regard to using Grade I and Grade II had been considered there was increasing agreement about the introduction of grade II in reading from the start. The aim of the scheme was to reduce the perceptual and cognitive load of the young reader beginning to use braille. Four story sequences were composed each centred round an imaginary family. The first books used a vocabulary that did not involve words needing contractions and which were drawn from the first three of Tobin's word lists. The four schemes were parallel in their gradual and agreed introduction of words involving the use of contractions. Attention was given to the presentation of the books which were small for braille books, 22 cm X 14.5 cm, and thus not too heavy or difficult for the young reader to handle. It was made clear that in order to use the readers the pupil must already be able to recognize the braille symbols as letters of the alphabet. In the first books of the series the phonic method of reading was the underlying principle. This sounding of words letter by letter with the construction of the word from the sounds is to some extent dictated by the fact that the fingertips touch the symbol one at a time in braille.

Attention was also given to sentence structure and to punctuation in the attempt to graduate the difficulties of the reading material. It is emphasized that pre-reading activities, including left to right movement of the hands, are essential as the specialized reading scheme does not attempt to introduce braille signs according to ease of recognition by touch. The gradual introduction of contractions for whole words such as 'and' or 'the' involves a 'look and say' element in reading. The later books in the series represent an attempt to introduce the complexities of Grade II braille in relation to the child's perceptual and cognitive development. The order of these consists of the introduction of pronouns, conjunctions, word sings, abbreviations, followed by an increasing number of more difficult contractions. Those familiar with the braille code and the rules for contractions and the word signs in the Grade II form will appreciate the difficulty of balancing the demands of the vocabulary level of the child, with the level of difficulty of the Grade II braille rules whilst maintaining an interesting level of material in the text. The authors of this scheme would not claim to have solved all the problems but they have developed a lively and by now widely used early reading scheme which gives realistic attention to the particular problems of braille reading for a young beginner.

Supplementary material for use with the reading scheme

The sighted child usually has his first reading books decorated with colourful and attractive pictures and it was felt that the blind child misses a delightful and motivating element in the absence of these in his braille boks. Consequently an imaginative approach was made in devising supplementary material which hopefully would serve the function of increasing motivating, giving direct preparation for the next reading stage, adding material for slower readers and extending the range of the readers' experience. Greenwood (1975) was instrumental in devising and making prototype material consisting of additional tape-recorded stories, small models of villages, and large soft dolls representing the characters in the stories. The combined effort of practitioners and researchers in the development of this scheme and its supplementary material is of more than local interest. The rationale of the scheme has been referred to in some detail since it exemplifies an approach to the teaching of braille which evidences not only a knowledge of the problems involved in its teaching but also a lively awareness of the developmental needs of children as they learn to read. The practice of using the *Standard English Braille Primer* as a basis for teaching primary school children to read braille with its seven-line system and rigorous practice exercises, is by contrast quite inappropriate.

Braille reading as the pupil progresses through school

The addition to the staff of an ordianry school of 'a braille instructor' is equally dubious, since if a child's vision is so poor that he needs to use this medium for communication in reading and writing he is likely to need help from a teacher or adviser in areas that extend well beyond a knowledge of the braille code.

The young reader who has completed a specialized reading scheme can progress to a transcribed reading scheme and to a variety of reaidng material since it is essential to remember that braille is not literacy but rather represents the gateway to literacy in providing the means by which the blind pupil can obtain information and derive enjoyment from books. There are some excellent readers available in braille at primary school level which can be obtained from one of the branches of the National Library for the Blind and suggestions with regard to these are outlined in *Books and Blind Children* (Chapman and Wilson, 1970). It can be useful for the pupil on an individual basis to have two braille readers in his possession. One well within the scope of his reading level to get on with in his own time, in addition he can have a slightly more difficult text for which he can enlist the teacher's help during class reading periods. A regular period in the day or week when part of a book is read aloud gives shared enjoyment and pupils should be encouraged to take braille books home at weekends and to have them available in the evenings to 'find out what happens next' and dispel any impression that reading is simply for the classroom.

The need to give specific attention to braille reading and writing even in the secodnary school years, is emphasized by both Mommers (1975) and Lorimer (1975) whilst Myers (1975) noted improvements in the ability of multiply handicapped blind youths to read braille if they had continued instruction even after they had left school.

The reading problem of the late blind child is a complex one, and individual teachers have worked out their own schemes. Tobin (1971) has an excellent programme based on taped material designed for the adventitiously blind adult but useful for later blind adolescents and older senior pupils.

Technical advances in tactile reading

Modern technology has been used in the production of braille material and the computer has been utilized in this connection.

Braille textbooks and readers are available from the Royal National Institute for the Blind who publish a list of available titles. The University of Warwick has initiated a scheme of braille transcription from printed material for blind clients and many schools and advisers are indebted to voluntary transcribers for help in brailling texts.

However, the Vernon Report draws attention to the difficulties in supplying an adequate number of braille books for school use promptly. This is a problem which has already received serious attention but it remains an outstanding area of concern for the teacher who needs to be sure that the books required following a particular syllabus are available at the time when they are needed.

A technical development which holds promise for tactile readers is the machine known as 'the Optacon.' This sophisticated piece of apparatus can convert ordinary printed images into a corresponding tactile image, with the advantage that it is therefore not restricted to any particular type-style or language. The apparatus consists of three main sections composed of a miniature opto-electronic camera, an electronic section, and a tactile stimulator array which consists of 144 small metal rods placed in an area of about 1 cm by 2 cm and arranged in 6 columns across and 24 along. The miniature camera is able to travel along a line of print and is connected by a light cable to the electronic section of the apparatus. When the machine is in operation it is able to convert the image of the printed letter into a pattern of vibrating rods which can be interpreted by the finger. Tobin *et al.* (1973) reporting on trials of this machine consider that initial and continuing practice with graded materials on a regular basis is necessary and that learning its usage is in the same order of difficulty as that presented to some adult readers in learning braille. Younger readers given the opportunity of a daily basic training period with additional free practice might gain benefit and pilot schemes are in operation at the grammar schools for blind pupils.

Successful use of such equipment brings a new dimension of experience to blind readers and necessitates the development of new educational techniques. However, whatever means are used for the transmission of written symbols to the reader the need for sound basic educational principles continues with the encouragement of motivation towards reading and the development of good levels of comprehension with regard to the material presented.

Learning to write braille

Many teachers begin the process of braille writing with their pupils at the same time as they begin reading. Most pre-reading activities are simultaneously pre-writing activities. The time spent in exploring shape and texture and in interpreting and discriminating sounds is helping to give the child something to write about. If the young visually handicapped child has had the advantage of early opportunities in associating words with objects and actions he will have a start in his reading and writing readiness programme. A sense of pattern and an association of pattern with meaning will have to be developed. Pittam (1965) outlines an approach in which patterns which will later represent braille letter combinations can be used. In addition to tactile and, if circumstances permit it, visual enhancement, auditory readiness needs to be developed. Story telling by the teacher, re-telling of the story by the pupils, gives attention to the building up of sequence. The acting out of stories can be tied in with the actual and imagined events in the child's life, and it must of course be ensured that the visually handicapped. Child has enough opportunities of real conversation with adults outside the classroom as well as with his playmates. This is a particular challenge to be met in the residential situation where the ratio of adults to children in out of school hours may be much lower than in the family situation.

Indeed in considering some of the difficultieis involved in the writing of braille by beginners. Hechle (1975) concludes that an understanding of language structure is a vital element which may have to be built up over a period of careful and considered tutelage. The mechanics of the process of writing braille offer fewer problems now than in the past in that with the use of an Upward Braille Writer such as the Perkins Writer, the dots are embossed on to thick manilla paper in the same form in which they are read. Previous methods involved indenting the dots with the necessity for the learner to memorize the characters in reverse for writing. Some senior pupils and students still find a use for a stylo and small hand frame for note-taking when the use of an upward writer would be inconvenient, but the use of a portable tape recorder has minimized this need.

Hechle however, exposes a central difficulty which teachers may encounter when children wish to write a sentence that is within the structure of their spoken language but which involves a complex use of contractions that lie beyond the range of their reading experience. He refers to the three ways in which this eventuality may be met as being to allow the child to write as he thinks fit without undue attention to correctness in the braille form or to show the child the correct form even if this involves difficult contractions at the limit or beyond the limit of his comprehension. Finally an attempt may be made to restrict the child's writing within the structures and attainments of his reading levels. The blind child is less likely than the sighted to encounter the written word incidentally and he is also restricted by the fact that finger reading reduces predictability. Over-restriction to ensure correct braille forms in the ealry stages of writing is undesirable and the use of a scheme such as *The Family Books* as a test on which to draw for practice in written answers to questions is helpful in that it embodies the controlled introduction of contractions.

Oral and written communication should develop side by side. The correction of mistakes in written braille needs to be undertaken on an individual basis and with care not to discourage the fluency of imaginative content of the pupil's expression. Blind pupils often appear to enjoy using the braille upward writer and learn to handle it with skill. Whilst encouraging accuracy and speed in the use of the braille code in all its complexity the pupil's creative expression must not be stifled. Exposure to correct forms of written braille and ample opportunity to practise writing it are vital aspects in helping the pupil to use this medium effectively to convey his thoughts in symbolic form.

PRINT READING AND WRITING FOR PUPILS WITH DEFECTIVE VISION

Visual skills involved in reading print

In a classroom where children with defective sight are using printed books, not braille, for reading, we might find John whose near vision is very poor so that the page of his book is held so close in reading that it touches his nose; Bill who has cataracts but is receiving treatment for this condition with a consequent improvement in the amount he can see; Jill who is an albino and who hates books with bright shiny pages, and Kim whose eye condition involving macula degeneration affects his central vision. In addition to these physically based visual problems the teacher suspects that some of her pupils have specific reading disabilities not entirely attributable to their visual defects. Also, Bill's hospital attendances have meant rather frequent absence from school, Kim comes from a socially deprived area, and Jill, although an albino, is an immigrant child with a limited vocabulary in English.

But all these pupils will need to develop comparable basic skills in order to use print for reading. They will need to be able to select a figure from its background, a letter, a group of letters or a word or phrase from the page. They will need to perceive constancy of shape in the case of letters and words presented in different sizes and type styles and to discriminate between letters that are similar in appearance. Besides developing sequential memory for visual and auditory symbols and the ability to discriminate and blend sounds, their skill in eye-hand co-ordination will need to be established and strengthened. All these skills are among those recognized as underlying the complex achievements of reading and writing and are largely associated with processes of visual perception. But the teacher concerned with reading and writing for visually handicapped pupils will want to know if there are any general principles applicable in teaching these skills to such children and if there are any specific approaches of benefit to pupils with particular visual problems.

Reading achievement in partially sighted children

One needs initially to consider whether visually handicapped children have been shown to have problems in reading greater than those of the non-handicapped child. It could be expected that visual defects limiting the visual field might well have an effect on speed and fluency. It is not surprising that research evidence shows a variety of conclusions when one considers the heterogeneous nature of visually handicapped pupils and the number of variables which, in addition to their defective sight, might influence their reading achievements. In reviewing the literature on the attainments of the partially sighted, Lansdown (1975) finds in general terms a range of evidence with regard to the learning achievement as well as to the social adjustment of these pupils. He cites several workers including Eames (1937), Park and Burri (1943), Schonell (1948), and Vernon (1971) who associate low reading ability with poor vision. There is also some evidence that partially sighted pupils may be older than fully sighted children in the same class. Peck (1925), Benton (1963), and Birch *et al.* (1966) show studies spanning the years which give confirmation of this tendency. However, complexity is introduced into the issue by the findings of such workers as Tinker (1936) and Douglas *et al.* (1968) who recorded exceptionally high reading rates among myopic children. As a sequel to his comprehensive review of previous studies a further one was undertaken by Landsdown himself (1975) with subjects from schools for the partially sighted in London matched with fully sighted pupils attending ordinary schools. His result showed no significant difference in the reading competence between the partially sighted and the fully sighted subejcts but there were indications of a slower rate of achievement in other tasks involving visual perception, for instance in the copying of shapes, in which the partially sighted showed some lag. The small classes in the special schools for the partially sighted and the availability of individual help from the teacher were consider to the possible factors contributing to the relative success in reading by the partially sighted group in the study.

Visual perception in print reading

Carroll and Hibbert (1973) also draw attention to the varied nature of the problems of partially sighted pupils and the difficulty of establishing from previous research either generalized or widely accepted conclusions about the attainments of these pupils as a group. Their own study indicated that in a sample of 13 partially sighted pupils of infant and junior age the mean scores on conventional intelligence tests were slightly below the means of the comparison group. Although the sample here is small the results give some support to Fine's (1968) survey of 1,374 partially sighted pupils in special schools in the UK which showed a comparable tendency to score below the average. Carroll and Hibbert are intrigued by the possibility that perceptual ability and visual capacity could be related.

Whilst there is criticism of the approach to training visual perception from some workers, evidence such as that contributed by Carroll and Hibbert suggests that the teacher of reading to visually handicapped children needs to give attention to perceptual training as part of the teaching of reading.

A reading scheme such as *Racing to Read* devised by Tansley and Nichols (1962) offers both these elements, and is well suited to partially sighted readers in its presentation which is in a clear format, well spaced and with simple illustrations.

Reading and Remedial Reading by Tansley (1967) again parents material useful in the early stages of reading, with its accompanying activities of matching, of left-to-right movement and emphasis of body awareness. In both these books the vocabulary and content are well suited to the developmental level of the children and the large work books and supplementary material, games and activities are manageable for many of the partially sighted.

The teacher has a difficult task in attempting to understand the visually handicapped child's difficulties in terms of the cause and nature of the visual defect and the probable influence it has on the child's visual functioning. It is not possible at the present state of knowledge to tie up specific teaching approaches and adaptations of material to match precisely the problems arising from specific visual defects.

However, there are some approaches in presenting reading materials which have been found in the experience of teachers to be helpful in relation to specific difficulties in seeing.

Difficulties resulting from specific problems of sight

For instance, pupils with a condition which affects the clarity of the area of central vision may be helped in reading by focusing their gaze just below the printed line rather than on it. Thus the top half of the letters which afford the most easily recognizable clues remain within the area of clearer vision. A child with this particular difficulty may also be helped by trailing a pencil or marker just below the line of print as he attempts to read it.

Some visually handicapped children may evidence low motivation towards using print, as a result of lack of encouragement or positive discouragement to use their sight for this purpose. Here again, the use of closed circuit television, the presentation of enlarged material on slide projectors, the use of flash cards, and language master machines which explose single words or short phrases from the reading book can help to concentrate attention. A simple exposure device in the from of a card covering the printed page with slit openings to reveal a controlled amount of text can also be used. Even the colour cue method of teaching reading such as *Words in Colour* (Gettengo, 1962) which at first sounds surprising as a teaching approach for children who do not see well, seems to help some pupils without impaired colour vision to concentrate on material presented in print form.

In the case of adult partially sighted readers, Shaw (1969) observed that those with contract were not helped so much by an increase in the size of print as by a slight increase in its boldness. Myopic subjects on the other hand found their reading facilitated by an increase in the size rather than in the weight of print but subjects suffering from glaucoma found that bold type was generally more helpful in their case. This study showed that an improvement of 35 per cent could be expected when the best features of typography were combined. The aspects exerting most influence on this improvement were size of type, which accounted for half of the improvement in legibility, increased boldness which added a quarter to the total factors of increased success, and finally a clear sans serif typeface which accounted for one eighth of the improvement noted.

Enlarged print

The question of enlargement of print poses a different set of problems in the case of children with impaired vision from those to be considred in the case partially sighted adults. The majority of whom are to be found in the middle and upper age groups. Children can bring their reading material close to the eye, thus affecting a spontaneous effect of enlargement since the lens is so flexible in its accommodation during this period of life. Over the years the possibility of discovering an 'optimum type' for school books has been considered by teachers, but no specific form or size of typeface has been found to be universally well suited to the needs of all visually handi-capped pupils. A slightly bolder than average Gill Sans Serif or Plantin typeface has been recommended as a good working presentation by some teachers of the visually handicapped. Typeface should not be too heavy, since the characteristic spaces in letters can be somewhat occluded if the presentation is too bold in the pattern of printed letters and words.

Lighting, magnification, and position of work

An experimental study has been followed up by a series of commentaries by Sykes (1975 and 1977). In total these give a comprehensive consideration of the question of print legibility for children with impaired vision. Comparing the effectiveness of standard print and enlarged print in facilitating reading skills he concludes that the use of large print in itself did little to help the young partially sighted reader but he suggests, as do most practising teachers, that attention should be given to the total layout of the print page in terms of the clear well-spaced presentation of material. Length of line and width of margin may also contribute to a well-displayed page. Attention is again drawn to the importance of appropriate illumination with a recommended level of fifty foot candles for low vision children who should be provided with portable reading lamps to permit regulation of intensity of light to suit their individual requirements. Photophobic children, such as albinos, will of course need to avoid glare and shiny light-reflective surfaces such as glossy pages and highly polished desk tops. The Department of Education and Science Bulletin No. 33 *Lighting in Schools* contains an appendix with particular reference to schools for the partially sighted, but questions of print presentation, illumination and teaching apparatus in reading should be considered for the visually handicapped pupil in any educational setting.

The position in which the reading material is placed also warrants attention. If the pupil needs to hold the material close to his eye, or if he uses a magnifier or how visual aid which necessitates a reduced focal length, his working position may give rise to tension or to bad posture unless care is taken to avoid this. If the reading book is placed on the flat surface of a desk or table top, the child may want to bend right over it in order to bring his gaze close enough to see it clearly thereby casting a shadow on to the page and adopting a stooped, cramped and uncomfortable position for reading and writing. A desk that is basically of the right size, and which has a sloping adjustable lid or the provision of a reading stand, can mitigate the difficulty of dealing with work at such close range.

The use of low vision aids or magnifiers can have some influence on the form of attack made on reading skills. A respected aim in promoting fluency in reading is one which emphasizes the ability to perceive words and phrases as wholes rather than concentrating on individual letters in succession. Visually handicapped children with a limited eye-span, or those using optical aids which only enable them to see one or two letters or part of a word at a time, may be expected to encounter problems with regard to fluency in reading. They can be helped by an approach which affords the opportunity for a period of word analysis followed by synthesis. However, Sykes (1977) in commenting on the child-centred approach to the teaching of reading which involves the learner in encountering written wrods from his own experience notes that the success of this method is dependent on the use of whole words, phrases and sentences. He draws attention to the fact that the phonic method which emphasizes the form and sound of individual letters and groups of letters, presents a more manageable task for some children with impaired sight, although fluency may be restricted because the analysis of words results in a slower rate of accomplishment. Thus it may be advisable to use either the whole-word method or the part method or even a combination of both according to the needs of the individual pupil; the possibility of introducing groups of letters notable for ease of visual recognition as well as frequency of use, is an interesting suggestion reminiscent of some of the teaching approaches in character recognition in braille.

Pre-reading activities

Whatever form the visual handicap of the pupil manifests, the complex process of reading for him, as for other children, will be rooted in speaking and listening. As for all children his ability to develop meaningful language and converse is likely to be enhanced by listening to stories, re-telling them and acting them. An information sheet for parents issued by the John Aird School for the Partially Sighted (1975) suggests ways in which opportunities for these activities can be encouraged at home. Children who do not see well will require pre-reading books with bright simple attractive pictures. They will need to be helped to realize the difference between reading a story and telling a story and to understand that the written words, not simply the pictures, convey meaning. Their wish to use books may need to be awakened and the first books they use should be accessible, attractive, and of a manageable size for them to handle. Children's libraries in the neighbourhood are an excellent source of well-presented story books.

The beginning of writing

Before the finer muscle movements involved in reading and writing are practised, the larger muscle movements need to be experienced and developed. Games involving imitative movements, including left-to-right movement of arms and hands, can easily be combined with practice in the spoken word. Nursery rhymes, singing games and action songs are important and enjoyable pre-reading activities for the visually handicapped child, who may need a good deal of free activity in gaining knowledge of the world around him before he begins to read and write about it.

These activities are a preparation for writing as well as for reading, since speaking, listening and movement are essential bases for this form of communciation. It is both important that the child has something to write about, and that he develops the technical skills that enable him to do so. The technical skills can offer some problems to children with poor vision. Manipulation of materials, pattern matching and recognition are necessary preskills in this area for pupils whose view of a figure is blurred or fragmented.

For the visually handicapped child who needs to work at close range in painting, drawing and eventually in writing, small easels or even blackboards give him the opportunity to make big bold shapes involving the use of arm and hand in a free and uncramped position. Linked patterns of undulating lines help to develop the 'feel' of fluent movements before actual letter shapes are attempted.

Attention to handwriting and to typing

The Marion Richardson scheme of teaching handwriting, growing out of patterns formed from letters is well suited to the visually handicapped in that the shape of the letters is represented and reinforced. Children who see poorly sometimes do not know where to start in the formation of a letter and a cursive rather than a separated script can be helpful to them. The use of closed circuit TV, enlarged material shown on a projector, or a close individual demonstration is necessary for such children who cannot easily see the process of drawing letter shapes. Practice in large movements making the shape of the letters and vocalizing the shapes and directions of movement may be needed before more conventional graphic forms are used.

Paper ruled with clear black lines give a guide to 'above' and 'below' line letter drawing. It can amuse and interest children to draw their attention to the characteristic letter shapes through describing them in terms of animation; the giraffe letters with their long necks above the line and the monkey letters with their tails curling below the line.

The use of a pencil which gives a heavy black line, and of felt tipped pens in clear bright colours enables the child to see for himself the shapes he has drawn and the letters which he has written. Both the thickness and the size of the written forms can be gradually diminished.

Using writing for names and labels, associating the written word with the person, the object, the action, is part of the beginning of written experiences. The difference between lower and upper case letters needs to be introduced carefully to avoid confusion.

The appearance of written work in a group of children with visual handicaps is likely to be very varied, from the minute style and tiny illustrations of some of the myopic pupils to the untidy apparently unco-ordinated attempts of some of the other pupils who find it difficult to reproduce a graphic shape. Every encouragement to write should be offered with the opportunities for the pupils to compile their own scrap books and story books.

It can be useful for the visually handicapped pupil to learn typewriting, since even wtih practice his handwriting may be relatively slow, and evidence his difficulty in keeping on a line. For examination purposes, typewriting is particularly useful. Nevertheless it does not replace handwriting as an art, and adequate time, and appropriate pre-writing activities and materials need to be employed in fostering this basic skill.

TEACHING OF MATHEMATICS AND NUMBER CONCEPTS TO VISUALLY HANDICAPPED PUPILS

Overcoming difficulties in basic mathematical concepts

Inability to see shapes clearly, or perhaps at all, with consequently a reduced opportunity to be aware of number groups, such as a clump of five trees at the far end of a garden, or eight seagulls bobbing on the sea in the distance, means that children with severe levels of visual handicap have a less informative and less inviting background against which to develop an interest in mathematical concepts than would be the case for children whose vision is not impaired.

It might be expected that total lack of sight, in particular, would be likely to presuppose difficulty, or at least delay, in many areas involving an understanding of relationships in number, size, and shape, as well as in spatial concepts. Just as the child with little or no sight has lacked or has received diminished incidental experiences in seeing printed or written words displayed in slogans and advertisements in his everyday environment, so children with little or no sight are likely to have a limited experience of visual pattern and shape of the kind econountered by the fully sighted child in graphic and pictorial material as well as in the object that surround him in his ordinary daily life. The round plate, the square table, the matching set of cutlery for each person at the table must be explored by the fingers or by the close gaze of the visually handicapped youngster. Not only in infancy, but as he is growing up too, his deprivation of the clear visual experience of form and shape may put him at some disadvantage compared with the fully sighted pupil. Even in the secondary school state Thwaites (1970) refers to the ways in which the visual stimuli of modern architecture and industrial design impinge on the minds of seeing children, and draw attention to the mathematical concepts at or near the root of the understanding of these forms.

The child who sees little or nothing will therefore not only need to explore and to discover the characteristics of shapes through tactile investigation, he will also need to build up a vocabulary of meaningful terms through which to express the result of his discoveries. Such words as vertex, edge, face and curve must be linked with tangible examples that evidence the characteristics which the terms embody. As the discoveries become more complex, so does the need for relevant vocabulary increase. Beginning with reference to shape and continuing with the critical features of shapes, a growing store of words to describe terms of weight, measurement, and amount is necessary. Reinforcement by tangible or, for children with some vision, by pictorial evidence of relationships is essential. The idea of fractions, for example, can be conveyed by halving and quartering stiff pieces of paper and giving names to the wholes and parts. The learning of number bonds from 0 to 20 can begin with tangibles and as in increasing understanding develops, the need for tactile verification will diminish.

In the case of the child using his vision, examples of objects that he can explore in tactile terms should be brought into a position for attentive gaze also. Eventually, attention must be given to ways of recording mathematical data that are appropriate for the child's level of seeing; but recording should follow a developing understanding of relationships and an increasing comprehension of shape and pattern gained through first-hand exploration. In short, the visually handicapped child, like the seeing child, should be helped to think mathematically, not simply to record symbols on one or more of the many ingeniously adapted pieces of apparatus available to him.

Nevertheless, the ability to transfer a visual problem into terms of symbols and equations, as well as the development of logical thinking and spatial sense are considered by Wilson (1968) necessary attributes for the pupil to be successful in mathematics. In the days when rather formal teaching of mathematics was current, it was optimistically stated in the *Handbook for School Teachers of the Blind* (College of Teachers of the Blind,

1956), that there were no difficulities inherent in the subject of mathematics itself which could not be overcome by blind pupils. The realistic teacher, however, will recognize that there are difficulties, particularly for the congenitally and totally blind child, both in the presentation of material and in the subsequent processes of understanding and recording results, but that these difficulties present challenges which do not prevent this subject from being a vital and interesting one in which high levels of success can eventually be obtained by some pupils.

Fortunately, many of the problems arising in the teaching of mathematics have been energetically tackled by teachers who, mindful of the limited experience of blind children, have developed and adapted concrete material in graded schemes of work to provide learning situations appropriate to the child's level of understanding.

In order to use these situations as effectively as possible, a good deal of discussion relating to the objects handled, as well as plenty of opportunity for tactile investigation and manipulation is required before the pupils are ready to collect data as a result of counting and sorting items. Beginning at a simple level the pupils are lead into the mastery of different ways of recording and representing mathematical problems and their solutions through increasingly complex stages. The attempts at recording should be introduced gradually as the idea of pattern and relationship develops, so that what is symbolized is understood, and the whole process of developing mathematical concepts is tied in with vital activity. As experience and understanding increase, more formal and more abstract work can be introduced, with problems posed, and solutions worked out with a decreasing need to refer to concrete examples.

Play activities leading to number work

Initially it is through play that objects are handled and examined, with colourful and visually attractive shapes giving as much invitation as possible to the child with a little vision to use it in increasing his sensory experience and fuelling his curiosity. Play, which begins at home and continues without much noticeable break into the early school years, can offer ways of helping the visually handicapped child to appreciate the code of relationships which underlies essential mathematical concepts. This view is put forward by Tooze (1967) in describing play situations in which the visually handicapped infant is led into discovering that some things are smaller than others, some heavier than others, and eventually that objects can be grouped into the patterns that we call numbers. Thus the beginning of basic number concept coincides well with an active play situation; it is important, however, to ensure that the material used is both manageable and distinctive in tactile terms, as well as colourful for children with some sight.

The building up of a programme involving an increasing awareness of numbers, shapes, and patterns should be an enjoyable exercise for both teacher and pupils. Many of the activities relate well to familiar play or domestic situations. The principle of one-to-one correspondence can be demonstrated by putting an egg in each egg cup when setting a table, then a knife by each plate. The idea of sets is now developing.

Sets and number relationships

Indeed in most children the idea of sets begins to develop intuitively as they start collecting things together, and progess as they sort objects out into collections with particular characteristics. The attention of the visually handicapped child may need to be drawn quite specifically to these characteristics. If a child meets several sets, in which the members of any one set can be matched one-to-one with those of any, other then this collection of sets possesses an abstract quality which is the cardinal number of the sets. Gradually the child becomes aware that different sets can have different numbers of elements, and this realization is related to the development of the concept of ordinal numbers. If sets are arranged in the order of an increasing number of elements (seriation) each set containing one more than its predecessor, the concepts of cardination and ordination are coming together. The difficulty for some visually handicapped children is that they are unlikely to be able to take in at a glance the information with which they are presented.

Sometimes ingenuity is needed in order to demonstrate a principle. Seriation can be evidenced in a tactile way through the use of nesting shapes and the handling and arrangement in graduating size of dolls or toy animals. Classification involving the mixture of two discrete elements can be introduced in terms of shape and texture, for instance in using six bricks of the same size, some of which are smooth, and some roughly textured. The contents of a box of mixed objects can be sorted, classified, and counted, with the groups of similar and then of identical objects totalled and compared. Equalization of groups can be demonstrated by dividing a pile of sweets exactly into two boxes.

Size, shape, capacity and volume

The beginning of an understanding of capacity and volume should have been forming as a result of such activities as sand and water play, with the filling and emptying of containers of different sizes. Simple comparison of lengths can be shown by the child measuring different fingers and book and desk lengths, but these activities are really quite difficult for a blind child and require practice from him as well as patience from his teacher. Games and activities which can help the visually handicapped child to sort and classify, according to a number of criteria, such as shape, size, and texture, can be started without the use of symbolic representation, and then lead into its use.

Adaptations in learning materials and in methods of presentation

Although many of the activities described appear comparable to those undertaken by fully sighted children, the teacher with a visually handicapped child or a group of such children in the class will need to give particular attention to some aspects of the work. In devising and selecting the material for activities, the teacher must bear in mind not only the goal of the activity, but its manageability in terms of the child who sees little or nothing. Control of material is more difficult for the visually handicapped child to achieve than for the fully sighted. Plastic containers or compartmental boxes can be used to hold small objects and units of material. Time can be wasted and confusion can ensue if pieces of material skid off the top of the desk or table while they are being handled, and it is essential that tactile materials should not only be accessible to the visually handicapped child, but also capable of thorough exploration by him. For example, although buttons and small objects can be mounted on cards foı matching numbers, objects should in general be presented in the early stages in such a way that they can be explored in all dimensions. The length of the sessions spent on specific activities warrants attention also. Some visually handicapped children can become bored and distractable whilst undertaking sorting and classifying activities if they are expected to continue doing so for too long at one time. These pupils need enough time to complete tasks, to explore and to investigate, but a new activitiy leading to a new concept should be introduced as soon as the pupil is ready for it. The goals which form the objective of each activity should be clearly set, and the progression ot activities matched to the developing capacities of the child's thinking. The teacher will need to keep a record of each individual pupil's progress, and to be alert to adapt any activities with which the child is having difficulties as a result of his sight defect.

Recording of work

Gradually the sets of facts discovered as a result of investigation and discussion can be recorded in a variety of ways, through speech, and later through permanent symbolic representation. Representation can be very simple at first, using pegboards or wooden blocks, with the introduction of braille or print numerical and operational symbols as the pupils begins to understand the principles represented. Histograms offer an effective way of beginning to use one object to represent several, and to show the early stages of collecting, sorting, and comparing data.

With regard to the progression of activities and the appropriate stages of introducing various types of recording in the primary school, reference can most usefully be made to the lively scheme of work for blind children described by F. H. G. Tooze (1967). The way in which this approach emphasizes the structuring of situations to enable the individual to make discoveries for himself does not preclude group work and the introduction of some formal learning, but it does emphasize the value of ensuring that the pupil understands procedures rather than simply repeating them, but the use of an organized system of number materials should be adopted.

Tooze suggests that, after the early play activities of the type described above, the use of colour factor rods should be introduced when the children are about six. A magnetized backing can be given to the blocks which can then be used on a steel plate to retain their position. Dienes logic blocks and multibase arithmetic blocks or Stern's apparatus can be used effectively with visually handicapped pupils also, although the blocks are somewhat less easy for those without sight to handle. Here again, it is important for the pupils to understand what the blocks are representing. The caveat which Dearden (1969) puts forward about the use of discovery methods in the early stages of mathematics teaching with sighted children has, if anything, even more significance in the case of the visually handicapped. His questions as to why wooden blocks should be seen as a concrete analogue of mathematical relationships if the pupil is not taught something of those relationships is even more cogent in the case of pupils who see poorly or who do not see at all. For these children especially, initiation must be undertaken in order to learn about concepts which are exemplified by concrete objects and the arrangement of representational forms.

Another form of representation which some blind children will be ready to use by this stage is the cubarithm board. This apparatus consists of a small, firm plastic board with lines of square apertures in which metal cubes can be fitted as required for recording or for working sums. These small cubes bear braille numerical and operational signs on each of their facets. Detailed instructions with regard to the use of the cubarithm board as well as suggestions as to the advantages and disadvantages of its use are given in *The Teaching of Science and Mathematics to the Blind*. In this, F. H. G. Tooze suggests a graduation of tasks of increasing complexity leading to the application of the four rules and of learned tables. The more formal approach is introduced when colour factor blocks are used for setting out and solving a problem and then the result is recorded by means of braille numerical symbols made on the Perkins braille upward writer. Side by side with the pupil's own attempts at recording work, brailled or clearly printed work cards can be introduced.

These are useful in providing problems for pupils to solve at different levesl of competence and understanding of mathematical thinking. In compiling such cards, clarity of content and presentation are essential.

Some of the pupils, including the totally blind, will be able to record work without much difficulty by using the Perkins upward writer when they are about 8 years old, although complete severance from the concrete will not have taken place in that colour factor blocks and the cubarithm board may still be used in the working out stages of a problem. Motivation in areas involving the four rules can be heightened and concepts reinforced by the pupils themselves making pictographs. The understanding of sequence and of number relationships can be shown by reference to the number line which is composed of linked units marked off with braille symbols; children will vary in their need to refer to such concrete evidence as a check during the processes of calculation. Indeed references to activities in mathematics as in other areas of learning for visually handicapped children should be considered as a guide line if suggested age-groups are quoted, since pupils are likely to span a range with regard to their readiness in understanding concepts. Tobin's study of the conservation of substance (1972b) shows this to be an important factor.

When the pupils are ready for a further form of representation in number work, the Cranmer abacus can be introduced. This is an adaptation of the Japanese abacus and works on a base of five. It is light and portable and the beads are easy to handle but do not slip about with the result that some pupils become very quick and adept in its use. Davidow (1966) gives a detailed but clear exposition of its use in full, but F. H. G. Tooze recommends it for addition and subtraction rather than for multiplication and division. He also suggests that in the later stages of the primary school pupils should construct three-dimensional forms such as the tetrahedron for themselves. Work of this kind involves the child in a disciplined study of shape including the investigation of edges and faces, thus giving direction and conclusion to earlier play with shapes. At the same stage and alongside this practical work increasing opportunities for recording the wording and solution of problems should be attempted. The cubarithm board and the abacus may still be used with something of the function of the pencil and notebook which the sighted child uses for jotting down interim stages of working. The use of the Taylor frame, another piece of specialized apparatus fulfilling a comparable role, is now seldom taught especially at primary school level. The ingenious but elusive small metal rods known as Taylor type are difficult for younger children to handle and involve the learning of an additional series of numerical and later of algebraic symbols.

The increasing availability and subsequently the universal usage of the Perkins upward writer which enables the braille symbols to be embossed on to paper, has diminished the need for using the Taylor frame, and enabled pupils to check their own work more easily. However, even now there is not a unanimous point of view throughout the schools with regard to the setting out of mathematical working in braille, and even a mathematical code which includes all operational, numerical and algebraic symbols has been subject to revisions and alterations that are not always adopted in practice.

Some teachers prefer a method of layout for mathematics in braille which follows as closely as possible to that used in printed forms, thus involving some vertical setting out in the process of working. Whittaker (1967) however, has devised a method of layout and working which has been referred to as the linear method. The figures and operational signs are set out along the line in horizontal form, and it is claimed that this minimizes the need for manipulating the Perkins by placing figures underneath each other. Whilst merit can be found in either of these approaches, teachers of blind pupils at secondary level are presented with a challenging task in dealing with a group of pupils who have come into a secondary class from different primary schools or departments using different forms of mathematical layout.

Mathematics for the secondary school pupil

Sims's (1967) studies of the teaching of mathematics to academically able pupils at the secondary school stage, show that the msot evident differences between them and sighted pupils of comparable age and ability was that the speed of calculation that could be expected from the blind pupils was slower, except in the case of mental arithmetic. The blind pupils in her experience had greater difficulty both in comprehending and in replicating diagrammatic work. She also considered that logical thinking was less evident than the result of repetitive learning in the case of the blind pupils.

Despite such problems, blind pupils of good ability have, with the help of skilled teachers, been able to achieve high levels of success in mathematics. The syllabus leading to external examinations at both GCE 'O' and 'A' Levels as well as the CSE, can be followed with adaptations in the presentation and recording of material, even with the sue of a 'talking computer', but with the examination content the same as for the fully sighted pupil. The value of the subject must not be under-estimated in terms not only of developing logical thinking and problem solving, but also in terms of opening up vocational possibilities and forming an essential skill in many areas of daily life. An understanding of the binary system, for instance, may be required in computer studies which are undertaken by some blind pupils at sixth-form level.

For the pupils who find abstract thinking difficult, opportunities for tactile discovery, comparison and reference should not cease at the end of primary school, since some blind pupils even at adolescence may show deficiencies both in the characteristics of objects and in spatial awareness. the need for pupils to be able to manage their own money, to plan ahead in terms of cause and effect, to budget and keep simple accounts is self-evident. Basic mathematical skills may have to be continued in the area of 'social arithmetic' throughout the secondary school years for some pupils who will need carefully graduated schemes and work assignments involving practical activities of weighing, measuring, and counting. Project and group work offers a useful opportunity to involve pupils in activities including construction and calculation.

Using residual vision for mathematics

The pupil who has useful vision should be encouraged to use this purposefully in his work in mathematics, although he should not be inhibited from tactile exploration and the use of concrete material which helps to clarify concepts. Suitable commercially produced material abounds in which clear diagrammatic representation and graded materials are available with teaching guidelines, pupils' workbooks and workcards. The material in such schemes is generally presented under broad topic headings which indicate the logical sequence of the work presented. Visually handicapped pupils relying on their vision may need plenty of practice at each stage and the general recommendations with regard to the position of work, lighting and demonstration of processes, even to enlarged drawing of geometrical figures and algebraic signs should be observed as for teaching of writing. Tables such as logarithms have been produced in large print form since the standard form presents so dense a page of figures.

In schools for sighted children there have been moves to replace logarithms by slide rules up of CSE and GCE 'O' Level Mathematics. Now the pocket electronic calculator looks like making both of these aids to calculation archaic at school level. The implications of this for the teaching of mathematics are hard to predict. In the case of visually handicapped pupils attention must be directed towards the development and production of instruments with an output that they can either read or hear.

Clear pictorial representation is well suited to pupils with enough vision to make use of this form of presentation. Data can be presented pictorially in such a way that attention is drawn to relationships that might otherwise be less clearly shown by a mass of numerals. A scheme which emphasizes the presentation of data in pictorial form, at the same time giving attention to the building up of a meaningful vocabulary of mathematical terms, is described by Lovatt (1970). He uses the Nuffield mathematics approach in work for educationally subnormal pupils, but the clarity of the presentation and the emphasis on simple graphical representation make this an approach that would be of value to less academic partially sighted pupils. A further advantage of such a scheme is that the individual and small group situations needed for a class of pupils of mixed ability and mixed visual competence would find in it work well suited to individual levels.

The Schools Council 'Look and Think' Project may have implications for the learning of mathematics by pupils with some vision, since its emphasis on shape discrimination, attention to critical features, and to symmertry and perspective, offer at least the possibility of transfer to situations involving the mathematical concepts of such phenomena as shape, pattern and sequence.

If a secure basis of experience and discussion with plenty of opportunity for practice is given to blind and partially sighted pupils during their primary school years, their secondary school programme in mathematics can approximate in content at least to that of fully sighted pupils of comparable ability. Teachers of blind and partially sighted pupils still confer in attempts to resolve some of the problems regarding suitable content and appropriate recording that still await solution, but the importance of mathematics presented at a level appropriate to the needs and abilities of visually handicapped pupils can be doubted by none.

MOBILITY ORIENTATION AND MOVEMENT TRAINING

Value of physical activities including sports

The thud of a large soft ball on a bat can be heard as a team of blind boys, some totally without sight, enjoy their game of cricket on an eighteen foot grass pitch. A spectator would note some adaptations to the traditional game; one bounce of the ball before a catch being allowed to those who do not see at all, and the ball itself made of white plastic and containing a handful of swirling roller bearings needs to be heard by the players. According to Raffle (1970) who enjoyed such games at school and later encouraged visually handicapped students to try it, one of the few drawbacks occurred when the equivalent of 'bad light' flew overhead or traffic noise at the bottom of the lawn masked the sound of the ball. The purpose of the game was exactly the same as for sighted boys—enjoyment.

Another sight that can surprise the visitor to a school for the blind is that of the pupils running flat out in track events, swimming and diving to competition levels, or spending leisure hours practising judo, wrestling or rowing. Schools for the partially sighted can also present an impressive list of the physical recreation activities which many of their pupils take up; the pursuits described by one school as being part of their programme included horse-riding, hill-walking, swimming in river and sea, canoeing in river and sea, rock-climbing and rifle shooting. There is a particular value in the sports and pursuits that a visually handicapped pupil will wish to continue after leaving school, both from the point of view of maintaining fitness, and making social contacts with people of similar interests. Consequently, it is undesirable that physical education and games times should be used by the visually handicapped child attending ordinary school as a time to have 'coaching' in work that he has found difficult to follow in academic lessons. The times of the day or week given to active participation in sport and physical activities are not expendable, and individual programmes need to be worked out for the visually handicapped pupil who cannot or does not wish to take part in team events.

Undue fears that the visually handicapped child may be in danger of damaging his sight further, particularly as a result of retinal detachment, are less frequently encountered than in the past, and if medical advice is sought and observed, activities can be adapted even for those few children considered to be at risk.

Early activities to develop purposeful movement

Easy and purposeful movement is not achieved however, by every visually handicapped pupil; early encouragement and opportunities to explore the physical environment together with training in orientation are necessary precursors to later achievement, and children deprived of these opportunities are likely to have difficulties in independent mobility later on.

Both the blind and the partially sighted child in his early primary school years will need the same large muscle and coordinating physical activities as the fully sighted child. Games which also include rhythmic movement such as clapping, skipping, and hopping are especially enjoyable. Interpretative movement can be difficult since demonstration cannot be seen or cannot be seen well, but action learning and kinaesthetic demonstration can help the children in animal games which include rabbit hops or duck waddles. Active outdoor play will provide opportunities for crawling and climbing but adult intervention to encourage and motivate this may be needed as the trees, blocks and tunnels of an adventure playground if not seen will be less inviting to spontaneous exploration!

Consequently, movement training for the young primary school child who sees little or nothing will need to be based on body awareness, movement in space, and movement that relates to objects and people. He needs to develop a knowledge and control of his arms, legs and body, and in exploring rather than shunning his physical environment he will gain experience in finding out what happens when he attempts to move himself about in relation to objects. Purposeful movement has to be developed according to the demands of a situation, so the visually handicapped child will need to move in as many different ways and in as many different situations as possible when his courage and initiative increase. Such activities will help him to develop awareness of the position of his trunk, head and limbs in space, both when still and in movement, increasing his ability to maintain balance, and developing his kinaesthetic or 'musclememory.'

Using all the senses in movement training

Without the co-ordinating sense of sight, the blind child, and especially the congenitally blind child, may show inept and uncontrolled movement; he may also fear space, and lacking a sense of direction, be unaware of directional change as well as being unable to correct or replicate a movement. In such cases there is clearly a need for timely and individual remedial work. D. Tooze (1967) traces such delays in readiness for purposeful movement to apprehension as a result of early limitations in the opportunity to play and explore actively. She considers that primary school work must lay emphasis on specific training in using the senses of hearing, touch and smell as cues in helping to develop orientation. Response to sound cues may be practised in chanting games, in following the sound of the teacher's voice and in games with large cane bell-balls that are easy to follow and to handle. The attention of the pupils can be drawn to the use of reflected sounds as a cue since some blind children will instinctively clap their hands or click their tongues when approaching a wall and the ability to respond to these cues can be improved with practice. Both Leonard (1967) and D. Tooze (1972) refer to the necessity for visually handicapped children to use their senses in an unusual manner—playing attention to the information gathered through the senses to an extent which the sighted child need not do. In locating places, for example, some shops notably a baker's or a fishmonger's, can be recognized by smell, as can the school dining-room. There are surface cues also, which can be noted and talked about, small slopes and changes in gradient, even within the school campus, about which the pupil can be alerted to feel the difference in weight and effort in moving up or down hill. A heightened awareness of the environment, and an increased ability to use many different sources of information when moving about will help to give a sound basis of training before formal mobility work begins.

Development of physical co-ordination and body awareness

Sensitivity both to the developmental readiness and the individual techniques which each child will develop is essential if an effective sequence of exercises concerntrating on body image, laterality and directionality is to be practised. In working out such programmes the screening test devised by Cratty and Sammes (1968) shows the extent to which the pupil can identify the parts of his body, the planes of his body (side, back, front, etc.) and left and right directionality. The progression of work from body-image training, through dynamic spatial orientation, to map-reading and mobility is outlined clearly by these authors. Carrying out verbal instructions with regard to bodily movement can be quite difficult for a blind child, and it is important that the instructions are clear and also that they are meaningful to him. Kooyman (1967) believes communication to be a fundamental aspect of physical education for pupils with defective vision. The relationship between the 'ego' and the external world is not easy for the blind child to establish, since he is likely to have less information, less control, less co-ordination and less stimulation than the non-handicapped child. He must develop an adequate and trustworthy relationship with his environment through movement, but his body may seem less useful, less at his disposal, than that of a sighted child, even seeming at times to be an obstacle rather than a means of expression. However the self-realization that can grow from meaningful communication and purposeful movement can be strengthened in active play and in mastery of the physical self.

Mobility as a school subject

Mobility has by now come to be considered as an essential school subject for blind children culminating in their ability to walk through familiar and unfamiliar environments self-dependently. The necessary competence can be broken down into sub-skills and taught to pupils in the same way as other school subjects. During the 1950s and 1960s both researchers and teachers in Great Britain became interested in the technique of using the long cane which had been so successful in the USA especially in the rehabilitation of war-blinded veterans. La duke, an American expert in mobility, initiated work in which two Liverpool schools for the blind were involved and in 1968 a special training centre for instructors was established now known as the National Mobility Centre. School teachers as well as social workers began to undertake this highly specific training in which a chest-high white stick is used in a series of sweeping movements to detect kerbs and obstacles. But the new techniques offered much more than that. The training was highly technical with its own terminology, such as 'lining up' and 'squaring off' being used to describe alignment and turning away from a fixture. Efficient ways of moving about indoors as well as out-of-doors were taught, including opening doors, locating chairs and tables, even retrieving lost objects from the floor with maximum safety.

Teachers, however, were increasingly convinced that the use of any mobility aid, especially one as useful as the long cane, could only be acceptable if training in its use was the culmination of a more basic course in orientation and movement training. The difficulty of time-tabling mobility with its need for regular individual instruction as well as practical sessions frequently outside the school campus was tackled in a series of conferences whose recommendations are published under the title *Mobility Training in Schools for the Visually Handicapped* (College of Teachers of the Blind, 1971).

In order to render such training programmes manageable Shannon (1971) suggests that an appropriately trained teacher should not only be responsible for the training of individual pupils, but a workshop project carefully developed whereby other teachers and house-staff can be instructed in pre-cane skills. Practical sessions using the blindfold with discussions to clarify and solve problems can be undertaken. Stress is constantly given to the necessity for early attention to body awareness, posture and gait before formal training in cane techniques. Directional techniques, protective techniques, familiarization with the environment and the use of a sighted guide follow this basic training.

Maps and diagrams in mobility training

The interpretation of tactile maps and diagrams in terms of orientation form a key feature of an effective mobility course. The pupil can be taught to plot his own chart with mapping pins as he recognizes landmarks and works out his direction of travel. Both research and practice have been directed towards co-ordination in the use of symbols in map-reading.

The question of standardization of design and symbolization in tactile route maps for the blind is analysed by James and Campbell (1975). They classify important landmarks under the headings of line symbols, point symbols, and texture symbols. The first group of these indicates such features as guiding surfaces, railings, walls and footpaths to the blind traveller, whilst the point symbols show the presence of possible obstacles or hazards, crossing points, and facilities such as telephone boxes. The last group of symbols gives information on the quality of surface under foot, the presence of parks, woods and grass verges. Questions of scale, coding space, information density and distinguishability are considered, together with the prime need to exchange information between all those concerned with the production of embossed maps, so that standardization is achieved in the way that information is presented.

Training in directionality and in tactile discrimination underlies the successful use of these presentations; it must also be concerned with demonstration and practice in the movements involved in handling the long cane.

Parental involvement in training schemes

Parental involvement in mobility training has been a challenging development in some schools for the blind. At Tapton mount School, Sheffield, for example, parents are trained by a mobility teacher from the school; their experiences under the blindfold as they negotiate foot and public transport journeys, walk along crowded pavements and weave through busy shops give them an increased and realistic understanding of the demands of mobility for the visually handicapped child. In addition, parental interest in this key area of training is likely to ensure that mobility practice undertaken by the pupil at school does not lapse during holiday times. Ideally this parents' programme should begin before the child comes to school, continuing through active play and pursuits which encourage freedom of movement throughout his school years and culminating in the formal mobility exercises involved in long-cane usage.

Mannerisms in visually handicapped children

Attention is given in the Vernon Report (1972) to the necessity for mobility training and the attempt to diminish mannerisms. Fine (1968) had drawn attention to the prevalence of mannerisms and poor mobility in her Survey of Blind and Partially Sighted Pupils in England and Wales. In this she recorded that 9.6 per cent of the partially sighted and 45 per cent of the blind displayed one or more mannerisms. Poor mobility which could not be ascribed to physical handicap was encountered in 4.5 per cent of the partially sighted and 25 per cent of the blind. Recent evidence (Jastrzembska, 1974) shows that there are some pointers which indicate that eye-poking is related more directly to visual impairment than other mannerisms such as rocking which is more likely to be associated with somatosensory deprivation.

Mobility training for children with partial vision

Nevertheless the observations in the Vernon Report (1972) with regard to partially sighted children show that their needs must not be ignored. The percentages of partially sighted children affected both by mannerisms and by poor mobility were not insignificant even though they were predictably less than in the case of children considered educationally blind.

The movement training and mobility skills required by children with enough vision to be considered as partially sighted has been less clearly defined both in research and in practical teaching programmes than the carefully structured training schemes for those who are considered to be dependent on their other senses rather than that of sight. This is emphasized by the use of the blindfold as a normal aspect of training procedure in mobility.

The individual differences in the way in which partially sighted children and chidlren with residual vision see means that each child will have a slightly different problem with regard to the extent and clarity of his visual panorama. Early training in body awareness and the relationship of the body to objects and its position in space is necessary, and specific training to help the child to make maximum use of his unimpaired senses by giving attention to cues transmitted by sound, touch, smell and kinaesthetic sensation can help him to locate and make use of directional information.

Dugmore (1973) gives examples of ways in which mobility training for partially sighted pupils ensures the opportunity for them to make the type of journey involved in going to work by public transport. This is essential practice in a residential school, but in many day-schools for the partially sighted pupils arrive by taxi or school bus and may not have had the chance to work out methods of independent travel in practical terms. Dugmore's scheme does more than simply expect the pupils to undertake public transport journeys of increasing difficulty. Tasks involving recognition of landmarks are set, problems encountered on the journey discussed later with teachers, and a methodical approach to overcoming difficulties is worked out with each pupil on an individual basis.

Specialized maps for partially sighted students have been developed and tested by Greenberg (1969) using white lines on a dark grey background; they were found to be useful to most of the pupils who attempted to use them.

Visually handicapped children in varied educational settings

Pupils in ordinary schools who are visually handicapped, blind and partially sighted pupils attending schools for the mentally and physically handicapped may need training in mobility too. It can be all too easy for them to depend on fully sighted friends for getting about, and to be left out of team games in sports because they are not good at them or do not want to take part. Much of the normal work in a physical eudcation programme can be of benefit to them but some of their needs in this respect are specialized and require the help of an advisory teacher for the visually handicapped.

On leaving school or further education it should be possible for the visually handicapped young person to choose whether or not be needs a mobility aid. If he does, there is a series of aids available to him. The long-cane for the use of which he should have received basic training while at school; the sonic torch—a rubber torchshaped device which emits signals indicating the position of obstacles; sonic spectacles which consist of a head-mounted device working on a similar principle; finally a guide dog who will provide a companionable means of independent mobility. But whichever means he chooses, the basic education he has received in mobility and movement training will be invaluable.

SELF-HELP SKILLS

Daily living skills

Breakfast time for most of us means taking the top off an egg, eating the egg with a small spoon, buttering toast, pouring out a cup of tea or coffee, adding just enough milk and one or two teaspoonfuls of sugar. What happens if we attempt to do all this under a blindfold? We are not in the same situation as the congenitally blind child who has never possessed vision nor the child with some sight, but this learning situation into which we can temporarily place ourselves highlights the necessity for giving practical training in the self-help skills of daily living to visually handicapped children by making us aware of the perceptual tasks involved in judging distances, balancing a weighted spoon, pouring liquids and locating objects without the guiding and co-ordinating sense of sight.

Training in social competence involves more than teaching the techniques leading to the mastery of such routine daily events as dressing, eating or finding and looking after one's belongings, but a reasonable level of adroitness in managing these skills can lessen the strain and anxiety for both the visually handicapped and the fully sighted since the sighted sometimes appear to be the ones who are ill at ease when a blind or partially sighted person puts salt into his tea or comes to work wearing a different coloured shoe on each foot. The opening-up of educational and vocational opportunities for the visually handicapped heightens the necessity for acceptable levels of personal appearance and the management of self-help skills. At the same time increasing emphasis on academic attainment as a passport to interesting jobs and tertiary education puts pressure on the time and energy of the blind and partially sighted pupil. Difficulties in managing routine social skills are likely to have been exacerbated if the visually handicapped child has been discouraged from doing things for himself at home or has spent years in an institutional atmosphere where many of his daily needs are catered for without effort or physical contribution being expected from him

Training in personal independence

Most schools for the visually handicapped do give attention to training in self-help skills (Childs, 1974) and many have worked out training in which both teachers and child care staff are involved. But if training in self-help skills begins when the visually handicapped child first comes to school it is already late, since the pre-school years embody the stages of perceptuo-motor development underlying the ability to perform simple tasks such as grasping, pouring liquids or lifting objects.

The school can face a diversity of problems when attempting to meet the needs of individual children in this area of training. The extent to which children have been encouraged to be independent in such matters at home will vary and some children will have had periods of illness or of being in hospital which may have emphasized their dependence; differences in the amount of vision and the way in which it is used may call for adaptations in the way some of the tasks are taught and undertaken; differences in the degree of developmental readiness will require the presentation of materials at the child's developmental rather than his chronological age. Finally, the ethos of the class or school will need to be such that training in self-help skills is considered vital, interesting and rewarding, not an unimportant 'extra' relegated to odd times and places so that it does not take time from more exciting subjects.

Systematic teaching is essential here although the child will need plenty of opportunities to find out for himself how to do things and to do them the way that suits him best, as well as having guided help in mastering techniques. A structured approach involving graded tasks of increasing difficulty and complexity can be undertaken. Simple activities such as spreading slices with butter and pouring milk into a cup are diversified until simple meals can be prepared and served. Eventually, in the last years at school, full meals can be undertaken with the necessary shopping, budgeting, and attention to nutrition forming part of the educational content. Cleaning and looking after a flat, laundering clothes, washing and making menus for a week, make such an essential course in domestic economy sound very like that undertaken by ordinary pupils at a comprehensive school. The end is the same but the means by which the pupils achieve these ends involve some adaptations in method, a few adaptations of equipment and systematic teaching in small groups or on an individual basis.

Graded checklists of skills

An attempt to relate the performance of specific day-to-day tasks to appropriate ages in the case of blind children has been made in the Netherlands by Van der Zwan and Heslinga (1970). It is stressed, however, that this checklist should not be considered as a test scale but rather as a means of enabling teachers to note, methodically, whether or not there are gaps in the ability of their blind pupils to perform self-help skills which it would be reasonable to consider within the competence of a blind child of a given age. The seven categories covered in this 'checklist' relate to eating, dressing, personal grooming, orientation, communication, household skills, and a final section headed 'miscellaneous' concerned with items such as using keys, putting a plug into a socket, packing a suitcase and wrapping up a parcel. Much of this training is scheduled to take place in the primary school years, and in the Dutch situation is carried out by specially trained youth leaders who have charge of the residential and leisure aspects of the pupil's school life. The emphasis is on learning through doing and the pupils are encouraged to take part in a variety of domestic activities such as cooking, doing small repairs under supervision, choosing and taking care of their clothes.

Analysis of tasks

Children with little or no sight find that the imiation of processes is difficult, so that even comparatively simple tasks taken for granted by the fully sighted will need to be analysed and broken down into manageable sub-skills. For example, in learning to pour out liquids it is necessary to place the receptacle on a flat surface, then the spout of the pouring vessel must be placed on the rim of the receptacle; both hands are used for this task, with one supporting the pouring vessel and the finger and thumb of the other hand steadying and controlling the spout of the vessel while the liquid is being poured. Another simple action, common to most meal times, involves holding a spoon steadily when it is full and being moved from the plate or bowl to the mouth; this action can be practised with a basin full of sand with attention being directed to the difference in weight when the spoon is full or empty.

A residential environment should give opportunity for systematic attention to this kind of training and the child-care staff have a major contribution to make here. Ideally of course, much of this training should take place at home but parents themselves may need help in knowing how to tackle the problems involved. The short length of the school day may make it difficult to include such work in a day school and the severely visually handicapped child in an ordinary school or one for other handicaps may be in a situation where his need for specific training in these skills is not realized or understood.

Home economics

Some of these skills can be dovetailed into a cookery and home economics programme. Simple cookery is a useful subject for blind and partially sighted children in the primry school since it is exciting and involves procedures of weighing, measuring, and attention to shapes and textures. If all goes well, it even has a consumable end product.

Groups will need to be small, since vigilance is needed to avoid accidents, and demonstration may be needed on an individual basis. Visually handicapped pupils will need time to find their way round the working room, locate equipment, learn to store materials in an orderly way and be alerted to any safety hazards such as power points and electrical equipment.

Visually handicapped pupils at secondary school level can undertake s home economics programme whose content is much the same as that for sighted pupils. Basic preparation techniques in cooking include rubbing in, mixing, beating, baking, and grilling, but not frying which is hazardous for those who do not see well. Commercial apparatus can be carefully chosen to help to minimize the practical difficulties of not seeing well, for instance a split-level cooker with eye-level grill, use of standard pinging electric timers and light brightly coloured plastic containers is recommended. The Disabled Living Foundation has listed apparatus and equipment especially useful for the partially sighted housewife and most of this is equally so for the pupil or student. Special equipment such as tea dispensers and milk savers can be obtained from the Royal National Institute for the Blind. Both gas and electric cookers can be fitted with braille markings. Teachers of domestic science in schools for the blind shared their ideas in adapting methods, for instance, in using homely measures such as teacups for measuring, (Chapman, 1970). Blind or poorly sighted pupils can be helped to use senses other than sight in locating and identifying ingredients. When containers are shaken, heavy syrup will sound different from a less viscous liquid such as vinegar. Smell, texture and weight all afford clues as to what a jar contains.

TECHNIQUES FOR VISUALLY LIMITED PUPILS

In this, as in other areas of learning, the pupil with some vision can be helped to use it as effectively as possible. Demonstration of tasks such as peeling a potato may have to be undertaken in small groups, even individually, so that the pupil can see the action of the hands and the knife. Closed circuit television can be a useful means of clarifying difficult or complex procedures of a practical nature. The workroom will need to be appropriately lit, shining light-reflective surfaces are best avoided. Labelling of equipment, cupboards and their contents should be done clearly with a black felt-tipped pen. Personal grooming and choice and care of clothes as well as the aspects of cleaning and maintenance of equipment should be embodied in an up-to-date housecraft course. A small but useful literature has grown relating to the teaching of these subjects to visually handicapped pupils which includes *Overcoming Handicap* (Hedley, 1972). Recipe books and books on housecraft have been transcribed into braille but the teacher will find it practical to use plastic cards with braille or clearly printed recipes as books may be cumbersome on a working surface. Small-scale projects can be practised in which the pupil will need to use initiative and develop powers of organization. Both boys and girls will need training in skills and techniques which are essential to independent living despite a visual handicap.

6

Deafness Among Children

A great deal has been written, particularly in the last few years, about the education and development of deaf children. Extensive educational research in different countries has been reported in many papers and books, and these have been (and are being) used to refuel longstanding and seemingly irreconcilable arguments about the educational needs of deaf children and the political rights of deaf people.

Psychological research undertaken through formal testing and laboratory experimentation has been dedicated to exploring and describing how deaf people think and, to use Conrad's (1979) term, has tried to discover what 'stuff' deaf people think in. Whilst the nature of this mental 'stuff' still remains obscure, there has emerged an increasing body of evidence showing that the majority of very deaf people do not think in words or 'internal speech.' Reasons—psychological, neurological and cultural—as to why this should be the case have been formulated and are still being debated. Psychologists, and members of other academic disciplines, have not been backward in coming forward with both criticisms of and suggestions for educators of the deaf. In particular, psychological and linguistic research findings have been used as a basis for recommendations to teachers about what methods of communication they should use to educate deaf children. However, surprisingly little attention has been given to the question of how teachers actually *do* teach and communicate with the deaf child.

This question is the main subject of our book. We explore it with a number of other questions in mind. Foremost amongst these asks: 'Why, despite years of teaching, do so many deaf children leave school essentially illiterate, with lower educational achievements than hearing children, and unable to understand or communicate with hearing people?' Educational, linguistic and psychological research has provided many insights into the problems facing those who attempt to prepare deaf children for life in the 'hearing world,' but not much consideration has been given to the issue of how and why these problems actually emerge and manifest themselves in classrooms. How *do* deaf children's communication and learning problems originate and what influence do these have on the processes of education and teaching?

One aspect of the problem of providing for deaf children's educational needs is the diverse nature of children labelled 'deaf'. There are marked individual differences not only in degree of deafness and vulnerability to additional learning, emotional, social and personal problems, but also in levels of academic and linguistic achievement. Whilst some of the 'organic' factors associated with levels of achievement, such as level of intelligence and cause of deafness, have been explored and measured, environmental factors have been less intensively studied. This is not surprising when one considers that even *describing* the social and educational environment in ways that might reveal potentially important developmental influences is a complex theoretical and empirical exercise. What do we look for in classrooms, for example, that might help to explain why a particular child is or is not progressing? What do we mean by 'progress'?

This book is also concerned with the study of individual differences both in the abilities and achievements of children and in the philosophies and 'styles' of teachers. Furthermore, we explore the relationships between these to see if we can gain some insights into aspects of teaching style that accompany and might be causally related to the *creation* of different children's linguistic and educational achievements. The pursuit of this aim is a far more ambitious, problematic and uncertain affair than that of identifying learning problems. We will often be cautious and even circumspect when we discuss educational 'causes' of achievement, since we are aware of the fact that many factors beyond our control (and that of teachers) and even outside our current knowledge might be far more important determinants of individual differences than those we are about to study. However difficult the task may be, we feel that it is time to start looking in detail at what actually *happens* in the education of deaf children and to try to sort out some of the social influences on children's development. Although we adopt a cautious stance we will draw on our observations, sresults and experiences in many different schools to give our views on changes or developments in educational practice that teachers and others can consider and, we hope, act upon, to discover for themselves whether or not any promise of progress materializes.

Throughout our work we have tried to keep an open but critical mind about the variety of practices we have encountered and sought to analyse. Of course, even with a will to be 'open-minded,' we cannot escape all the presuppositions, assumptions and 'biases' that constrain the very fabric of our perceptions and thoughts. Consequently, we need to say a little about our own theoretical background and our working assumptions.

Our theoretical 'roots' are to be found in the ideas of Vygotsky (1962) and Bruner (1966, 1983). We do not intend, however, to make this book an introduction to theories of child development nor consider the differences of opinion between various theories in any detail, although we shall consider the implications of major developmental theories for the formal education of deaf children. The central feature of both Vygotsky's and Bruner's approaches to the study of the human mind is a fundamental emphasis on the role played by adult-child interaction in the formation of intelligence and competence. Everyday interactions between parents and infants, for example, lay the foundations for the acquisition of language. Formal instruction in schools is the basis for the cultivation of rational thought and scientific understanding. Culture is transmitted from one generation to another through communications between those already embedded in that culture and new arrivals to it.

We bring this general perspective to bear on the study of deaf children's education. What impact does deafness exert on the processes of cultural and educational transmission? How are interactions between the mature and immature affected by the handicap? Our view is that many features of the development of communication and spoken language and of ways of thinking and understanding are threatened by childhood deafness. The study of disrupted adult-child interactions and the effects of such disruptions on the child's linguistic and educational development provide a major theme that runs throughout our writings. However, we are not only hoping to identify 'special problems' facing teacher and child. As we shall see, teachers adopt very different philosophies, methods and strategies when they interact with preschoolers talk to school-aged children and try to teach reading. By exploring differences between teachers and their effects on children's learning, we gain some insights into educational approaches that work relatively well and those that do less well. The reasons why some approaches work better than others are theoretically interesting and educationally important and will be discussed as we go along.

Anyone looking for a comparison of, or discussions about, different methods of communication in this book will be disappointed. We are only concerned with children who are being educated in 'oral' settings: special schools and units attached to ordinary schools. Our neglect of other methods of communication is *not* due to ideological bias. It arises from more mundane, practical limitations. First, the work we will discuss involves long periods of involvement in schools and the development of relationships based on mutual trust with teachers. The very nature of our approach to the study of education demands attention to *details* and a great deal of time transcribing, classifying and evaluating videotaped classroom interactions. Only by maintaining a relatively narrow focus on one method of communication were we able to find enough resources to complete these analyses. More recently, however, we have turned our attention to the study of other methods of communication. A second, practical constraint acting on us was the fact that, when we began this work ten years ago, few schools in the United Kingdom were using other than oral approaches to communication with young deaf children.

Anyone interested in different methods of communication will, we suspect, find themselves wanting to explore several lines of thought and debate should they bother to read this book. 'Would this problem happen if you *signed* to children?' will, we think, be a question raised in each of our chapters. Only rarely will we pursue such lines of enquiry here. There are a number of reasons for adopting this strategy. First, we did not want to make the book too long, nor to 'obscure' its main message. We believe that many arguments about *methods* of communication have taken place in the absence of sufficient knowledge about the *processes* of communication that they create. This is reflected in the often polemical and even irrational arguments that all too often characterize talk about 'methods.' By drawing attention to important features of communication and teaching processes we hope to provide new ways of evaluating different methods. In the final chapter, we consider a range of questions and issues that need to be addressed in arguments about methodology. Answers to these, we suggest, will provide more effective ways of deciding whether or not a particular appraoch to the education of a given child is or is not working well.

But the main reason for postponing discussion of communication is that we are still in the process of extending our analyses to children in schools using signed English and sign support for English, both in the United Kingdom and Australia. When the information provided by these studies is analysed, digested and evaluated, we will return to discuss and compare methods of communication currently being used in different schools.

Another limitation of the book is its 'audio-centric' orientation. We will be considering children's problems and capacities in relation to sound, talk and text. Although we will place considerable stress on the importance of preverbal and non-verbal communication in development, these will be discussed within a framework provided by knowledge of spoken language. It is important to acknowledge that analyses based on different frameworks and assumptions (e.g. on a theory of sign language and its structure) would probably reveal *different* insights into the processes we will explore and, perhaps, lead to different implications. No analysis, however 'objective' it may seem, can escape constraints imposed on it by the implicit and explicit assumptions on which it is based. We accept this view of scientific analysis and try, insofar as we can, to articulate some of the asumptions that shaped the way in which we looked at classroom interaction.

Finally, this book does not embody a detailed review of the literature on the development of deaf children. Good, contemporary, evaluative overviews already exist (e.g. Quigley and Kretschmer, 1982; Quigley and Paul, 1984), and we have no intention of trying to do what they have already achieved. We will concentrate on our own studies and their educational and theoretical implications, drawing, when appropriate, on other research both to explain and discuss our own work. Our main audience is addition to our colleagues (we hope) will be teachers of the deaf, speech therapists, educational psychologists and, perhaps, parents of deaf children.

ASSUMPTIONS AND HYPOTHESES

Articulating one's assumptions is a far more difficult task than announcing one's objectives. In this section, we try to spell out our own in terms of a series of propositions about the nature and development of deaf children. Thus, the reader may challenge our evidence not simply on the basis of its internal consistency, representativeness or robustness, but also in terms of the basic assumptions which attribute it with significance. In the book, we will examine both our own evidence and that provided by other studies in an attempt to show the force and value of these assumptions. Sometimes, we will argue that the evidence should compel us to accept their value but, at other times, we will be more speculative and discursive where the evidence is, in our judgement, less than compelling.

Proposition 1. Deaf Children Face Special Problems

To one outside the field of hearing impairment, this might sound like a self-evident and uncontroversial assumption. Why write a book about deaf children's education or provide special equipment, teachers and schools for them if they have no special problems? The issue is much deeper and more complex than such questions imply. Indeed, the stance one adopts in relation to these questions (as Freeman, Carbin and Boese, 1981, have pointed out in some detail) betrays one's basic image of the deaf person.

Many of the practical arguments about the educational needs of deaf children, such as where they should be educated, by whom they should be taught, what kind of syllabus they should follow and what methods of communication they should receive, are really based on answers to, or attitudes towards, certain key theoretical issues. Is the deaf child basically like all other children? In comparison to hearing children of the same age, are the 'lower' levels of educational and linguistic performance of deaf children simply the result of slower but essentially normal development? Or does profound deafness result in a different 'psychology' and a unique developmental path? If so, what are the special characteristics of this psychology, what needs does it give rise to and how might these be met? And when is a child to be considered 'deaf'?

Conrad (1979), for reasons explored later in the book, suggests that a child with an 'average better-ear loss' of 85 dB is unlikely to develop functional speech or literacy. Others (e.g. Meadow, 1980) argue that the threshold should be 70 dB, whilst some put the figure at 105 dB. Quigley and Paul (1984), who discuss the issue of classification in some detail, offer 90 dB as 'the most defensible criterion'. In this book, most of the children we will be studying have losses around or in excess of 85 dB. When referring to these children en masse, we will employ the collective terms 'severely or profoundly deaf' or, by way of shorthand, 'deaf'. However, we fully accept that classifying a given child as 'functionally' deaf or partially hearing is not an easy task. It is even more difficult to determine whether any special learning problems created by deafness occur only with a specific degree of deafness or whether deaf and partially hearing children suffer similar problems with differing degrees of severity. If the latter, when do we start making special provision for the child?

Another set of important questions about proper provision for children reflects one's views on the relationships between speaking and thinking. How important is langauge and, specifically, speech for intellectual functioning? Is speech the basis for various intellectual activities, such as mathematical computation, or simply one medium in which thinking can take place? We will consider these questions and discuss some of the proposed answers to them in the later chapters of the book. For the moment, we introduce them to underline the fundamental connections that exist between practical considerations such as educational provision and teaching methods on the one hand and difficult theoretical issues on the other.

What do we mean, then, by saying deaf children face 'special problems' and what educational implications stem from these? Well, imagine for a moment a child who is totally deaf. Such a person is indeed rare, since very few 'deaf' children are born with absolutely no hearing. Suppose our totally deaf individual is but six or seven months old. As we shall see in the next chapter, at this age, adults and hearing babies are already involved in structured interactions and are embarked on the early stages of communication. When involved in feeding, bathing or some other interaction, the adult tends to follow the flow of the baby's attention and to put into words what she thinks he is experiencing or feeling. From the first days of life, the hearing infant's activities are suffused with the sounds of human speech that overlay and often interpret his experiences.

Consider now the totally deaf infant. When he turns from the adult's face to an object, say, what sign does he have, not simply that the adults is still in existence (perhaps through touch, warmth and smell) but also that they are sharing and commenting upon the object of his attentions? Logically, the infant faces a problem of discovering what is largely given for the hearing baby. When the infant turns back to the adult, how does he construe the visible reactions he sees? Is it a new event? Or is it a comment that relates to what he has *just* experienced? How is the adult to help coordinate his experience of reality with the act of communication? Will this achievement not take more time and need more maturity and intelligence on the deaf baby's part than is demanded of the hearing baby? Will there not be, at least, some delay?

This is a logical point and derives any force it has both from a consideration of a very rare individual, the totally deaf baby, and from findings (largely Piagetian) about the cognitive capacities of young infants (i.e. that they find it difficult to coordinate experiences that take place at different times). When we come to consider hearing-impaired infants with hearing aids on, the issue ceases to be a logical one and becomes empirical. What level of assited hearing is needed before sound intrudes into the baby's consciousness? What information does an infant with a given level of hearing get from any sounds he hears? How far does the faintest murmur help him to discover the relationships between reality and communication?

For the moment, we provide this example as an illustration of one problem that many hearing-impaired children face, not simply at this stage of development but throughout life. To be sure, all the children we shall consider have some degree of hearing, so the problem they face may not be as severe as that faced by our hypothetical, totally deaf child. But, we will argue, many do face problems of this type.

A consideration of these and other specific problems facing the deaf child are a major focus of the rest of the book. The central questions to which they lead ask if, how and when they can be helped to overcome such problems.

Proposition 2. Many Problems that Deaf Children Face are 'Secondary' Consequences of Their Handicap

Deaf children, throughout their development, are likely to evidence an increasing gap between what they know, think and feel on the one hand, and what they can express, negotiate and communicate about on the other. This growing gap between knowledge and communication often dislocates processes of social interaction, teaching and learning. One problem facing teachers is, so to speak, to decide whather they should address and instruct the 'intellectual' child or the 'linguistic' child. To understand many of the problems that deaf children face, we need to examine the effects that their handicap exert on those hearing adults who are significant influences in their development

This assertion, too, may seem relatively uncontroversial, but it is not. Indeed, there are many possible bases for argument, as we shall see. For example, unlike Piagetian psychologists, notably Hans Furth (1966, 1971), we afford social interaction an important role in determining not simply what the child thinks about but also *how* he thinks. Piagetians argue that social interaction and language play no important role in determining the structure of thinking. We will be exploring the view that they do play such a role and that any problems of communication between adults and children are likely to have far-reaching, 'secondary' consequneces on development.

More importantly, however, we will argue that such secondary deffects, though a product of the handicap, are not inevitable. Here we will also find ourselves enmeshed in arguments about the role of social factors in the development of language. For instance, it is reasonably well established that in our sort of society, one finds close links between a child's stage of linguistic development and the language addressed to him by more competent speaker-hearers (e.g. Cross, 1978; Snow, 1979; Bruner, 1983; Wells, 1984). The issue is this: is such a close connection a *necessary* condition for linguistic development? If so, is it the child who paces the adult or the adult who leads the child? Such questions are of more than theoretical interest in any study of children with language problems. If the answer to the question just raised lies in the child, then adults may play a relatively minor role in mediating the effects of handicap on development. However, if adults lead, then any disruptions in their normal styles of interaction and communication may be causally involved in at least some of the problems the child faces.

We will explore this issue later in the book. We do so largely through the exploitation of two basic concepts—control and contingency. This is not the place to explore these concepts in depth, but a brief consideration is necessary to establish the basis for our third proposition.

Children learn most readily and generalize what they learn most effectively when the help they are offered is *contingent* upon their developing competence. Stated boldly, such a principle sounds commonplace and even banal, but its achievement, as we shall see, is hardly commonplace in schools. To be contingent upon a child, one must offer help and control when he faces difficulty, and relinquish control and provide opportunities for initiative when he shows signs of success. Consider what this involves. First, one must be aware of what the child is attempting to achieve, and be able to diagnose success and failure. This itself is not nearly as easy as it may sound. It demands attention to the child, observation and listening, both of which may be difficult to achieve in the classroom. Further, many 'errors' that children make are not due to inattentiveness, stupidity or ignorance. Rather, they are a natural product of their stage or phase of learning and must be interpreted as such. To take a specific example: if we look at a piece of writing from a deaf child, can we say with any confidence how far his departures from standard English are due to his stage of language development? Can we spot those 'errors' that are the product of a 'child grammar'? If so, when is the time right for control and corrective feedback? The issue is not easy. To diagnose and interpret the significance of errors and successes by a given child, we must have a valid psychological model both of the learner and what it is he is learning. Thus the way we interpret linguistic errors is determined by our theory of language and its development. Demanding corrections that are too far beyond the child's current level of mastery serves to demoralize him. Conversely, demanding too low a level of response is likely to bore him. The achievement of contingency is often formidably difficult in schools and especially so with the deaf child.

Proposition 3. Secondary Problems can be Ameliorated

This proposition, certainly no less controversial than the preceding ones, forms the pedagogical 'heart' of the book. We will show first that the incidence of control and contingency often varies from teacher to teacher. More important, we will identify several predictable effects of different teaching styles on children's learning and their use of language and will try to tease apart cause and effect to show that teaching style and not simply factors 'in' the child mediate these effects. We will also look at individual differences between children of similar hearing loss and intelligence to reveal some marked differences in language ability and educational achievement. Although such studies demonstrate that degree of deafness and intelligence are not the only determinants of success, it will be left to the reader to judge how far our evidence supports the view that teaching philosophies and styles are other important determinants. Our evidence is not compelling, but it is highly suggestive and consistent with knowledge about the course of human development.

7

Teaching Language

IN the next two chapters we will identify and discuss some of the stages that young deaf children pass through as they make the transition from 'pre-verbal' communication to when they begin to understand what is said to them and to produce words themselves. We will also be looking more widely at the deaf child's experiences in nursery school, examining some aspects of the impact of deafness on teaching-learning interactions. We attempt to outline and discuss observations of young children in school and start to 'measure' their school experiences against their communicative and wider developmental needs.

In this chapter, we begin by discussing the early stages of language development in hearing children. Why, one might ask, start with hearing infants? Well, in the first place, recent studies have shown how the emergence of a child's first words represents the *culmination* of a process of communication that begins at birth. The importance of this work, for our purposes, is the lessons it holds for the management and teaching of young deaf children. When the hearing baby is developing the pre-verbal foundations of communication he is largely immobile, attracted to human faces and limited in his thinking to what fills his senses. As we shall see, many deaf preschoolers are still in the pre-verbal stages of development when they enter nursery school. They are mobile, interested in many things and likely to have plans and intentions. Establishing the conditions for contingent interactions to foster the development of verbal communication is far more difficult when a child's intellectual maturity is so far in advance of his communicative development.

The acquisition of speech involves much more than the ability to hear others talk. We shall argue, following Bruner (1983) and others (e.g. Lock, 1980), that such pre-verbal communication provides the child with 'keys' to unlock the meanings of speech.

Although the importance of pre-verbal communication is becoming widely recognized amongst educators of young children, we will argue in the next chapter (and later ones) that many features of teaching *practice* are still at variance with this knowledge. In short, teachers often attempt to get deaf children to 'listen' and 'speak' without due regard for the processes of *communication* which lend sense and significance to language.

One way of looking at research into early language development is as an illustration of its 'multisensory' and 'interactive' nature. For words to take on meaning for a child, they must be integrated with what he sees, feels or in some other way 'senses' in the world. To take on communicative *significance* words must refer to something perceived, remembered, imagined or felt. Words are also 'shared symbols' and for successful communication they must invoke similar percepts, ideas or conceptions in both a speaker and listener, they are 'socially constructed, shared symbols'. Thus, to understand what a word means to a child and to study its acquisition by that child, our observations must be rooted in social interaction. Similarly, the study and evaluation of the deaf child's experiences of language must look beyond what the child is saying or doing to consider the social practices in which he participates. If language arises through communicative interaction, then problems in acquiring language may reside, in part, in the nature and structure of such interactions. Here, too, we will be arguing that teachers are often concerned with the quality of a child's language or his ability to comprehend speech without paying due regard to the social practices that lend meaning and significance to utterances.

Finally, towards the end of the chapter, we consider two issues that are central to the educational concerns of our classroom research and this book. How far or in what sense do adults 'teach' children language or provide the basis for its development? Is there an 'appropriate' way to talk to children to assist language learning? More specifically, should the immature speaker be exposed to relatively 'simple' speech in order to foster that learning?

These, then, are some of the principle reasons for beginning our study of the spoken language development of deaf children by considering the transition from pre-verbal to spoken communication in hearing children.

SOUNDS AND MEANINGS

In this section, we examine some of the achievements made by young hearing babies in their first year of life. We cannot hope to provide even a modest overview of the voluminous research into this period of human development; rather we shall examine some important 'landmarks' in the growth of infant competence.

Systematic observations of babies within hours of their birth have demonstrated their remarkable powers; powers that are soon exploited in their contacts with adults (usually, of course, their mothers). Newborn babies, or neonates, show considerable powers of *discrimination* and *organization* that are either present at conception or developed in the womb. They react selectively and (often) predictably to many sensory experiences very early in life. For instance, a touch on the neonate's cheek will usually elicit a 'rooting reflex'; any ensuing contact with a suckable object will then evoke highly organized sucking behaviour. Although not so predictable in their effects, sounds will also occasion movements of the (supported) head and, more often than chance allows, the infant will turn *towards* the sound source, showing both that he can hear and that the ability to locate sounds is innate or developed during intrauterine experience (Crassini and Broese, 1980). The baby also responds selectively to different sounds. Loud, percussive noises startle whilst gentle, low frequency, repetitive sounds tend to soothe. Although the baby's responses to sound are not totally predictable (depending, for example, on how alert he is) they are at least partially structured (a fact that is exploited by microprocessor-controlled units such as the Linco-Bennett cradle for neonatal screening for deafness) (see Stratton, *Psychobiology of the Human Newborn*, in this series)

The neonate is also selective in his responses to certain smells. Offered a choice between his own mother's breastpad and that of another lactating female, the infant will usually turn to his mother's. Similarly, although the neonate can only focus on an object a few inches from his face, he is able to bring both eyes into focus on an object at that distance and show marked preference for the sight of the human face. The human voice is also accorded preferential treatment. The *combination* of human face and speech, for a baby who is reasonably alert, is almost irresistibly attractive (Brazelton, 1982).

Adults soon 'exploit' the privileged status afforded them by their look, smell and sound. When they hold the baby, bring their face close to his and talk to him, they are likely to be rewarded by intent attention. They may also exert some control over the infant's state of being—helping to rouse the sleepy baby with movements, an animated voice and face, and to soothe the agitated one by holding him close and uttering low, soft, repetitive sounds.

Because babies are, so to speak, functioning on all sensory cylinders, there are many 'avenues'—touch, smell, sight, sound and taste—whereby they can become attached to and familiar with those in frequent contact with them. Perhaps this is one reason why sensory handicaps in young babies are so difficult to detect: the infant always has other ways of coming to know the world and of establishing interactions with others.

The infant's 'love affair' with the human face lasts until around four months of age when his attention becomes monopolized by objects. Those long, sustained periods of looking at faces decline and the characteristic responses of the adult change in ways that reflect the baby's interests. He may look intently at an adult's face for a time, then turn away for a period before coming back into eye contact. The adult, meanwhile, is likely to be looking at the baby all the time. When she addresses the infant, it is usually to talk *about* him. The baby's changing facial expressions, movements and sounds are likely to be *interpreted* as 'meaningful' events by the adult and put into words.

By making their reactions and sounds *contingent* upon the baby's initially spontaneous activities, adults help to endow these with 'meaning.' The infant begins to reciprocate by *repeating* a movement, gesture or sound which 'caused' an adult response. If this, in turn, leads the adult to respond again, the baby may try again, thus, building up the foundations for *communicative* exchanges.

Once the baby produces an action and shows clear signs of *expecting* a response, he must have at least a rudimentary *knowledge* of the likely actions of another person. By three months of age the infant has almost certainly built up such expectations since, if his partner (usually the mother) does *not* respond as she usually does, the baby shows signs of unhappiness, withdrawal, surprise or alarm (Cohn and Tronick, 1982). Well before the emergence of the first word the baby is thus playing a part in communicative exchanges in which he 'expects' certain things to happen as a consequence of his own *actions.*

When, at about four months, the infant's attention turns to objects and happenings in the environment the patterns of interaction change. Typically, when adult and baby are together, the infant's visual exploration of the environment is 'mirrored' by the adult, who probably looks where the baby looks and talks about what is being looked at (Collis and Schaffer, 1975). By following the infant's line of attention, drawing inferences about what he is looking at and may be feeling, the adult may put into words that which is likely to be of interest to the baby. More remarkably, at around the same age, the baby begins to follow the *adult's* line of gaze when they break eye contact (Scaife and Bruner, 1975; Butterworth and Cochran, 1980; Churcher and Scaife, 1982). How babies achieve this feat is not known, but it increases the probability that adult and child will be looking at the same things.

Such shared attention to common objects and events has been called the 'reference triangle' and identified as the basis for the development of shared meanings and, eventually, words. If both partners look at the same thing whilst one talks about it, then the chances that the baby will discover the relationships between words and things is increased. The adult spontaneously helps to bring the infant's experiences into conjunction with language. Even before the baby recognizes or produces words, the intonation or 'mood music' supplied by the human voice, which has already become significant for the infant, may play a part in providing an *interpretation* of the significance of different experiences. Sounds of surprise, caution, delight, fear or whatever may 'infect' the infant's feelings whilst he looks at the object of communication. Thus, the beginnings of verbal meaning reside not so much in the significance of individual word sounds but in the personal, social and emotional 'tone' that is communicated by the intonation of the voice. Put another way, the baby is introduced to 'interpretations' and not only single word-object relationships. Because the infant's state of being can be controlled by the tone of voice, so his feelings can be affected in the presence of different objects and events. We can thus communicate feelings of security, fear, surprise to the infant before he understands individual words.

In the first few months of life, then, the infant is playing an active, reciprocal role in interaction. He has come to recognize and respond selectively to the voices of familiar people, such as those of mother and father. In his sound making, early coos and gurgles are giving way to babbling. Comparisons of the sounds made by babies in different cultures reveal that the *intonation* patterns found in the six-month-old's pre-speech sounds begin to resemble those of his host language (e.g. Menyuk, 1971). Thus, by six months there is already some convergence between the infant's sound making and aspects of the speech system that he will eventually master. Similarly, by eight months of age babies respond differently to various patterns of intonation *addressed* to them. They react in different ways, for instance, to questions and statements. Though they may not recognize words, they show some discrimination between intonation patterns (Kaplan, 1969).

After a period of rapt attention to the human face and the beginnings of interest in things and events in the immediate environment, the infant begins to 'integrate' the world of people and objects. For example, when, around ten months or so, the infant looks at the mother whilst *pointing* to an object, he almost literally 'draws' a 'triangle of reference' which involves the object of reference and two minds trained upon that object. Similarly, in 'give and take' games, an object plays a role *within* a social exchange. As both Lock (1980) and Bruner (1983) have argued, the emergence of such gestures and games is an indication of the development of intentional acts of communication by the baby. Thus the scene is set for the acquisition and use of vocal symbols. A word or utterance that is used in response to or in parallel with such non-verbal gestures is likely to be interpreted by the baby as a reference to the activity that is uppermost in his mind (and that of the speaker).

Before moving on to look in a little more detail at the emergence of speech in the child, we pause to draw attention to some general features of pre-verbal communication that will figure in our analyses of teacher—child interactions with pre-verbal deaf children. First, an obvious but important point: during the early interactions we discussed the infant was drawn 'naturally' to the human face. During most or all of the period we have been discussing, babies are incapable of moving their bodies around in space. They are not easily 'bored' by repetitions of simple routines. The natural attraction of faces lends the adult significance and provokes the necessary attention for the growth of communication with the baby. His immobility means that the adult, in interactions with the infant, is likely to find the object of the child's interest 'obvious.' The infant's stage of development is such that what he is aware of will be present in the immediate context. Infants' 'tolerance' and enjoyment of simple, repeated sequences of interaction also provide a 'natural' starting place for the discovery of regularity and predictability in their experiences, which forms the basis for communication.

If the child's development of pre-verbal communication is 'delayed' for any reason, each of these conditions is likely to be violated. If the face has to compete with other, more attractive objects; if the child is able to formulate relatively long-term plans and desires; if he is mobile and difficult to follow or easily bored by simple repetition, then the problem of achieving mutually satisfying pre-verbal communicative exchanges becomes increasingly difficult.

Two other points need to be raised as preliminaries to our considerations of communicative development in deaf children. These concern the achievements which accompany the development of 'reciprocal interaction.' As the baby comes to anticipate the structure of recurrent events like feeding, undressing, playing and so forth, he discovers how to 'take turns' in interactions. Once he expects his actions to result in some predictable reaction from another, he is participating in turn-taking routines in which, so to speak, he leaves 'gaps' or 'pauses' to be filled by the anticipated response. Bruner (1983) has argued that such 'formats' in early interaction engender the development of 'conversation-like' exchanges in which mother and baby take turns. Although there is still debate as to exactly when and how the baby can be said to be a truly 'active partner' in turn-taking, infants have almost certainly mastered the rudiments of this ability before they begin to talk.

One final point concerns a general feature of adult responses to young infants. From the start they respond to the child *as though* he has intentions and as *if* the child as controlling them. Similarly, when, later in this period, they talk about what the child is looking at, they make what they do and say *contingent* upon their interpretation of what is in the child's mind. Thus, not only do they help to bring the child's experience into conjunction with speech sounds, they also offer the infant an opportunity to *control* what happens next. For the infant, the growth of communication and of 'self-efficacy' are thus closely intertwined—something we return to when we discuss the 'control' of deaf children by parents and teachers.

Having identified some of the more general features of early, pre-verbal communication that will inform our discussions of deaf children, we will go no further into the development of pre-verbal patterns of interaction, although many other achievements occur en route to the development of speech. We turn our attention now to the child who is beginning to talk, to consider the early stages of speech development. Again, the reason for looking selectively at aspects of language development is to identify features of the process that are relevant to our considerations of deaf children.

LANGUAGE: 'TAUGHT' OR 'CAUGHT'?

As Bruner (1983) points out, two theories of language acquisition have dominated research in the past. One (called by Miller the 'impossible' theory) held that language was *taught* by exposing children to simple associations between 'words' and 'things' (Skinner, 1957). The other view (the 'miracle' theory) held that language was simply *caught*, rather like an ailment, by exposure to speech. Because the child was born with an innate 'Language Acquisition Device' or 'LAD' (Chomsky, 1965), there was no need for either teaching or 'privileged communication with another speaker.' More recently, although arguments about the precise roles of innate abilities and environmental influences in promoting language acquisition persist, most students of child language have come to accept an 'interactionist' perspective in which both the child's natural capacities and interactions with more mature speakers are important in development. The child may catch' language, but, to abuse the metaphor perhaps, adults tend to make sure he is in the right place at the right time to catch the verbal ball.

When the infant begins to use sounds 'meaningfully' (the first sounds used communicatively by a baby are not, of course, 'adult' words) a number of important changes occur in the reactions he receives from adults. Studies of adult talk to children undertaken in several countries have revealed some common (though perhaps not universal) phenomena. Adults in different parts of the world, when talking to infants, tend to talk about similar things connected with 'universal' aspects of child care such as feeding, dressing and so on. Thus, the vocabulary addressed to babies is similar across many cultures. Adults also begin to use 'simpler' language than they used previously when talking to the pre-verbal baby. Utterances tend to be articulated relatively slowly, they display a fair degree of repetition and are characterized by exaggerate intonation patterns at relatively high speech frequencies in comparison to talk between adults and older children.

Such features of adult talk to infants have been called 'motherese', labelled the 'baby talk register' or described as a child's 'primary linguistic data.' Since adult talk to children tends to become more complex, less repetitive and less intonationally inflected as the child gets older, the term 'grammatical fine tuning' has also been coined to mark the complex 'adjustments' found in adult speech as children become more verbally competent. Similarly, what is *talked about* changes as the child gets older, more knowledgeable and mature.

I here has been a great deal of debate and research about the generality, cause and significance of such findings. Some theorists have argued that 'fine tuning.' for example, represents a form of indirect language teaching whereby adults present children with examples of language that are just 'beyond' their current levels of production to help 'model' or provide support for the next steps in their progress (e.g. Snow, 1979). An alternative interpretation of the same phenomenon places far more emphasis on the child's naturally developing abilities. Basically, the counter-argument to the 'teaching' view is that changes in adult speech represent '*accommodation*' to the child's developing competence (Gleitman, Newport and Gleitman, 1984). From this perspective, adults change what they talk about and how they talk to fit in with the child's abilities to understand, but such adjustments follow rather than lead the child on to the next stage.

We enter into this debate later in the chapter. First, however, we consider some of the evidence relating to claims and counter- claims about 'motherese' since the importance we attach to parental speech to children will clearly inform the ways in which we examine attempts by teachers to 'teach' deaf children language.

THE MORE THE BETTER?

Several researchers have studied the language of parents to young children in terms of how often they use certain language structures. Differences between parents are then compared with what their children say some time later in development. Is children's progress in mastering the language structures studied related to how frequently they hear those structures?

Generally speaking, the answer to this question is 'no' (Gleitman and Wanner, 1982). Mere frequency of exposure to grammatical structures does not play a vital role in their acquisition by children. We suspect few people would doubt the fact that some *minimal* level of exposure is needed; however. The implication is that the hearing children in these studies all encountered adequate levels of exposure to various structures and, therefore, all acquired them. We can, however, reject the notion that children who acquire a given structure of language quickly are those who hear it most often; mere 'amount' of exposure is not a good basis for explaining the phenomenon of language acquisition.

Before moving on to consider the lessons we might draw from this conclusion, we need to draw attention to two other important findings that have emerged from child language research. The first addresses the theory that hearing 'simple utterances' is the key to early language acquisition and the second illustrates how the 'natural' working of the auditory system rather than any environmental experiences constrain the way in which children discover aspects of linguistic meanings. Again, this is grist for the 'miraculists' mill.

THE SIMPLER THE BETTER?

The finding that adults tend to use relatively simple grammatical structures when they talk to young children has been used to support the notion that language is taught; teaching starts with the simple and moves on to the more complex. This proposal, however, is weakened by two lines of evidence: one from studies of talk to children and the other from experiments in computational linguistics (i.e. attempts to program computers to 'understand' language).

Although, as we have just seen, there seems to be no general relationship between the number of times children hear various language structures and how quickly they learn them, one less obvious connection has been found both by researchers who support and those who deny the fine-tuning hypothesis. The finding in question concerns children's acquisition of auxiliary verb phases such as 'I will . . . ' . In adult speech, such a combination of a pronoun and auxiliary verb is often spoken in the contracted form 'I'll. . . ' . Children only come to produce such contractions relatively late in language development after a period of using the non-contracted forms. Thus, although children often hear contractions, they do not produce them until they are 'ready' to do so (Gleitman, Newport and Gleitman, 1984).

There is one type of utterance, however, in which adults cannot contract such pronoun-auxiliary pairs. These involve two-choice questions such as 'Will I have time. . .?' or 'Will-you please . . .?'. Children whose parents ask relatively large numbers of such questions begin to use *statements* including the auxiliary earlier than those whose parents ask fewer. The implication is that children discover or lerarn how to use auxiliary verbs not by hearing adults use relatively simple, declarative statements but the grammatically more complex question form. This finding might also imply that children, in some intuitive sense, 'understand' the grammatical connections between the auxiliary verb systems in questions and statements. If one accepts this view, then one is attributing sophisticated, early knowledge of language *strcuture* to very young children—something that those who believe in the child's 'natural' language acquisition capacities are likely to use as evidence for their views.

The point we wish to underline, however, is that children appear to be exploiting quite *complex* linguistic structures to inform their 'theory' of language at a very early stage. Thus, the notion of 'simplicity' in adult speech is not as simple as might appear.

This observation has received support from designers of computer 'language learning' programs (Gleitman and Wanner, 1982). Without delving into details, they have found that a computer exposed only to simple language (e.g. Mary hit John, Anne went to town, etc.) is unlikely to 'discover' the grammar of English because a large number of grammatical rules could account for such simple constructions. However, if the machine is also presented with examples of more complex language, these narrow down the number of possible rules that can 'explain' how the language is structured. This discovery from computational linguistics, in company with studies of child language, seriously undermines the view that *exclusive* exposure to 'simple' utterances is the best way to learn language.

Another line of evidence also questions the 'language is taught not caught' theory and helps to shed some light onto the specific speech acquisition problems of deaf children. We have already taken note of the fact that young hearing children do not utter linguistic contractions like 'We'll. . .' until relatively late in development. This phenomenon is part of a general feature of the early stages of language development in which children seem to work on the assumption that anything that sounds like a *single sound unit* in speech also functions as a single *element* of meaning. Many words are, of course, single-meaning elements (e.g. cat, house, large, etc.). Many, however, are not. For example, words like 'un-friend-ly', 'cat-s,' 'un- prepare-(e)d' contain two or three elements of meaning. Furtherore, the meanings of some of these elements, like '-ed,' are grammatical in nature. Children may utter words containing such 'grammatical morphemes' early in development (e.g. says, cats, walked, etc.) but only use them generatively or in a 'rule-like' way in all relevant contexts after some time (Brown, 1973; Bowerman, 1982). How and when do children come to appreciate the grammatical significance of prefixes and suffixes?

The answer to this specific question has general implications for language development. One could argue that children learn *first* those prefixes and suffixes which they hear most often. Alternatively, it might be the case that some suffixes or prefixes are easier to learn than others because they express 'simpler ideas.' For example, it might be the case that it is easier for a child to learn the distinction between one/many (cat/cats) than it is to learn the difference between perfective (walked) and progressive (walking) verb forms, because plurality is a 'simpler' idea than the state of actions. Third, children may learn some things before others because they are acoustically more salient. The first explanation—frequency—does not stand for similar reasons to those discussed earlier. The second—intellectual difficulty—may well be true of some features of language development (DeVilliers and DeVilliers, 1979), but the third explanation—acoustic salience—seems to play a major role in the acquisition of grammatical morphemes like '-ing', '-ed,' 'un-' and '-s', for example (though most of the evidence comes from studies of languages other than English). Briefly, children appear to learn first those prefixes and suffixes that are most *stressed* in speech (Gleitman and Wanner, 1982). For example, '-ing' is almost always learned before '-ed.'

Such findings add weight to the view that the course of language development is not determined as much by factors 'outside' the child, such as how often he hears things said, as it is by factors 'inside', such as how *sailent* things *sound*. The implications of such findings for the linguistic development of deaf children and, in particular, the problems they face in learning about tense and aspect (e.g. progressive versus perfective verb forms) will be explored later.

It seems clear that any theory that seeks to explain language development in terms of *teaching* ignores important, 'natural' factors that are part of human nature. Thus, we are not advocating, and will be arguing against, the idea that language is, in any simple sense, 'taught' to children. However, we shall also reject the idea that all we need to consider in understanding what deaf children understand of language is the view that language is usually 'caught' by children. The relationships between linguistic experience and language development are more complex than either extreme view allows. That complexity, we suggest, is best studied by examining language in use for purposes of communication, i.e. discourse, coupled with attempts to describe the deaf child's 'theories' of language.

COMMUNICATION AND DISCOURSE

Although there are diametrically opposing views about the importance of adult talk to children in facilitating the course of language development, there seems to be widespread agreement that the child's discovery of relationships between sounds and meanings is facilitated by pre-verbal communicative interactions such as those outlined earlier. However, the relationships between *communication,* on the one hand, and grammatically structured *speech,* on the other, are still being debated. Unfortunately, attempts to explicate the relationships between talk addressed to children and rates of language development have been too curde in conception to shed much light onto the processes involved. Whilst ruling out the importance of sheer quantity of exposure as an explanation for rates of acquisition, they have failed to look at the *processes* of language use in way that might be more revealing. Our own view is that any attempt to study the facilitation of language development that neglects the *structure* of the interaction and discourse within which language is embedded is doomed to failure. We need to consider, for example, not how often parents use a given linguistic structure when talking to children but also *how, when and where* they talk and *what* they say in response to children during conversation. Furthermore, we will question attempts to study language development that concentrate on syntax to the exclusion of all else. Studies by Wells (1984), for example, have been far more concerned with the study of how parents *respond* to what their children say and how what they say *relates* semantically (i.e. at the level of meaning rather than syntax) to the child's perceived meanings. Parents who were more likely to respond *contingently* to what their child was trying to say and communicate, to build upon or extend what the child was talking about or to negotiate with the child about what both of them were trying to communicate, facilitated their child's linguistic development more than less contingent parents. Studies by Cazden (1977) have also shown that when children are treated more like 'equal partners' in discourse, where what they say is used as a basis for conversation, children show more rapid language development than do children who have what they say repeated back to them in 'better grammar', for example.

Any attempt to study the acquisition of language without due attention to interactions between speakers, in our view, misses the very thing it seeks to study. Throughout this book, we shall concentrate upon language in use and the structure, content and function of conversations between adults and children for this reason.

Before moving on to the study of deaf children entering nursery school, we undertake a brief review of some of the research into the development of communication between deaf babies and their mothers. It is not our intention to attempt a comprehensive overview of the findings and issues raised by this research, but to provide some sense of 'life before school.' Gregory (in preparation) will be presenting a detailed study of parent—child interaction in the first three years of life, and Bishop and Gregory (in preparation) will discuss the transition of the deaf child from home to school.

SOUNDS AND THINGS

Earlier, we used the medical metaphor of 'infection' to characterize what happens in the infant's experience when people talk to him about what he is looking at or experiencing. Sounds signifying, for example, reassurance, surprise, shock or concern may be communicated to the baby before he understands individual words. Imagine a deaf baby with little or no awareness of sound. Assume that he does not hear (though, eventually, he may be able to listen). When he looks at an object or event, he receives none of the 'mood music' that accompanies the social experiences of the hearing baby. Suppose he looks from an object of his attention to turn to an adult who is 'sharing' the experience with him and the adult talks about what he has just been looking at. Is it obvious to the child that what they are doing is an *act of reference?* Does the infant even realize that *communication* is taking place? To discover the relationships between a word and its referent, the deaf infant has to *remember* something he has just observed and deliberately *relate* this memory to another observation. In short, the deaf child with little or no auditory awareness has to do by intellect, *in sequence,* what 'happens' to the hearing baby in parallel. An adult can take the responsibility for timing and adjusting the act of communication to fit the hearing infant's attention. The deaf baby has to do much more, 'discovering' the relationships between two very different visual experiences that are displaced in time.

The problem of 'divided attention' provides an explanation for a number of features of the deaf baby's social experiences that several different observers have reported. In comparison with encounters between hearing infants and their mothers, those between hearing parents and deaf babies have been described as more likely to be 'emotionally negative' (e.g. Schlesinger and Meadow, 1972). Signs of frustration for both parent and child are more frequent. The reason usually given, not surprisingly, concerns differences in the quality of communication and two-way frustration at not being able to achieve mutual understanding. Gregory's (e.g. Gregory and Mogford, 1981) research indicates that even with babies in the pre-verbal stages, mothers have much greater difficulty in establishing turn-taking and reciprocity when their baby is deaf. The reason for such findings we believe lies in the general role that sound usually plays in establishing and maintaining contact with the infant and in 'sharing' the object of his attention. Unlike the hearing baby, the deaf baby's experience of objects is not 'infected' with human sounds, so the process of communication is more difficult even before we would expect his understanding and use of speech to emerge onto the scene.

One common and perhaps 'natural' response by hearing adults to the problem of achieving mutual understanding with their deaf infant is to become more 'controlling' (Goss, 1970; Mogford, Gregory and Hartley, 1980). We suggest that such control is a byproduct of efforts by adults to 'simplify' the child's task by trying to manipulate his visual attention in some way. They may, for instance, turn the infant's head towards them, try to insinuate their face into his visual field or take objects from him to bring them close to their own mouths. Each of these common responses results in a more intrusive parental style and much higher levels of external control over the infant's experiences. They are, we suggest, consciously or unconsciously designed by the adult to overcome the problem of divided attention. They are also counter-productive. Even when the adult 'demands' or 'grabs' the child's attention or takes objects close to her face the infant still has to *work out* what is going on. Indeed, rather than making the child's task *easier* it renders it more difficult, as we shall see later.

Thus, whereas adults interacting with hearing babies often make what they say and do *contingent* upon their interpretation of what the child is seeing or thinking, when hearing adults interact with deaf babies they often demand that the deaf baby attends to *them* and the baby has to work out what they mean. Put another way, the deaf baby is often 'expected' to make *his* thinking contingent upon the intentions of the adult. We believe that this demand is totally unrealistic and cannot be met by infants of this age or, as we will see, by children who are considerably older. If attempts to 'help', direct and control the child result in frustration and tears, it should come as no surprise, given the difficult demands being placed upon the child. Consequently, we suggest that the deaf child may be frustrated not only by any lack of success in communicating his own needs and intentions but also by the demands placed on him when adults try to help him communicate by overcontrolling his actions and attentions. He is also likely to be frustrated in attempts to achieve his own intentions when the adult 'cuts across' his path of activity by 'distracting' him from his own purposes.

Other researchers have argued, however, that such parental responses to deafness are not universal and that given early diagnosis of infant deafness, provision of good amplification and effective parental support, contingent interactions between very deaf babies and their mothers can be established (Tucker and Nolan, 1984). We will consider the theoretical and educational significance of these arguments in the final chapter when we have described our own work. For the moment, however, whilst we accept that very deaf infants with useful levels of auditory awareness do exist and also acknowledge the fact that such awareness (by definition, in our view) overcomes or at least ameliorates the problem of divided attention, the majority of children whom we have studied and who are the subject of this book are not so fortunate.

Given the fact that very few deaf babies are diagnosed or studied in the first year of life, we have no firm information about their social or communicative development during this period. There is no reason to believe that the deaf neonate will not display the usual attraction to the human face, so initial attachments to parents may take place. However, Gregory (in preparation) suggests that by ten months of age when, normally, the baby begins to integrate the world of people and objects and is participating in activities like 'give and take' games, differences between deaf and hearing infants are detectable. This is consistent with the view that voice sounds have already 'infected' the hearing child's experiences to provide a 'bridge' between objects and people. But what of those deaf children who, aged three years or so, enter special nursery provision? What stages of development have they reached?

8

Pre Primary Education of the Handicapped

THIS chapter is concerned with a number of questions and issues relating to the 'quality' of deaf children's experiences in special nursery school groups. More generally, it reports an attempt to describe the structure of adult-child interactions and to relate these to the child's developmental needs and progress. What developmental 'tasks' are facing severely/profoundly deaf three-to five-year-olds in classrooms? What are their educational, social and linguistic needs and are these usually met? How can we evaluate a child's progress during this period and assess the relevance or value of the experiences he is having?

In an attempt to answer these questions, we have undertaken three lines of research. We have observed children in their classrooms, studied attempts to teach deaf preschoolers a difficult construction taks and filmed a group of twelve children at regular intervals in interactions with their teacher. Each line of research has raised common issues concerning the communication and learning problems facing the deaf child and the difficulties and challenges these problems create for teachers. In addition, the longitudinal study of twelve children (Tait, 1984) yielded detailed insights into some of the stages the preschool deaf child passes through in attempting to communicate, acquire speech and learn.

INTO THE NURSERY

Studies of young deaf children in preschool groups are relatively rare, and most of the research that has been done has concentrated mainly on children at play. Since the pioneering observations by Heider and Heider (e.g. Heider and Heider, 1941) a number of studies have painted similar pictures. Their play is often characterized as rather 'literal' and concrete, repetitive, non-symbolic, largely non-social and disjointed. So, for example, whilst one may observe deaf children involved in imitative role play or making 'appropriate use' of toys such as tea sets, hairdriers and cars, one sees little evidence of symbolic or representational play in which objects and toys are exploited for more fanciful or imaginative uses (as when, for instance, a child uses a broom as a horse or a matchbox as a car). The deaf child's play tends to be more solitary than that of similarly aged hearing preschoolers, and any interactions with peers are less likely to be sustained, involve make-believe, negotiation or playthemes not directly related to objects in the 'here and now.'

In our experience of preschool groups, the organization of activities and choice of materials in special nurseries are similar to those in hearing nurseries or playgroups (see Sylva, Roy and Painter, 1980, for a description of life in preschool groups). Children are usually left largely to their own devices in 'free-play' periods. They are encouraged to involve themselves in art and craft activities and to participate in adult-directed group activities: listening to stories, holding group 'conversations' and so on. Whilst the amount of time spent in such activities varies from classroom to classroom (as it does in hearing groups) a similar diet of materials and opportunities are provided.

In our observations, however, we have noted some important differences in the interactions that take place in hearing and deaf nurseries which have been replicated and extended recently in a larger-scale study (Gross, in preparation). The deaf child, throughout his day in school, has many more encounters with adults than is usually the case in hearing groups. The more generous adult-child ratios in special nurseries, coupled, perhaps, with a teaching philosophy amongst teachers of the deaf that puts more emphasis on the importance of adult-child interaction, probably explain such differences. However, whilst the higher levels of contact in the special groups may be consistent with the goals of teachers, more detailed examination of the duration and 'quality' of these interactions shows that they are not, in our view, compatible with the goal of encouraging the development of communicative competence in deaf children. Although more numerous in free-play activities than they are in hearing preschool groups, adult-child contacts in special nurseries are brief (as they usually are in hearing groups too). The majority of contacts do not last over ninety seconds and involve only two or three 'turns' in an interaction (typically, the teacher says or does something, the child responds, the teacher responds and the contact breaks). Such contacts are best described as 'encounters' not interactions.

Encounters *between* children are also generally brief. Extended periods of cooperative play are relatively rare and, in Gross's observations, show little increase over time. In other words, the child who is rising five years is not involved in many more sustained bouts of cooperative play than he was at the age of three. in our earlier observations (which, unlike Gross's, were not longitudinal but involved different children at various ages) we found a dramatic increase in the frequency and duration of child–child interactions at around six years of age. This is, of course, the time when opportunities for child–child interactions in the classroom are inhibited by changes in school timetable. More about this later.

In addition to our studies of deaf children in nursery schools, we have also been involved in detailed analyses of interactions between hearing preschoolers and adults in playgroups and nurseries (Wood, McMahon and Cranstoun, 1980). Some of the conclusions we drew from our observations in that research are relevant to our considerations of special nurseries. Broadly speaking, many of the relatively brief encounters between adults and children in 'free-play' sessions are managerial in intent, although this is not true of all classrooms. When one records what teachers are saying to children, the focus of the interaction is often to with activities like putting on aprons to paint, access to equipment, toileting, ensuring fair turns for all and preventing hostility from breaking out. When adults do become involved in children's play or constructive activities and attempt to help or to converse with them, the interactions often become adult dominated and revolve around question-answer exchanges. We pay a great deal of attention to the issue of questioning children in the next two chapters. For the moment; the point we wish to underline is that, despite advantageous adult-child ratios in special nurseries and notwithstanding the much higher frequency of adult-child encounters, the opportunities for sustained, genuinely cooperative interactions between teacher and child are not often exploited. Although there are some important and informative differences from classroom to classroom there is considerable scope for improvement if the goal of the teacher is to promote productive interactions with the deaf child. We return to more specific suggestions about how such opportunities might be seized later in the chapter.

When we were working in hearing nurseries, one response we met to our emphasis on teachers and their interactions with children was an ideological one. There is a strong tradition in British nursery schools favouring non-directed, free-play for children and a view of the preschool child's needs that largely 'prohibits' adult involvement. Although we agree that preschool hearing children enjoy and benefit from interactions with each other and learn through self-directed activity, we also believe that adults have an important role to play in developing the child's communicative and intellectual abilities. Though this is not a relevant forum to debate this complex issue, we raise it to illustrate the ideological constraints that underline any attempt to 'evaluate' educational provision. Our theoretical framework leads to a strong emphasis on the central importance of adult-child interactions in promoting development. Consequently, we strongly challenge the view that any young deaf child who is manifestly incapable of achieving productive, sustained interactions with his peers can benefit from a 'non-interventionist' approach, for specific reasons that we turn to below. At the same time, however, we are not advocating that teachers adopt a didactic role or try formally to *teach* children language or concepts. The role of the adult in fostering the social, emotional, intellectual and communicative competence of preschool children is a far more subtle, demanding and skillful affair than either the 'laissez-faire' or 'didactic' philosophies imply.

The teachers of the deaf with whom we have worked do seem to share our view that they should play a vital role in helping children to learn and communicate. Indeed, every classroom we have observed used group 'conversation' sessions and many also encouraged one-to-one interactions between teachers and children. So it could be argued that free-play should be relatively 'free' from adult interaction because other activities on the timetable are dedicated to such goals. However, for reasons that we now identify, we question the wisdom and validity of this view. Crudely, we feel that many of the group sessions and one-to-one encounters that take place with young deaf children do *not* meet their communictive or social needs.

CONTINGENT CONTROL OF LEARNING AND COMMUNICATION

In this book, we introduced the concept of 'contingency' to characterize adult responses to infant activities that are likely to foster the development of self-efficacy, understanding and communication in babies. It is a concept that we will use frequently throughout this book and one that we think is central to the facilitation of independence and learning at all stages of development. When we began our work with preschool deaf children, the issue of if and how hearing adults could achieve contingent interactions with deaf children was, and still is, one of our major interests. Since we had already undertaken a whole series of experiments with hearing preschoolers in which we had described and evaluated attempts by parents and other adults to teach them, we decided to undertake similar studies with preschool deaf children. The specific task involved was a pyramid to be built up from 21 square blocks, which fitted together via pegs and holes into five layers of four blocks each. This task is a very difficult one for preschool children. Eight-year-olds find it far from trivial when they are asked to build it alone with the aid of pictures or filmed instructions (Murphy and Wood, 1982) and three-year-olds can only master it if they are taught well (Wood, Wood and Middleton, 1978).

The first question we asked was whether preschool deaf children aged three to five years could be taught the taks at all. In our previous work, we found that adults use frequent verbal instructions with young hearing children, so we were not confident that the twelve very deaf children we worked with, all of whom had severe or profound losses and little or no expressive speech, could be taught how to do the task. Although our experiment involves a rather arbitrary problem, the question it addresses—'Can we *teach* pre-verbal deaf children?'—is a very general one that tests our confidence in the young, pre-verbal deaf child's ability to learn from instruction. It is relevant to the issue of 'expectations' of deaf children. It also provided us with a way of investigating the teaching process that could be related directly to similar studies of hearing children. Thus, we were able to gain some insights into the effects of deafness on teacher behaviour and explore the impact of the handicap on teaching-learning processes. We ourselves learned a great deal from the experience, not least from the reactions of the teachers who took part, as we shall see.

We asked teachers of nursery-aged children to teach individual children how to do the task (having first shown the teachers how to do it) and emphasized that we wanted them to teach in any way that *they* felt would help the child to understand. When they had completed the taks with the child, the blocks were taken apart again and the child was asked to put them back together with no additional help. The whole process was videotaped for later analysis. Our analyses relate the teaching process in the first stage to the child's successes and failures when he or she attempts the task alone. To make sense of these analyses, however, we need to say a little about our methods for describing and evaluating teacher behaviour.

Table 8.1. Levels of intervention in the pyramid task

LEVEL 1	General verbal encouragement
LEVEL 2	Specific verbal information
LEVEL 3	Assists selection
LEVEL 4	Prepares material
LEVEL 5	Demonstrates

In Table 8.1, we present the outline coding system for the analysis of teacher instruction. Note, as you read down the list, how the categories of instruction become more specific, informative and controlling. If the teacher says, for example, 'Now you have a go' (Level 1), she provides the child with no specific guidance as to what he should do nor how he should go about it. If she says 'Get four big ones' (Level 2), she provides an explicit goal verbally but does not help the child to 'unpack' the instruction, as she does if he points to or helps to select blocks that are implicated in the word 'big', for instance. If she actually chooses material for the child (Level 3), then she solves the problem of selecting what blocks to work with next and the child is left with the more constrained task of deciding what to do with them. Orienting the blocks (Level 4) ready for pushing together obviously solves many more problems! If the teacher demonstrates an operation (Level 5), she takes total responsibility for and control over the particular phase of the task in question. In addition to coding each teacher instruction into one of these categories, we also note whether the ensuing responses by the child are successful or not.

How, then, do we turn this analysis of teacher—learner interactions into a 'measure' of effective teaching? Well, how would you, reader, define effective teaching in such a situation? We define it according to two rules. If, following an instruction, a child does *not* succeed, then he should be given more help, or increased control *immediately*. For example, if a specific verbal instruction fails, the appropriate next move is to indicate the relevant blocks to the child or help him by selecting them. Alternatively, if the child *succeeds* in following an instruction, only general encouragement should be given until he encounters a problems that he cannot solve. At this point the teacher should increase help/control until he is again successful, when she again relinquishes control, and so on. By following these two rules, we argue, the teacher maximizes the chances that a child will be confronting problems at the appropriate level of difficulty. Increasing help when he is struggling gives him a more manageable problem. Stepping back when he has shown some degree of success implicitly demands more of him. This is what we mean, in this context, by 'contingency'. The teacher's instructions should always be contingent upon the momentary successes and failures of the child, thus serving to avoid demanding too much or too little of him, neither over-nor underestimating, overwhelming nor boring him.

We have tested the notion of contingency in a number of different experiments involving parents, teachers and adults unfamiliar with the child-learner, and always found the same result. Children who are taught contingently learn much more about the task than children who are not.

When we observed interactions between teachers of the deaf and their children in this situation we found, as with hearing children, that some of the preschoolers did well after instruction, managing to assemble the pyramid alone, whilst others seemed to have learned practically nothing and managed to do little more than fit pegs into holes as if at random. However, when we employed our usual measure of teaching efficiency we found, for the first time, that it did *not* predict how well children did alone after instruction. Why? We thought it unlikely in the extreme that the more successful children could have figured out how to do the task for themselves since, as we have already said, eight-year-old hearing children find the task difficult even when they have pictures to help them. Teaching must, then, have taken place, but it was evident that our analysis was not revealing *how* it took place. How were the successful teachers getting the message across to their children?

VERBAL AND NON-VERBAL COMMUNICATION OF INSTRUCTIONS

From our inspections of the videotapes it was clear to us that the twelve deaf children who took part in this study were generally more difficult to be 'contingent upon' than most hearing children (about 180 in all) in our previous studies. We considered the possibility that the difficulties presented by some children might be so great that, however well they were being taught, they learned little. If so, this might obscure any clear effects of teaching. Three children in particular showed very different 'styles' of responding to teaching and these styles were a reflection of their different capacities in handling the problem of divided attention.

One child, call him Peter, was 'engaged' in his attentions to the teacher but almost to the exclusion of attention to the task. At one point, for example, the teacher asked him to 'Find four big ones.' His eyes never left her face as he moved his hands around on the floor even, at one point, feeling *behind* his body to locate blocks. Despite being one of the least deaf children (75 dB) he was the most 'teacher bound' in his attention. The teacher managed to overcome the problem he posed by looking away from him after giving instructions to look at something else—at which point he paid attention to the blocks and performed quite well. He was reasonably successful, though extremely reluctant, when he was asked to do the task alone.

Another child, Paul, was 'task bound' and his eyes almost never left the blocks. He was very deaf (102 dB) and showed signs of hyperactivity. He worked furiously with the blocks but to no avail. He never looked for instruction and, at one point, the teacher tried in desperation to get into his field of attention by squirming her head along the floor into his field of view. Given this child's seemingly non-existent knowledge of the process of communication it seemed impossible that, even with the best will in the world, the teacher could achieve a contingent interaction with him. All the teachers who knew this child told us that he was a most difficult child to engage in any interaction.

Our third case study, Stephen, was also very deaf but, unlike his two peers, showed tremendous skill in 'incorporating' the teacher into his activities and exploiting her help. Although he had little intelligible speech at the time, it was quite clear that he was learning from the teacher in this situation. In the early stages of instruction, he would look to the teacher, almost invariably having completed a successful operation, as it 'inviting' her to comment. Similarly, if he got into difficulties he would look to the teacher for help. He provided clear and interpretable openings for confirmation or instruction, into which his teacher could offer congratulations or give further suggestions. His ability to distribute his attention between task and teacher made it possible for the teacher to establish a turn-taking structure in their interaction. Stephen met her more than half-way. After instruction, he managed to complete the task on his own and took visible pleasure and pride in doing so.

Around the same time as our experiment took place, we observed these three children, amongst others, in the classroom for a total of six hours each. What we had observed in the experimental situation was reflected in these observations. Peter, for example, spent almost all his time watching the teacher, even when she was on the other side of the room working with other children. Stephen, on the other hand, occupied himself, quite well when the teacher was not attending to him, but, unlike Paul, he almost always responded to her proximity by attending to her and providing opportunities for interaction.

These very different levels of 'teachability' in young deaf children illustrate the interplay between educational 'readiness', the problem of divided attention and the difficulties facing the teachers of some young and very deaf children. As yet, however, our analyses have told us nothing about the nature of the teaching process. Should we conclude that the processes of effective instruction in similar task circumstances are very different for deaf and hearing children?

We were entertaining this possibility when we 'de-briefed' the teachers about the results of the experiment. As part of this process, we produced an edited film showing episodes of each child's session which we called 'the social contract.' This was designed to illustrate the problems of divided attention and its impact on the communication process. Around this time, Margaret Tait (who eventually became one of the research team, completed doctorate and is joint author of this chapter) made a major criticism of our analyses. Having read a preliminary account of the experiment incorporating the coding system outlined in Table 8.1 she was convinced that we had failed to come to grips with the essential nature of her interactions with children. Specifically, she was critical of our notion of 'general verbal prompts' and 'specific verbal instructions' because she felt that they ignored what she was *doing* when she talked to children. She was conscious of the fact that she gave postural, facial and other non-verbal cues to children to help get her message across when talking to them.

In response to her criticisms, we retreated back to our ivory tower and decided how we might test out her intuitions. The solution was obvious (but took some time to figure out nonetheless). We re-examined the video-recordings with the sound switched off! Immediately we did so (and our response was immediate) we were made aware of a wealth of non-verbal communication that, in our attention to speech, we had overlooked. Accompanying our so-called 'verbal' instructions were non-verbal cues and action sequences that were often readily interpretable to us. Let us provide just two examples to illustrate some aspects of the processes involved.

Stephen has just selected four blocks and is attempting to put them together. He has matched them for size but is attempting to assemble two pieces that will not fit together because he has the wrong combination of pegs and holes. What he needs to know is that he must reject one of the pieces (that has a peg on it) in favour of another that contains a hole. He realizes that he has a problem and looks at the teacher. She says: 'You don't want two pegs. You need one with a hole.'—a 'specific verbal instruction' giving information about 'connectives.' However, whilst she says this, she selects two other pieces of matched size that also have the 'wrong' connecting pieces. She holds these and Stephen looks at her hands whilst she 'taps' the two pegs together. he returns to her face and she smiles and shakes her head. This non-verbal 'display' takes place in the same instructional 'turn' as the verbal prompt but we, in our original analysis, had not noticed the non-verbal component that served to draw the child's attention to the crucial features that he had overlooked. He went on to assemble the four pieces with no further problems and then generalized' the experience to another four.

A second example shows how *not* to do it. A child has just selected two blocks but they are not matched for size. The teacher takes the smaller of the two from the child and holds it beside her face. The child points to himself, perhaps intending to communicate the fact that the block belongs to him. Certainly, there was no evidence that he understood the teacher's intended message. The teacher said: 'This is not right. It's too small. You need a big one.' However, when we viewed this instruction without sound, all we saw, ignoring lip-patterns, were several shakes of the head which we might interpret as 'This block—no.' Because there was nothing to compare the block to, the critical feature being discussed—'size'—received no non-verbal definition.

When we reanalysed all the teaching episodes without sound and classified the non-verbal instructions in terms of a revised coding system that paid attention to such phenomena, we found that the children who received the most contingent instructions *non-verbally* were usually the ones who learned more of the task. Therefore, the feature of teacher communication that facilitated mutual understanding and learning—contingent responses to children's signs of success and failure—was essentially the same for deaf and hearing children.

To explore the question of non-verbal communication further, we decided to reanalyse a sample of our original recordings of preschool hearing children being taught by their mothers (Wood, 1980). These, too, were analysed without sound and when we examined them we found similar (though less obvious and more fleeting) examples of non-verbal equivalents of verbal instructions to those used with the deaf. The non-verbal contingency measure was also strongly related to how much the hearing children learned. Indeed, the relationship between non-verbal contingency and learning outcomes was much stronger for the hearing than the deaf sessions. More important, however, were marked differences in the relationships between our *verbal* and *non-verbal* measures. In the teaching sessions with hearing children these were very closely related. In short, a mother who was contingent on the verbal measure was also contingent on the purely non-verbal one. The opposite was true of the deaf sessions—the teacher most contingent non-verbally was least so on the verbal measure. Why should the relationships between verbal and non-verbal aspects of teaching be so very different for deaf and hearing groups? The answers, for there are several reasons, are subtle but important. One reason has already been hinted at above. The separation of verbal and non-verbal control is a symptom of the problem of divided attention facing the child and a conseqeunce of counter-productive responses such as taking material out of its task context to 'talk' about it. When a hearing child faces such problems the adult (mother, teacher or whoever) typically marks her doubt with sceptical 'Hmm's', 'Well's' or explicit comments like 'I don't think that looks right'. If the child is not looking at her, the adult will often point to the problem and perhaps elaborate, saying something like: 'This one is bigger than that. You need two the same size.' Not only can the child hear the explicit verbal instruction but he may also be helped to *understand what is said* by what the adult *does*. Indeed, we have argued that such non-verbal support for verbal instructions illustrates how the task-specific meanings of what is said are transmitted to the child (Wood, 1980). If the hearing child looks up to the adult, verbal instructions are accompanied by slight nods of the head or eye movements which 'point' to the things being referred to. Contrast this with what happened above with a deaf child. By taking the offending block out of its task context, the child was robbed of any *non-verbal* support for understanding the teacher's instruction. He was doubly handicapped in comparison with the hearing child both by not understanding what was said and having no non-verbal cues to support what was being communicated. Another study that we have undertaken showed that hearing children who are taught this task purely verbally with little or no non-verbal support find it extremely difficult (Wood, Wood and Middleton, 1978). Ironically, deaf children are more likely than hearing children to be robbed of such non-verbal communication because of the strategies teachers use to try to over-come the problem of divided attention.

In summary, then, when one simply looks at what teachers *say* to young deaf children, one may obtain a false impression of what is actually being communicated, not simply because the child does not hear or understand what is said but also because the non-verbal cues and signals that the teacher provides may be impoverished, non-contingent and even misleading. Deaf children can be taught quite difficult practical tasks but, like hearing children need contingent instruction. However, the fact that the child has to divide his attention between teacher and task creates problems for him that are often reflected in the actions of the teacher. However, some teachers are able to bring off successful interactions with children and they do so by making what they *do* contingent upon the child's level of understanding.

We have already acknowledged that the teaching situation we have been considering is artificial and 'unnatural.' However, it provided us with opportunities to explore the impact of what we think is a general communication and learning problem facing the deaf child and to demonstrate that this problem generates a range ot teaching strategies, some of which are counter-productive. It also illustrates how hard it is to maintain a teaching role with young deaf preschoolers and draws our attention to the central importance of considering the interplay between verbal and non-verbal aspects of communication.

We turn now to a far more elaborate, 'naturalistic' and telling line of research that arose as an indirect consequence of the experiment we have just outlined. We have already mentioned that Dr. Tait became a member of the research group after we had worked in her classroom for some time. We encouraged her to become involved in research of her own, hoping that she would explore further our mutual interest in the non-verbal foundations of verbal understanding and help to show how these might profitably influence classroom practice. We were somewhat surprised when she decided to do research into the role of singing (no, the 'n' and 'g' are not misplaced) in the education of preschool deaf children. The topic of singing and its roles is the subject of a booklet written by her (Tait, 1985). Fortunately, we were able to persuade her to compare her singing sessions with 'conversations' to see how far the comparisons of children in the two situations might lead to insights into the structure and development of turn-taking in communication (since singing is a form of vocal communication that people do together rather than in turns). In the event, two goals were achieved. One was a detailed analysis of the stages involved in the transition from pre-verbal to verbal communication in preschool deaf children. The other was a demonstration of the multifaceted and multipurposed value of singing for deaf children. We turn now to the stages of development.

FROM PRE-VERBAL TO VERBAL COMMUNICATION IN DEAF NURSERY SCHOOL CHILDREN

In the following quotation, Conrad (1979) speculates about the communicative competence of very deaf children when they enter school around the age of five years or so. Note that he predicts not only that such children are likely to be unaware of speech sounds *per se,* but that they will also lack fundamental knowledge about the fact that verbal communication (and its non-verbal accompaniments such as lip movements) exists at all.

> (Deaf) children . . . reach school age with little concept of the existence of verbal language and effectively no experience of it. They may not even know that the facial gestures centred on the mouth that they see around them are accompanied by sounds and are used to effect comunication . . . . They will not know that objects have names: that they can be referred to when they are not immediately present.

There has, in fact, been very little systematic, detailed research into the early educational experiences of deaf children and none, as far as we are aware, that has looked analytically at the child's 'knowledge' of communication. We present evidence relevant to this question here. Over a period of four years, every severely/profoundly deaf child entering a special nursery for the deaf in an inner city area was included in a longitudinal study of communicative development. Only children with losses in excess of 80 dB (the mean hearing loss of the group was 104 dB) and suffering from no known additional handicap were included. Twelve children fell into this category and these were filmed at three-monthly intervals beginning after they had been in school for a minimum of three months and ending when they moved on to primary school. Children were filmed with their teacher in one-to-one 'conversation' and singing sessions and also in group sessions. These sessions were not 'special' (apart from filming) but a part of the school routine. The teacher herself (Tait) arranged the video cameras which were in place most of the time. Children seemed to 'forget' the presence of a camera.

Although some of the chldren were speaking in single words on entry to school most were not. They understood little or nothing of what was said to them. Thus, they were at different stages of linguistic development on entry, despite being a reasonably homogeneous group in terms of hearing loss. Not all the children were at the 'earliest' stage outlined below on entry. Individual differences in levels of communicative competence will be explored later.

What changes occurred in children's communicative competence during the twelve to eighteen months spent in the nursery and what inferences can we draw from these about their progress?

Stages of Pre-Verbal Development

Before we consider some of the results of the study we need to say a little about our use of the term 'stage.' We are *not* using it to denote very clear-cut, independent periods in children's progress. The stages often 'overlap' in the sense that children are at certain stages in some familiar situations while they are less competent in other, less familiar or more problematic ones. Another term we use interchangeably with 'stage' is the notion of 'developmental tasks.' Children have to overcome certain 'tasks' before they begin to talk. But these tasks often recur when they find themselves in new relationships with unfamiliar people in unusual circumstances. If, as we did in the block study above, we place the children into new, difficult and initially stressful circumstances it is likely that they would seem less competent than they do in more familiar and predictable settings. The notion of development tasks and their recurrence when new demands are made on children are important ones that we explore later.

Stages 1 and 2. 'Disengaged' and 'Engaged'

Consider the two transcripts given below. (Note that the child's contributions, nonexistent at this stage, are in these transcripts presented in parallel to, and below, the teacher's utterances.) The transcripts involve the same teacher and child and were recorded twelve weeks apart. Initially, we represent only what was said. On this criterion, the child seems to have made no progress.

DISENGAGED

→ Teacher	Look, lets go—round and round and round and round . . .
→ Child	
→ Teacher	One . . . Two . . . tickle! Do it again? . . . Round and round . . .
→ Child	

The teacher does all the talking and the child makes no vocalization—a typical state of affairs with this child (age at the time 31 months; hearing loss 110 dB). Now the second transcript.

ENGAGED

T. You tell it, say 'come on!' . . . I'm going to say 'Come on'.
C.

T. train' . . Ch-ch-ch-ch-ch . . . Oo! . . . Ow! It bumped me! . . . It's
C.

T. going to come and . . . bump you!
C.

Again the child remains silent, but the nature of his involvement in the interaction has, in fact, changed considerably and positively. To detect such changes, however, we have to attend not only to what the child says (or, in this case, does not say) but also where and what he looks at. We now reproduce the transcripts with two important additions: representations of where both the teacher and child are looking throughout the interaction. The straight line placed above the speech of either partner remains high when they are looking *at* their partner, and drops down towards the verbal transcription when they look away, when what they *are* looking at is written in above the line.

DISENGAGED

T. Look, let's go—round and round and round and round . . .
at hand / outside
C.

at C's hand
T. One . . . Two . . . tickle! Do it again? . . . Round and round ...
at video / outside / at table
C.

ENGAGED

on train / train

T. You tell it, say 'come on!' . . . I'm going to say 'Come on

aside / at train

C.

train

T. train' . . . Ch-ch-ch-ch-ch . . .Oo! . . . Ow! It bumped me! . . . It's

train train

C.

train

T. going to come and . . . bump you!

train

C.

Now the differences between the two episodes should be clearer. In the first transcript, the child's attention patterns are totally unpredictable. He shows no evidence of knowing that communication is taking place, though whether this is due to the fact that he is still new to and overawed by school we cannot say. However, twelve weeks later, his pattern of attention shows a marked change. He is now almost totally 'engaged,' either looking at the teacher or at the object/event being talked about.

In both sessions, the teacher's attention is directed almost totally at the child. This may seem a banal point, but it is crucial to the role she is playing in helping him to discover the act of communication. In an early session, for example, when the child was almost totally disengaged, she managed for one brief period to gain his attention and foster interaction. He was given a drum which he duly banged. The teacher feigned alarm and he looked at her. She held a 'shocked' face for a time and he watched her as he banged the drum again. She responded in turn with another expression of shock. The episode only lasted a few seconds, but was made possible by the fact that the teacher was observing the child closely and prepared to respond immediately and contingently to any action that he made which might conceivably be endowed with communicative intent. In the first weeks, she seldom succeeded in earning his attention, however. Her actions and reactions usually went unnoticed by the child because he was not often looking at her at the right time. Eventually, however, he did begin to watch her reactions and started to paly a more intentional role in their interactions.

Note what the child is *not* doing on the second transcript. Although he is distributing his attention between object and person, there is little or no correspondence between where he looks and the *structure* of the interaction. For instance, he is almost as likely to look away whilst the teacher is in mid-utterance as he is when she ends her verbal 'turn.' In short, his pattern of attention displays no real appreciation of the 'turn-taking' character of verbal interaction. He is also silent. As we shall see, these two features of interaction are not unrelated.

Stage 3. 'Structured Attention'

In the next episode filmed 24 weeks later we see two new and important features emerging in the interaction. The teacher and child are looking at a picture of an umbrella in a book, and this is used as a springboard into conversation. We will talk about the content of conversation a little later. For the moment note how the child's attention is beginning to reflect the structure of the discourse. When the child looks away during a speaking turn (as he does when the umbrella is *mentioned*) it is usually a fleeting affair and is relevant to the focus of discourse. As we saw in this book, here too we find the emergence of a 'triangle of reference' in the child's distribution of attention. Also note how, when the teacher mentions the fact that they were unable to go outside when it was raining, the child looks outside, again reflecting knowledge of the topic of discourse.

T. My big umbrella, and it's blue (at picture) And . . . Yes, (at picture)
C. boo boo

T. It's blue. And you held the umbrella because it
C. boo

T. was raining. Yes it was raining. We couldn't
C. rai

T. go out, could we? No. It is raining

outside

C. uh (shakes head)

outside

T. today? No, it's stopped.

outside

C. 'op.

The teacher is still subtly orchestrating turn-taking. Although she usually finishes what she has to say (not, for example, stopping talking when the child glances away) she is prepared to postpone or relinquish what she has to say when she perceives that the child has something to contribute. For instance, when the child twice says 'boo', meaning blue, whilst looking at the book (and hence not hearing the start of the teacher's next contribution 'And . . .') the teacher pauses, acknowledges the child's contribution and only then proceeds to complete her own turn. Establishing such contingent patterns of responding to children is not easy and requires a good deal of vigilance and self-control on the teacher's part.

Another important achievement is illustrated in the transcript. When children show clear signs of having discovered the turn-taking structure of discourse and are able to distribute their attention between the speaker and object of communication, they usually begin to vocalize. There was, in fact, a close relationship across the group of children between the development of visual attention to the teacher during speaking, on the one hand, and the emergence of child vocalizations, on the other. Only when attention to the teacher was sustained and that to objects of discourse relatively fleeting did vocal communication emerge on the scene. The integrated character of attention, turn-taking and vocalizations are compatible with Bruner's theory of the relationships between pre-verbal and verbal communication which we mentioned in the last chapter. Their interrelation is also evidence that however unintelligible the child's speech may seem to an outside observer, they are beginning to make vocal acts of communication.

Stage 4. 'Structured Vocalization'

Because the development of structured attention and vocalization are closely related and, in some children, almost seemed to emerge simultaneously on the recordings, it is questionable whether we should talk about structured visual attention and vocalization as distinct stages. However, we decided we had to discriminate between them because some children displayed relatively skillful patterns of attention for some time before beginning to vocalize with any frequency. Although vocalizations to the teacher occurred only very infrequently *before* attention patterns were structured with any child (i.e. achieveing reciprocal attention was a precursor to the emergence of vocal communication), the 'delay' between structured attention and predictable vocalization varied considerably from child to child.

On the first recordings, made when children had been in the nursery for a relatively short time, they only made a vocal response to the teacher (i.e. took a vocal 'turn' in an interaction) about 25 per cent of the time on average. On their final recordings, as they approached the end of their time in the nursery, this had risen to 75 per cent. Looking at individual children: the most vocal on the early recordings responded to a little over half the opportunities to talk; by the last session, one child missed not a single opening in ten minutes of conversation. At the other end of the scale, five children were virtually silent on the first recordings; by the end, no child was totally silent but two still took up less than half the opportunities given to speak.

Although these children are a relatively homogeneous group in terms of age and hearing loss, there were marked differences both in the readiness with which they developed through the pre-verbal stages of interaction and in the time-lag between the development of structured attention and frequent vocalization.

Stage 5. 'Conversational Partnership'

Children who had clearly reached Stage 5 by the end of the study had become real partners in conversation. Some of what they said was genuinely informative (i.e. not obvious from the context), sometimes amusing, on occasion a blatant lie and occasionally a little rude!

The stage of conversational partnership is marked by the emergence of several quite different achievements, and is best viewed not simply as the product of one development or discovery by the child but as an opening up of many new lines of progress. It is, so to speak, more of a 'watershed' than a single stage. All the achievements that we noted after Stage 4 did not emerge immediately for each child, hence we use the term stage very loosely in this case.

One of the most important things that emerges in Stage 5 is an increase in the *range* of discourse functions or types of linguistic 'move' used by children. For example, one of the most verbal children (aged four years eight months and with a hearing loss of 108 dB in one ear and 104 dB in the other) began to 'disagree with' and 'correct' the teacher, as in the following excerpt. They are discussing a visit that the child (Hazel) had made to a friend's house (Susie). (Note: in these and all subsequent transcripts, the teacher's and the child's utterances are presented in turn.)

CONVERSATIONAL PARTNERSHIP

C. Sarah house, Sarah. (shaking her head)
T. Wasn't Sarah there?
C. (shakes her head)
T. Wasn't she? Was Pamela there?
C. I SUSIE friend (i.e. not Pamela's nor Sarah's who are Susie's sisters).
T. I know, you're Susie's friend. Was Pamela there?
C. Pamela school.

Here the child is holding her own in the conversation. When the teacher asks 'Was Pamela there?' (really wanting to know!) the child does not answer immediately, being determined not to let the teacher get away with what she (the child) sees as a misunderstanding. First, then, the child 'refuses' to answer a question because the thinks that the teacher has the wrong end of the conversational stick. Later, she goes beyond the force of the teacher's two-choice question 'Was Pamela there?', not simply saying 'no', a minimal response, but to say where she *was* at the time. Thus, the child starts to argue, attempts to correct what she perceives as a misunderstanding, negotiates rather than 'slavishly' answering questions and elaborates beyond the force of specific questions to provide relevant information. Her role in conversation has become one of initiator and not simply one of acting as a respondent which was a characteristic of earlier interactions. She also shows clear signs of taking conversational initiative. As we will show in the next two chapters, not only is such a display of initiative rare in deaf children, it is also very dependent upon the style and technique of the teacher.

Other signs of autonomy and confidence emerge. These include 'interrupting' the teacher. Whereas, in Stages 1 to 3, any vocalization by the child during a teacher's speaking turn was usually uninterpretable and appeared to have no communicative significance (e.g. a 'spontaneous' noise), the content of interruptions by children in Stage 5 show that they are contributing to the *theme* of conversation. They may lack finesse but they are following the topic.

T. You'll be a very big girl . . . .
C. (interrupting) Same as Sarah.
T. Pardon?
C. Sarah four.
T. Oh, Sarah's four, of course she is, yes. And YOU'RE four, and when you're five . . . .
C. (interrupting) Susie six.
T. Pardon?

Note not only how the child is volunteering information and showing initiative but also how, characteristically, the teacher is prepared to 'relinquish' the control of the topic, again responding contingently to any offering by the child. Had she not done so, as we will see in the next chapter, it is highly likely that the child would have shut up.

Hazel could speak about 40 to 50 words when she entered school and on the first recording took up about 40 per cent of the openings to speak offered by the teacher. Therefore she was already into Stages 3/4 early in her school life. By the end of the period of study she was taking up about 90 per cent of all openings, but, most important of all, the *range* of the responses changed dramatically from largely *responsive* utterances solicited by the teacher to the use of such autonomous conversational acts as just illustrated.

One final example is taken from the final recording of another child, Andrew, who also became a ture partner in conversation before leaving the nursery. Somewhat older than Hazel when he left (five years six months) he had a better-ear loss of 102 dB when he entered school at four years, but this had 'risen' to a 96 dB loss by the time he moved on. Like Hazel, his conversation shows signs of autonomy, initiative and loquacity. He interrupts, elaborates on his answers to questions and volunteers information spontaneously. Here, too, the teacher usually responds contingently to his acts of communication to enable him to hold the conversational floor as much as possible. In the first extract, the child introduces new topics of conversation:

T. Look at what the train's doing now.
C. He happy.
T. Yes, he's happy because he's in the tunnel.

At this point, Andrew starts to point out features of the picture being studied which he thinks are being overlooked. Meanwhile the teacher is saying . . .

T. Look at her (i.e. the train) now! All clean! Isn't she?
C. It my blue.
T. That's you with your blue jumper, yes.

In the next episode he goes beyond the force of teacher questions, interrupting the teacher to continue his answer:

T. What does Lynnette do?
C. She Lynnette cry.
T. She does . . . .
C. (interrupting) She poorly, Lynnette.

Not all children achieved this degree of loquacity, independence and initiative by the time they left the nursery. Two children were still in Stage 3. However, the growth of signs of autonomy in terms of introducing topis, elaborating on answers, interrupting and so on increased across the group as a whole and were clearly evident in the final recordings of several children even though, like Hazel and Andrew, they were very deaf children.

Another feature of Stage 5 conversations, as much to do with the skills of the teacher as with the capacities of the child, is an increase in the volume of 'decontextualized' talk. By this we mean talk about objects, happenings, experiences and the like which are not present in the immediate context. Once deaf children start to play an active role in conversation, there is no reason to suppose that they can only take part in the 'concrete' interactions commonly encountered in schools. Restricted verbal demands such as 'Show me your shoes,' 'What colour is your dress?', 'What's this called?', 'Give me the car' are not only likely to inhibit the young child from talking but they also offer little scope for truly *functional* and interesting communication. In our studies of hearing playgroups and nurseries, we found that children in conversation with teachers were likely to be talking about events at home or in the future that had some real *significance* for them. There is no reason to suppose that deaf children would not be similarly motivated about things that matter to *them*. Once children achieve Stage 5, their language begins to catch up with their 'thoughts' and they are 'ready' for genuine conversation. Whilst the teacher may use props or aids (like photogrpahs and toys) to initiate topics there is no reason, once the child has reached this stage of communicatvie competence, for discourse to remain context bound.

We would like to make one final note about other developments that occur with some children around this time to do with 'auditory awareness.' We have already noted that Andrew's audiogram, like that of several other children, improved with time in the nursery. They were making better use of their hearing in hearing tests and this was reflected in their conversational activities. Some of the children began to look away from the teacher *during* her speaking turns. This was not due to 'regressions' in their stage of development, as they continued to respond appropriately to what she said. We believe that this phenomenon, not found in the less verbally able children, was due to the developing use of residual hearing to monitor voices. Although very deaf, it seems likely that these children were able to hear elements of intonation and stress, together, perhaps, with the start and end of vocal turns.

We developed a simple test in which the teacher stood behind the children and asked them to give her familiar objects whose names they already knew. These were included in a set of objects placed on a table in front of the child. Although they could not lip-read the teacher, since she was out of sight, the children who were showing signs of auditory awareness in conversation scored well above chance levels of success in picking out named objects. Thus, they were hearing and understanding something of what was being said to them. Children who were not showing signs of awareness in conversation could not do this task.

We cannot prove what we are about to say next! We believe the development of auditory awareness, when it occurs, arises in discourse and conversation. One important facet of the teacher's behaviour has yet to be underlined. When we examined the structure of her conversational style on the first and last recordings we found some marked similarities. She was offering very similar numbers of openings to both the non-speaking children and those in Stage 5. She asked similar numbers of questions and so on. Even when children were disengaged, she tended to act 'as though' they were participating in discourse. Studies of interactions between mothers and pre-verbal hearing babies have produced similar findings. Adults orchestrate interactions with babies to produce 'pseudo- conversations'—responding contingently and swiftly to movements and vocalizations from the baby to make it appear that the infant is taking turns in the interaction (Elias, 1983). Thus, both the teacher and parents act out a form of 'self-fulfilling prophesy.' They provided predictable conversational framework into which the child is eventually 'recruited' as a partner.

Let us return to the children who displayed some auditory awareness. Our interpretation of this finding is that by maintaining a 'normal' conversational framework for children, even with those in Stage 1, the teacher provided conditions for their *discovery* of pre-verbal, verbal and acoustic aspects of language. Some children, even with losses as great as 110 dB, showed signs of making *sense* of what they were hearing and of exploiting it in conversation. It is almost certain that they could not function without lip-reading and other non-verbal cues, but there is evidence that they also exploit their hearing too. We suggest that this is because their experience in discourse with the teacher made what they could hear *meaningful* and significant, because it was encapsulated within interpretable social interactions.

EDUCATIONAL IMPLICATIONS

In both the experimental teaching study and longitudinal observations, we have drawn attention to the importance of sustained, projectful, contingent interactions with young deaf children. We have also argued that we must attend to pre-verbal and non-verbal aspects of what both teacher and child are doing to understand if, when and how communication takes place and to evaluate the value of any activity or interaction. Similarly, if we want to chance any progress made by the child in the early stages of linguistic development, a consideration of his patterns of attention and their relationships to the communicative activities of his partner in interaction are a *sine qua* non for success.

At the beginning of this chapter we commented on the concrete, literal and rather asocial nature of children's encounters with their deaf peers. This is fully understandable and predictable when, as is usually the case with pre-school deaf children, they are in Stages 1 to 3 (and, perhaps, 4 too). How can we expect deaf children to maintain extended and productive play themes with each other when they are unable to participate knowingly in interactions with communicatively skilled adults? We also said that we found very dramatic increases in child-child interactions around the age of six years. This is also predictable for those children who achieve Stages 4/5. Once they can develop the ability to construct mutual understanding in communication, they begin to hold sustained interactions with each other. Consequently, we would argue that any benefits likely to accrue to children from peer group interaction and play are most likely to occur not at the age of three or four years but around the age of five years onwards. Paradoxically, however, when children are five or six, they have usually been moved on to more 'formal' educational experiences. In our view, full-time formal teaching, be it concerned with reading, counting or whatever, is only likely to prove beneficial to children who have consolidated their ability to play an active, sustained and competent role in discourse.

Young deaf children can, however, be recruited into 'projectful', constructive interactions in which they help to *do* something with an adult, as we argued in our teaching experiment. The joint completion of projects not only helps to develop and sustain the deaf child's abilities to concentrate, plan and solve problems but also provides a context for reciprocal, contingent interactions. The most important single resource in the classroom is, for us, the teacher and other adults. But are such human resources always used effectively? We think not.

As we also said early on in the chapter, most adult interactions with deaf children in the classroom either take place in groups or tend to be fleeting in character. Group sessions have a role to paly but *not* in developing conversational competence in young children. Young hearing children in preschool groups, though relatively fluent verbally and skilled in one-to-one conversations, face considerable problems in 'group talk.' Playing a productive role as listener and contributor in a group demands a range of conversational skills (Wood, McMahon and Cranstoun, 1980) that many preschool hearing children may only just be working on.

Groups have an important part to play in activities like singing (Tait, 1984) and story telling, in which either all participants contribute *in parallel* rather than in turns or all attend together to a drama or story. In the next two chapters, we will look at some of the problems and pitfalls associated with teacher-led group 'conversation' sessions. To our mind, these pitfalls are far too deep for the young deaf child to be exposed to.

The young deaf child needs a great deal of *individual* attention and the kind of experiences in which the more mature create an enabling and contingent framework to facilitate the development of interaction and communication. At the end of the last chapter, we explored some of the problems facing hearing adulsts when they attempt to communicate with the pre-verbal deaf child. These arise in part, we argued, because of the greater maturity of deaf children (in comparison with hearing infants) when they are in the pre-verbal stages of development. We now examine other factors that are likely to contribute to these problems and inhibit the chances of producing a contingent learning environment for the child. The three most important of these are the fact that children are in groups, with teachers and in school.

Language development in hearing children is a remarkably robust process that is difficult to stop (though it can be impeded). The most formative stages take place in the family and community, in interactions with individuals who are centrally important to the children and who know them intimately. Children are not expected to acquire their mother tongue in groups; nor are they sent to a special room or building to do so. What they communicate about tends to be of immediate significance and personal concern. Topics of talk are not decided by external authority but arise 'naturally' as a consequence of living with other people.

Work with preschool hearing children (Tizard and Hughes, 1984) has shwon that interactions between teachers and hearing nursery school children are generally less frequent, less sustained, more context dependent and less linguistically and intellectually challenging than those between mothers and the same children. To a large extent, such differences are likely to be attributable to the less favourable adult-child ratios in school. They also hinge, perhaps, on the philosophy of many educators who hold that an important (if not the most important) experience provided in preschool settings is not adult-child contact but the opportunities provided for pet group interaction. Another important factor stems from the differential nature of the adult-child relationship and the context within which that relationship usually functions. The sustained, verbally elaborated and intellectually stimulating conversations that preschool children have at home revolve around happenings and social practices in their everyday lives and are stimualted by events in their environment. Wells (1979), in a study of language in the home, reports that the three-year-old child *initiates* around three-quarters of the verbal interactions with his parents. *He* chooses what is going to be talked and thought about. In the study by Tizard and Hughes conversations about such things as 'why Mummy gives money to the window cleaner' led to extended and interesting discussions between mother and child about why people need money, what they do with it, what would happen if they did not have any and so on. The child's induction into monetarism and the language of economics arise out of such seemingly banal events.

In school, such discussions are relatively rare, although, interestingly, we have found that the most common topics for extended conversations between the teacher and hearing preschooler often centre on such familiar ingredients as happenings in the child's life at home (Wood, McMahon and Cranstoun 1980).

Schools did not evolve as institutions designed to foster language development in children. The education of very young children in groups, looked after by specially trained adults, is still a relatively new experiment in social engineering, conceived a little more than half a century ago. Only recently has the preschool environment been afforded an explicit role in developing children's language and it should, perhaps, come as no surprise to find that it has yet to prove that it can fulfil such a role. Schools were never designed to foster the intimate, two-way, reciprocal and contingent interactions that seem best suited to the development of communication between adults and children. Indeed, they are more likely to achieve the opposite state of affairs by demanding that children 'pay attention' and pursue goals established by adults. The child in such a situation must often make *his* thinking contingent upon that of the adult (Wood, in press), and not the other way round. The history of schools, their curricula and architecture; the teaching role and training of teachers are still rooted in a technology given over to the socialization and education of children which is based on the adult leading and the child learning how to follow. If a child is to be helped to learn how to communicate in a school setting, then many of the implicit and explicit assumptions underlying the historical definition of the teaching role must be questioned and changed. Truly productive use of teacher time with young deaf chidlren will look suspiciously like fun and games to an outside observer. However, the teacher and the more acute observer will realize what tremendous levels of skill and constraint underlie the achievement of any such enjoyable, reciprocal, contingent interactions.

9

Communicating with Deaf Children

IN the last chapter, we outlined and discussed several stages in the transition from pre-verbal to verbal communication and found, by Stage 5, that children were starting to participate in conversation. We now move on to study the structure and function of conversations involving children aged from five to fourteen years. In fact, we devote three chapters to the topic. Here, we look at 'pragmatic' aspects of teacher—child conversation, examining both the ways in which teachers manage conversations and children's reactions to different conversational 'moves' and management styles. Analyses and comparisons of the conversational styles of different teachers, talking to both deaf and hearing children, enabled us to identify those features of teacher talk that promote extended verbal responses from children and influence the amount of verbal initiative children display. These results led us to mount a series of classroom intervention studies in which we asked teachers to change their styles of talking to children in order to test our predictions about the effects of different teaching styles on children's receptive and expressive language. These studies, which were designed to help identify strategies for achieving sustained and productive conversations with children, are outlined in this chapter. In Chapter 8 we look in detail at grammatical features of teachers' talk to children and compare these to aspects of deaf children's understanding of English grammar (which are the subject of Chapter 1). We ask, in Chapter 2, if teachers regularly expose children to examples of language use that might help foster language learning.

CONVERSATION

Conversation is one type of discourse. We do not, for example, regard verbal interactions concerned with naming objects or describing them as conversation. Whilst discovering the names of things and how to analyse and label their properties is obviously an important element of language development, particularly in the early stages, it is not, by our definition, conversation. When talk serves to relate and *share* past experiences, plans for the future, life in other times and places or what might come to be, then it becomes a conversation.

Basically, then, we see conversation as talk about things that are *not* in the immediate environment of the talkers and listeners. Though conversations may, and with young children often do, arise out of talk about objects, pictures or happenings in the shared context, it is when talk moves on to memories, plans, experiences and aspirations that a conversation is born.

Conversation is also to be distinguished from debate and teaching. In 'teaching' discourse, there is an implicit assumption that the 'direction' for and evaluation of what is said will be largely the responsibility of the person in control. In conversation, roles are more 'equal', and what is considered worth saying can be decided by any participant.

Conversation is also different from debate, where there should be a 'tacit contract' accepted by all participants to 'keep their minds' on a specific topic, to 'edit' what they say in order to minimize the introduction of irrelevancies and so forth. In conversation, there are fewer constraints on the topics that may be introduced, and what is considered 'legitimate' talk is less clearly circumscribed. This is not to say, however, that conversations are 'unstructured' or take place without (unspoken or tacit) rules. Indeed, productive conversation is constrained by several types of rules. These include a need to 'take turns', for speakers to make what they say coherent and accessible to their listeners, for listeners to provide indications that what is being said is being *listened* to and to respond to speaker contributions in some intelligible fashion.

Participation in converesation demands knwoledge, not only in the construction of intelligible, coherent and linguistically acceptable utterances but also of interpersonal and social skills. Interpersonal understanding is needed to appreciate how one's ideas must be organized and disciplined in such a way that they can be understood. Some things have to be explained before others can be grasped, and so on. It is also necessary for a speaker to monitor his listener's non-verbal and verbal responses for signs of comprehension or misunderstanding, interest and boredom. Thus, participation in conversation provides one route towards an understanding of other people and how they think. A skilled conversationalist cannot be too 'egocentric,' taking account only of his own perspective and needs. He must 'put himself in his listener's shoes' and see the situation from their perspective.

To adults who have become practised in the art of conversation, it is easy to overlook the intellectual and interpersonal demands facing the less mature and inexperienced. Some demands they face are linguistic (e.g. using pronouns appropriately) but others concern the need to relate experiences in a sequence that is comprehensible to their listeners (Wood, McMahon and Cranstoun, 1980). When young children remember a vivid experience or scene they tend to put into words the more salient events that are, naturally, uppermost in their minds. They often do so before 'setting the scene' so that what they say is not easily understood. Coherent conversation contains elements of 'story telling' which help to form a bridge to literacy.

Conversations between more than two people also demand 'group talk' skills which take time to develop. A child will often answer a question addressed to someone else, for example, or interrupt another's speaking turn when a dramatic idea comes to him. Self-restraint, monitoring and listening to others, knowing when to 'come in' and when to wait demand a degree of knowledge and self-control that does not 'come naturally' but demands experience. In short, conversation provides opportunities to discover many aspects of what is involved in 'becoming a person.' It demands not only a grasp of grammatical procedures but knowledge of when, in what manner and to whom one speaks. Many social practices, rules of etiquette and intellectual abilities are implicit in conversation, participation in which promises many developmental rewards.

Becoming a *partner* in conversation demands not only an ability to contribute and question but also the capacity to listen and interpret. For very deaf children, it also demands knowing how and when to maintain one's visual attention on a speaker. Even in two-person interactions where talk is largely about things in the immediate situation and takes place in partnership with a 'skilled' adult, knowing when and how to take turns in talk presents difficult problems for deaf children. When talk moves on to conversation, any support from environmental and non-verbal cues to meaning is reduced (though, as we shall see, they do not disappear entirely). The would-be conversationalist faces a number of intellectual, social and linguistic demands. He must learn what is involved in keeping two or more minds 'focused' on a common topic and discover how to play a part in constructing a shared 'realm of discourse' that 'grows' as conversation develops. He has to learn how to refer, relate and integrate each new item of information to what has already been constructed. This, in turn, involves skills at a number of levels.

At one level, for example, the child must understand how words like pronouns serve to refer back or forward to past and future utterances. He has to realize how words like 'that' can be used to make reference to a previous idea, as in 'I don't agree with that.' He may have to draw implications from what has been said to make sense of a new question or contribution. To take a simple example, if someone has said 'We went to town yesterday (meaning the speaker and another person), we did some shopping and had tea in a little cafe. What did you do?', the 'timeframe' being referred to in the question is established, implicitly, in an earlier contribution. Many, more subtle aspects of meaning rest on the ability of a listener to interpret a new conversational move in the light of what has been said or implied in previous ones. In addition to paying attention and understanding individual utterances, then, a child has to learn how to participate in the construction of realms of discourse.

Most conversations between teachers and children, as we shall see, are characterized by question-answer exchanges, in which almost all the questions come from the teacher and nearly all the answers from the children. One 'advantage' of such a strategy is that it enables a teacher to establish and develop the 'theme' of conversation and to maintian coherence in discourse. Her questions produce the 'framework' into which a child's responses fit and can be related back to preceding utterances. Questions may establish who or what is being talked about (the topic) and then proceed to establish things about that topic, such as who did what, when, to whom and with what consequences. From the child's point of view, this means that he can often participate in the interaction by attending to each question from the teacher as a single event, taking little or no responsibility for the task of constructing a *coherent* conversation.

Questions, by their nature, are 'demanding' and 'controlling.' They have to be listened to and thought about. Indeed, as we have seen in Chapter 1, a child's ability to answer teachers' Wh-type questions (who, what, where, when, why and how) with appropriate and relatively long replies is usually a good index of his linguistic competence, including his reading ability. Eventually, however, if the child is to become a truly 'equal partner' in conversation, he must learn how to attend to longer *sequences* of utterances and discover how to integrate and remember them. He also has to work out how to use this accumulated information as a basis for questions or contributions of his own that are sensibly and coherently related to what has gone before in the conversation. Constant cycles of question-answer exchanges, we will try to demonstrate, are unlikely to provide conditions for a child to learn how to develop such skills and abilities in creating realms of discourse.

Conversation provides a means to many developmental ends, but it is not, educationally speaking, the terminus of communicative or linguistic competence. Being able to attend to and understand teacher 'monologues' when she is 'transmitting' knowledge and information creates a new set of demands which, we believe, grow out of and extend abilities founded in conversation. When the child is exposed to long sequences of monologue (or 'autonomous' speech; Romaine, 1984) he has to maintain his attention on the speaker for relatively long periods of talk and try to recreate from sequences of utterances the structure of the 'story' being told. The information is not 'broken up' into a series of relatively simple utterances, as can happen in conversational turn-taking. Nor are there as many opportunities for mutual checks of understanding that the two-way exchanges in conversation permit. If the child is to be capable of transmitting information himself, he must develop the capacity to present ideas not simply in grammatically well-formed, single utterances but in a sequence that honours his listener's needs. He must also monitor his listener for indices of comprehension and signs of perplexity or misunderstanding. Faced with a breakdown in mutual understanding he may have to supplement, paraphrase or explain what he has already tried to say in order to reinstate it.

Becoming skilled as a listener to, and presenter of, such 'autonomous' discourse is clearly a difficult task. Indeed, it is one that many hearing adolescents (and, we suspect, adults too) have not mastered (Brown *et al.*, 1984). Our own classroom recordings contian very few examples of deaf children even attempting to produce 'autonomous' discourse.

But isn't it unrealistic to expect such achievements of deaf children who have so much difficulty in understanding the 'basics' of language? At present, given the general character of school discourse involving deaf children, it probably is unrealistic to expect children to develop into 'autonomous' communicators. Indeed, as we shall see, many deaf children do not become effective partners in conversation. However, we will be arguing that not all the reasons for this state of affairs reside 'in' the child. Rather, the way in which teachers 'manage' conversations often provides little or no opportunity for children to learn how to become good conversationalists. Whether this is a direct and inevitable consequence of children's deafness remains to be seen. We suspect, however, that it is not. It is possible to create productive, coherent conversations with deaf children, but doing so demands hard work and considerable skill on the part of teachers.

However, we move on too fast. For the moment, we hope that this short essay on the importance of conversation explains and justifies our emphasis on its value, not simply as a way of encouraging a chld to watch, listen and verbalize but also as a source of opportunities for him to learn many other features of what it is to become a competent listener, talker and thinker. But, as we shall see, it is hard to hold productive conversations with deaf children. There are, in fact, several sources of difficulty considered in this and other chapters. Some of these, such as speech that is often difficult to understand, arise 'directly' out of the handicap. In the last chapter, for example, we presented a few extracts of conversation between a teacher and her children. In one sense, such transcripts give a misleading impression of what is taking place. Having the luxury of a videotaped recording enables researchers to go over a child's utterances many times, to consult colleagues or the child's teacher to help work out what is being said as fully as possible. This, of course, is far removed from the 'reality' of the interaction and a poor reflection of the tacher's task. He or she must respond in 'real time' to what a child says, with only 'mental' re-runs of the interaction for consultation. Though their knowledge of the child should provide them with a better basis for understanding than an 'outsider' (without a recording), they may still find it difficult to comprehend what is said to them.

One arises as an 'indirect' product of comprehension problems. Generally speaking, in everyday conversations, when we do not understand what is said to us, we are likely to take *control* of the interaction to seek clarification, a paraphrase or explication of what has been said. Deaf children offer many opportunities for such episodes of 'listener control,' which, exploited in excess, can have marked negative effects on a child's desire to communicate.

A second cause of problems stems from the nature of teaching and schooling itself. When we have considered our formal analysis of conversation between teachers and children in the classroom, we will argue that they resemble not conversations so much as 'pedagogical' discourse. Such 'teaching talk' is not designed to fulfil the roles played by conversation. It does not encourage talk from children nor facilitate their attempts to discover how to make themselves comprehensible. If anything, it achieves the reverse, as we now see.

TEACHING AND CONVERSING

When we began to consider ways of trying to describe the structure of conversation, we were working both in schools for deaf children and in nursery schools and playgroups for preschool hearing children. Most of the teachers in both these settings considered talking to and with children an important part of their work. The general climate of opinion in early childhood education includes a stress on the importance of communication and language in helping children to become competent individuals and effective learners. In recent years, research into the processes of language development and the study of individual differences in children's acquisition and use of language have reached almost epidemic proportions (e.g. Tough, 1977; Blank, Rose and Berlin, 1978; Wells, 1979; Tizard and Hughes, 1984; to mention a few). The emphasis on the importance of language in education is commonplace in many countries.

Working in twenty-four different preschool settings for hearing children and in six schools for the deaf over a period of a year or so, we were struck both by marked similarities between and revealing differences across the various settings. In some classrooms, children seemed relatively active, loquacious and responsive. They talked a good deal, asked questions and contributed to discussions. In others, children seemed rather reticient and unforthcoming. They spoke little and often in short phrases or even monosyllables. Although the deaf children were considerably older than the hearing preschoolers, they were, as one might expect, far less verbal. Most of the deaf children in our studies had better-ear hearing losses of at least 80 dB, but we were still struck by marked variations in the language of deaf children with similar hearing losses but in different classrooms.

The basic idea behind the system we eventually devised to try to capture the essence of differences and similarities across settings suggested itself when one of us was listening to a conversation between a teacher and a group of children from outside the room in which they were talking. Although not able to see the participants, he was struck by the fact that each time the teacher talked, there was little doubt about what sort of response the children were likely to make next. Anticipating how the teacher would react after the children had spoken was a little more uncertain, but still usually possible. The structure of the interaction was so predictable, we felt, because the teacher's different verbal 'moves' towards the children exerted so much *control* over the children's part in 'conversation.' Unless they were to ignore her or strike un a topic of conversation outside the one she had initiated—which, as we shall see, children are unlikely to do—then their pattern of response was usually preordained.

This led us to the notion of 'control' in conversation. Subsequently, we were to find (as one usually does in research) that several other students of classroom discourse had come up with very similar ideas (*e.g.* French and MacLure, 1981; Dillon, 1982). In fact, a number of quite detialed and elaborate systems exist for describing and analysing such discourse. Our aim, however, unlike that of most researchers in this area, was not to develop a comprehensive, linguistically sophisticated analysis of discoruse. Rather, we wanted to find a way of describing the interactions that would explain why children seemed more or less active and loquacious in different interactions. The main categories of the system we developed are shown in Table 9.1.

Table 9.1. Levels of control in conversation

	Level of Control	*Examples*
1.	Enforced repetitions	Say 'I have one at home'.
2.	Two-choice questions	Did you have a good time?
		Did you go with Jim or Pete?
3.	Wh-type questions	What happened?
		Where did she go?
		Tell me about Sunday.
4.	Personal contributions, comments, statements	Where did she go?
		That must have been awful!
		They call it a zoom lens.
		I love the lakes in Scotland.
5.	Phatics	Oh lovely!
		Super!
		I see. Hmm.

The person or people *listening* to these moves are being cooperative and compliant, attempting to meet the 'force' of any requirements laid down by the current speaker. After the first, most controlling move (an enforced repetition) the response of our compliant listener is fully predetermined. Within the limits of his receptive and expressive language ability, what he says next is fixed. The next move, 'two-choice' questions, specify at least one word that the listener should respond with. Should he so wish, he can meet the 'force' of this move with a single word (which, as we shall see, children usually do). The next category, 'Wh-type questions' also dictates the natue of the ensuing response. If the listener understands the move, the 'semantic focus' of his response (e.g. where—a place or location; when—a time; who—a person) is predetermined. The current speaker still controls the direction and content of the conversation.

After a 'contribution,' however, the listener is left with a number of alternatives. He may simply acknowledge what is said in some way (perhaps saying nothing, just nodding), he might ask a question, continue with the theme or make a contribution of his own. The speaker tacitly offers the listener a chance to take over the control and direction of the subsequent conversation. The final category, 'phatics,' includes any move that fills a 'turn' without offering any substance or direction to the *content* of discourse (unless, of course, it involves irony, sarcasm or some other 'hidden' meaning). It may signify reception and comprehension of what is said, but leaves the next person to speak with control of the conversational floor. If *he* then responds with a phatic move of his own, this may be a signal that the current focus or topic of conversation has been exhausted (e.g. John: 'I went home then;' Mary: 'Oh really;' John: 'Yup'), in which case someone may introduce another topic, ask a question or they may part conversational company.

In the study of children in nursery schools and playgroups already mentioned, we found that preschool hearing children acted like compliant listners most of the time when in conversation with the teacher. In other words, they responded to different types of teacher moves in the manner described above. This led us to some very specific measures of child *initiative* in conversation that we need to consider before discussing conversations with deaf children. What does it mean to be 'active and forthcoming' in a conversation? Well, for us, it involves the following ingredients. An active participant will sometimes take *control* of the interaction by asking questions. They will also *contribute* readily and frequently after a contribution or phatic from their partner. They will extend the theme being discussed and occasionally introduce new topics of talk. Finally, when they answer questions addressed to them (particularly two-choice ones) they will characteristically not do so with a single word but will go on to add further information (i.e. make a 'double move' by answering *and* contributing to the topic).

As we shall see, whether or not children are active and forthcoming in conversation depends mainly upon the ways in which teachers manage the interaction. What about older deaf children? Do they understand enough of what is going on even to be 'compliant listeners?

When we first posed this question (see Wood *et al.*, 1982) we were unsure of the answer we would get. For deaf children to be influenced by different structures of conversation in the same way as hearing children, they must be 'aware' of the basic force of different moves from the teacher. They would have to be able to discriminate questions from statements and phatics, for example. They would also have to be able and ready to follow the less controlling moves from the teacher (e.g. contributions) by saying something themselves. If they do not readily take initiative in conversation (by saying something or asking questions after a contribution or phatic) then it may be the case that teachers have to 'question' deaf children in order to encourage them to play any role in conversation at all. We were not sure what the answer would be.

In fact, we found that deaf children's patterns of response to different teacher 'moves' were almost identical to those of hearing children. they did, as one might expect, tend to confuse different 'Wh-questions' more frequently; otherwise, their reactions were the same.

Having established this level of competence in children, the next question was asked was whether different teaching styles had similar effects on the two groups of children. Did the way the teacher controlled the conversation influence how much children said and how much initiative they showed? It did.

TEACHER POWER, CHILD INITIATIVE AND LOQUACITY

The conversations that we analysed were based on audiotaped (hearing groups) and videotaped (deaf groups) interactions between teachers and children in their own classrooms. With the deaf groups, these involved 'news sessions' in which teacher and children talked about what had happened, say, over the weekend at home. Having transcribed the interactions 'verbatim' we classified teachers' and children's turns into the move categories shown in Table 9.1. These also include a number of 'hybrid' moves such as 'tag contribution' ('Strawberries are delicious, aren't they?') that are not illustrated in the table, but which are available in the Appendix.

The principle measure of teaching style, 'teacher power,' is simply the proportion of each teacher's conversational turns that end in a controlling move (questions and enforced or requested repetitions). A second measure (more sensitive with preschool children) also includes all 'tag' moves since young children tend to respond to these as two-choice questions. A teacher who asks questions and/or demands repetitions frequently at the expense of other moves, thus gains a 'high power ratio'; one who asks relatively few gains a low ratio.

We measure children's responses in two main ways. One is an assessment of how much 'initiative' they show, the other estimates how talkative or loquacious they are. The most general measure of child initiative takes into account a number of features of children's talk. How often does a child not only answer a question but go on to elaborate on his answer by making an unsolicited contribution? How likely is he is make a contribution after the teacher has made either a contribution or has simply acknowledge what he has already said? How often does he ask questions?

Broadly speaking, what we find is that this measure of child initiative in conversation is related *negatively* to teacher power. Consequently, teachers who ask the most questions are least likely to gain elaborated answers from children, receive spontaneous contributions or be asked questions by them. Thus, children become increasingly passive as a teacher increases control via questioning.

Another way of examining the child's involvement in the conversation is to see how *much* he says. On average the deaf children in our studies produce responses of between two and three words (or word-like sounds) in length, but how much they say in each turn depends upon what the teacher has just said. They offer short responses after two-choice questions (they only elaborate on them about 25 per cent of the time) and relatively long ones after contributions and phatics. Thus, where controlling moves are frequent, children's turns tend to be short. In sessions where teacher control starts high and stays high, children become progressively less likely to show any signs of verbal initiative and their responses become more and more terse. Thus, if we want to understand why some children say a lot in conversation and others very little, it is not enough to consider the relative talkativeness or linguistic competence of the children. What they say and how much they talk is also strongly influenced by the conversational style of the teacher.

Teaching style also influences the readings with which children talk to (and hence listen to) each other. When teacher control is high, children seldom address comments or questions to their peers. However, when control is low, children are more likely not only to contribute comments and questions to the teacher but also to converse with each other. Thus, the whole 'tenor' of a group conversation is directly influenced by very specific, and very simple, features of teaching style. In the next chapter, we offer some examples of conversations to illustrate these general principles.

If a teacher wants to get children talking and showing initiative, she should be prepared not only to question but also to inform, react, listen and acknowledge. Rather than directing the conversation by questions or trying to use it to 'improve' language (we shall return to this topic later) she needs to become more contingent upon and accepting of what the children have to offer. Of course, if the goal is *not* to get children showing initiative and being talkative, all this goes by the board.

WHY ARE CHILDREN SO PREDICTABLE AND WHY DO TEACHERS ASK SO MANY QUESTIONS?

Children are not generally noted for their predictability. Teachers, however, are widely known for their questions!

Usually, when we compare the activities of children of very different ages we find marked differences in their performances. Yet we have found that the way in which children of very different ages and even cultural backgrounds respond both to different types of teacher move and to the overall structure of discourse is remarkably similar (Wood and Wood, 1985). *What* is talked about varies with age, as does the complexity of the language involved. But the 'typical' style of teacher talk is independent of the age of the children involved, and the ways in which children respond to each type of teacher move and different styles of management are remarkably consistent. Why? What implications might the answer to this question have for attempts to help deaf children acquire language?

One of the main reasons why patterns of children's responses to teachers are so similar despite great variations in age and background stems from the fact that, unlike teachers, they seldom make more than one 'move' in *their* conversational turn. Teachers typically utter a string of moves ('Oh, that's nice. I went to town on Saturday and I bought some new shoes. You've got some new shoes, haven't you? Did Mummy buy them for you?'; and so on). Young children, deaf or hearing, rarely act in this way. Thus, if you ask children questions you tend to get what you ask for but little else. They can be encouraged to show more initiative and make multiple moves, but only if questions and enforced repetitions are relatively infrequent. The reason why multiple moves are so important is that they almost invariably introduce new topics, themes or information into the conversation. They are a source of 'surprise' and offer new conversational avenues for exploration. Responses to teacher questions, on the other hand, usually help to fill conversational 'gaps' that she has opened up. They can, of course, lead to new lines of thought but tend not to do so if they are used in excess (as we see in this chapter).

Although children are 'compliant listeners' (most of the time) it is important to realize that compliance, as we have defined it, is *not* the only option available to competent listeners if they have equal 'status' in the conversation.

For example, in everyday conversations questions are sometimes followed not by answers but further questions. Imagine, for instance, a woman asking her colleague 'What time are you going into town?' and getting back 'Why do you want to know?', then responding 'Oh, I need a lift,' to which is said 'Well, I could get away by noon.' When a question meets another question as a response it is usually a signal that 'negotiation' is taking place and that there is a degree of equality in the interaction. If answering a question may lead to important and potentially undesirable implications, we usually ask another before answering it to ascertain what the implications are.

The 'rules of engagement' in classroom conversations are relatively specific and limited. Children seldom 'negotiate' with teachers through questioning because of the asymmetry of power in their interactions. Classroom discourse does *not* normally provide children with opportunities to explore a range of functions served by language, for these often rest upon particular personal relationships. Indeed, we suggest that children's responses to classroom discourse are deeply rooted in and symptomatic of their *relationships* with the teacher and in the relative 'status' of teacher and pupil.

WHY DO TEACHERS ASK SO MANY QUESTIONS?

The teaching role, as we argued earlier, has not 'evolved' to foster language development in young children. Where a teacher is faced with the task of imparting knowledge to large groups of children, then one obligation may be to keep 'all minds trained on the same topic.' Attempts to gain and maintain control over the attention and thought of group of learners is often sought through questioning. Indeed, the use of questions and the expectation of appropriate responses to them are 'sanctioned', even demanded, by the school as an institution. Reflect, for example, on the very different relationships and interactions that tend to take place between teachers and children *outside* school, on visits, after-school activities and the like. The 'group rules' that underlie discourse in the classroom are 'special' and often different in a variety of ways from those implicated in most everyday interactions (e.g. French and MacLure, 1981; Mercer and Edwards, 1981). She who can question and remain more or less confident of getting a predictable answer is in absolute conversational control. She is likely to be teaching, interrogating, interviewing, cross-examining or in some other position of authority over the other participants in dialogue. She is also the one upon whom all others must be contingent.

We have already mentioned that when hearing children are learning to converse at home it is usually they themselves who initiate the majority of verbal interactions (Wells, 1979). What is talked about is usually contingent on their interests and uncertainties. In school, however, it is more often the case that children must take the lead from and be contingent upon the plans and direction of the teacher. This 'reversal of contingency' offers one explanation for children's apparent 'compliance' in classroom discourse.

There is currently a good deal of debate about the importance, quality and functions of question—answer exchanges in classrooms (Dillon, 1982). One obvious function served by questions is to keep the minds of a group of learners (hopefully!) focused on the same theme or topic. Whether or not such questions 'work' in facilitating subject learning is not at issue here, but their role in facilitating language development is. When a teacher is confronted with thirty or forty pupils, it is perhaps inevitable that he or she must lead classroom discourse through questions. Although the teachers in our studies were *not* confronted with thirty children, but between two and eight, they still seemed to manage the interactions *as though* they were working with large groups and attempting to 'teach.' We question the wisdom and value of this 'carryover' of the teaching register *if and when* the aim is to help children benefit from conversation.

Perhaps they lack the linguistic or intellectual resources to do otherwise. For example, do children know how to respond to questions with a question of their own? Are they insensitive to the fact that answering questions may have implications for what may happen subsequently and, in consequence, do not think before they answer? Perhaps they are not intellectually advanced enough to participate in such complex interactions, and that is why they are so predictable in discourse.

We suspect this is not the reason for their compliance. We have already said that our system of analysis has been used with much older pupils, and others have used it to study tutorial discussions involving university undergraduates and found similar results (Kingdon, 1983). the 'typical' structure of teaching behaviour was remarkably similar across these different contexts, as were the patterns of pupil responses to them. Unless we are to assume that university undergraduates also have limited linguistic resources, cannot anticipate and so on, we must conclude that the relationships between teaching style and pupils response are most likely to be a product of the asymmetry of power implicit in the teacher/learner relationship. Whether young hearing children and deaf children also have a wider range of linguistic resources is a question explored in the next chapter. It is worth noting, however, that Wells (1983), discussing our speculations about hearing preschoolers, argues that their preformance in contexts other than school (when they are embedded in different personal relationship) displays a much wider and less 'predictable' range of verbal responses.

So far, we have emphasized the basic similarities between the structure of conversations involving deaf and hearing children and the commonalities across teacher behaviour in the two contexts. But there are some important differences too. These, however, revolve more around the *purposes* being pursued by teachers rather than in the exercise of control.

WHAT DO TEACHERS USE CONVERSATIONS FOR?

Teachers of the deaf are specially trained to 'teach' or, perhaps, to help children acquire language. How do they go about it? There are, as we shall see, 'special' features of teachers' talk to deaf children. Are these a product of training and of benefit to the child? Perhaps the differences we found are a reflection of the expertise of teachers. Before addressing these possibilities, however, we need to outline the system of analysis we developed to explore such differences (Table 9.2).

REPAIR

When a conversation is running smoothly, most of the 'moves' made by speakers will be 'substantive' in nature. Contributions that develop, elaborate and extend the topic at hand and questions designed to solicit additional information or elaboration will usually be serving *substantive* functions. The listener, meanwhile, when not asking questions designed to solicit substantive replies, will be showing non-verbal and verbal signs of attention, interest and understanding. If the conversationalists are achieving mutual understanding, then 'continuity' moves from the current listener (such as 'Mm,' 'Really!,' 'You don't say!') help to fulfil their obligations to the speaker.

Table 9.2

Function	*Examples*
Substantive	Tell me about your dog. What happened on Sunday? I like cream cakes too.
Continuity	How nice. Oh, it was red, was it? Yes, I see..
Repair	What? Say that again. Say 'I have one at home'. I don't understand. Wait a minute, you saw a *train* or a *crane*

Occasionally, however, the listener may be distracted or not hear what is said. Or they may lose the thread of conversation, finding something ambiguous or unintelligible. In these circumstances, the listener is likely to take control over the interaction, 'stop' the flow of conversation and try to 'repair' the breakdown in understanding. They may do so by asking a repairing question 'Did you just say . . .?', a repairing phatic (e.g. 'Sorry?', 'Pardon?') or with a repairing contribution such as 'I didn't understand what you just said.'

When we examined a series of conversations involving teachers with hearing children and compared these to classroom conversations with deaf children, we found, perhaps unsurprisingly, that the greatest difference between the two lay in the incidence of 'repair'. However, less obviously, most of the repairing moves came from the teachers and not the children. Although the children involved were very deaf, they seldom exercised 'listener control.' Either they were understanding everything said to them (which seems rather doubtful) or they did not know 'how' to seek clarification; or the asymmetry of power between teachers and children inhibited them from taking control of the conversation. We shall show in the next chapter that the letter explanation is most likely to be the case.

A lot of teacher repair with deaf children arose as a 'natural' product of unintelligible speech and ambiguous utterances from children. Other repair sequences, however, seemed more 'pedagogically' inspired to help children improve their utterances. When we measured the frequency of repair by teachers of hearing children in classroom talk, we found between 6 and 10 per cent of their moves were repairing. Although repair of deaf children by their teachers was more frequent, we found very marked individual differences between teachers of the deaf in their readiness to repair children's utterances. For example, one teacher with a group of children with average hearing losses of 83 dB displayed 14 per cent repair. Another teacher, whose group had average losses of 87 dB, made 68 per cent repairing moves. Whilst some teachers seized almost every opportuntity to clear up ambiguity or to check the meaning of an unintelligible utterance, others did not. Also, some teachers made more frequent demands for 'enforced repetitions' which, by their nature, always go 'backwards' and serve a repairing function.

Enforced repetitions are extremely rare in interactions between hearing children and teachers. They may occur occasionally in play (e.g. the teacher says to a child 'Say goodbye to Uncle Fred for me'), in 'lessons in etiquette' (e.g. 'Say please') or in teaching songs or nursery rhymes. Some teachers of the deaf (though by no means all) use such moves relatively frequently when talking to deaf children. One teacher, in our initial study, employed them in 43 per cent of her turns. For example, one child having said 'Yesday—Mother Day,' his teacher responded with 'Say, "Yesterday was Mothers' Day".' We presume that the purpose or function underlying such tactics is to 'teach language,' but syntactically motivated repair is uncommon in the speech addressed to hearing children. As Roger Brown (1977) observes somewhat wryly, we often repair childen's meaning but almost never their grammar, yet they grow up to tell lies (violate meaning) but with a capacity to speak in well-formed utterances!

Our notion of 'repair' thus covers two main activities: the deliberate modelling or teaching of 'better English' and also natural reactions to the handicap. In all cases, however, it is a hallmark of repair that it goes 'backwards' into previous conversational territory rather than moving it, or permitting it to move, on.

REPAIR AND DIFFERENT MOVE TYPES

One important feature of the relationship between repair and 'move type' needs to be underlined because it highlights specific problems that many deaf children face. When a listener does not fully understand what a speaker has said or there is some 'mis-match' between what the listener was tacitly expecting and what was said, repair may be achieved *with any move type.*

Herein, we believe, lie many pitfalls in talking to deaf children. Our 'natural' response when we do not understand is to stop the proceedings and repair the break in mutual understanding before proceeding further. Where this is done speedily and effortlessly (on both sides) it prevents the accumulation or perpetuation of ambiguity and misunderstanding. It is also the case, however, as we have seen in this chapter, that the *way* in which children are repaired influences the development of communicative (*Misprint*) children provide so many potential opportunities for misunderstanding that, should we seek continually to clear up, check and disambiguate every ambiguous move from them, we are likely to find ourselves, as some teachers were on our recordings, not so much involved in conversation as embroiled in cross-questioning and cross-checking.

As we indicated above, repair (like other functions) can be achieved in many ways using any type of move (questions, contributions and so forth). In some classrooms we also found that teachers were most likely to repair the deafest children. In so doing, we argue, they were magnifying rather than overcoming the communication problems of these children. Not only does the child have to work out what *type* of move he is facing and strive to understand its force and content (e.g. is it a contribution or a wh-type question?), he must also, more often than his less deaf or hearing peers, work out whether that move is going *back* over previous territory or *forward* into new areas.

In such encounters children often appeared bewildered and baffled. They did not seem to know whether or not the teacher was really asking for the *same* thing again; whether she did not hear what he had just said or had misunderstood it; if he himself had misunderstood what was asked on the last occasion; or whether a completely new element had been introduced into the conversation that he had just missed.

Another counter-productive aspect of repair is the way in which it tends to be associated with increased levels of teacher control which, in turn, breed further repair. Some interactions with deaf children are characterized by ever-increasing spirals of control and repair. Although repair can (and we will argue in the next chapter usually *should*) be achieved by contributions ('I don't understand that') or repairing phatics ('Pardon?'), teachers are most likely, once in a repair sequence, to resort to questions. Thus, teacher power increases with the effects we have already outlined above.

CAUSES AND EFFECTS: WHO DOES WHAT TO WHOM?

Teaching styles, which we have described in terms of power and function, are highly correlated with a number of features of children's responsiveness and productivity in conversation. Certain aspects of teaching styles, we have argued, stem from implicit or explicit theories about how language should be 'taught.' Others are responses to the *nature* of the handicap and the way in which it is likely to distort the structure of interactions by evoking *natural* but often counter-productive responses from the hearing adult. The fact that teachers vary substantially in the way they control conversations and in their levels of tolerance for ambiguity in children's language suggests that high power and frequent control are not, however, *inevitable* outcomes of conversations with deaf children. But, you might well ask, are teachers different simply because their *children* are different? In our analyses of interactions, we differences in the amount of teacher control. But it is still possible that factors located 'in' the child—such as native linguistic ability, natural loquacity or desire for initiative—explain why teachers vary in style. Perhaps they are simply responding to such differences between children?

One way to investigate this possibility is to examine the effects of very different styles of teacher conversation on the *same* children. If the arguments we have been putting forward here have any substance, then it should follow that as teachers decrease control, for example, children should start to show more initiative and become more talkative. We turn to a test of this hypothesis in this chapter. We also take up the thorny questions—'What is a "good" conversation?' and 'How is it achieved?'.

10

Role of Questioning

CAN teachers *change* the way in which they 'normally' talk to deaf children? If so, do their pupils reciprocate in any systematic way to become more or less talkative? In this chapter we look at two studies where teachers did try to change their styles of talking. We examine the effects of different styles on the same children and begin to etch out the 'role' and place of different types of conversational move towards children. 'When is a question fruitful; when is it stultifying?' is one issue we address. Our comments on such issues leads us on to one of our major concerns: what does a 'good' conversation look like?

Another question we explore has already been considered to some extent in Chapter 9. If high teacher control inhibits children from talking when the goal of the teacher is to *encourage* them to talk, why do the majority of teachers ask so many questions? We have already suggested that problems arising from the nature of deaf children's speech and language provide one possible explanation and that the 'teaching role' is another. In this chapter, we will explore other reasons.

CHANGING STYLES OF CONVERSATION

When we were beginning our stuaies of conversation with deaf children, we outlined our plans for research and the ideas behind them to a conference for teachers of the deaf. We were approached by one of the teachers, Jean Lees, who was already beginning to study her own style of talking to children and exploring ways of modifying that style to explore the effects of change on children's responses. She had already attended a course based on the work of Joan Tough (e.g. Tough, 1977) which focused on aspects of children's language development and the role played by teachers in facilitating it. Having recorded examples of her classroom conversation, she decided that she was asking too many questions and doing rather a lot of 'checking' of what children said to her. She eventually joined the team and undertook a systematic study in which she modified her style of talking to children in a number of ways, maintaining each style for several weeks and recording and analysing interactions with children en route. Basically, she found that as she questioned children less and made more contributions of her own, children displayed greater initiative in conversation, said more and were much more interesting to listen to.

Lees' (1981) research inspired some confidence that children will respond predictably to changes in teacher style, but she was already more or less convinced that they would do so. Perhaps children sensed her enthusiasm for her own preferred approach and responded accordingly. Was it her style of talk *per se* that was instrumental in bringing about change? Further, was Lees unusual in being *able* to change her style? A second consideration in trying to evaluate what happened as she changed style was the time scale involved. Lees employed different styles over periods of three weeks or so, providing children with ample opportunities to discover the rules of each new linguistic 'game'. How long does it take for children to respond to changes in a teacher's style? As we shall see, it takes a lot less than three weeks.

In parallel with Lees' research, we were beginning to undertake similar studies with both hearing and deaf children. We recruited teachers and illustrated five different 'strategies' of conversation. These were modelled on the five main categories of level of control described in this book. We asked the teachers to try to bring about ten-minute conversations (that we videotaped) in which they biased the interactions towards each different move type in turn. Thus, with each teacher, we recorded *enforced repetition, two choice question* and *Wh-type question* sessions, together with one loaded with *contributions* and a fifth high in *phatics*. These sessions, recorded on different days over a period of about four weeks, were 'sandwiched' between two 'normal' conversations in which the teacher did what came 'naturally,' albeit in front of a camera.

We have done this study with a total of five teachers: one with six hearing children (four of whom were learning English as a second language), the remainder with deaf children aged between three and eleven years. The original studies, outlined in Chapter 9, were concerned with deaf children aged six years and upwards, and we will focus in this chapter on sessions recorded by two teachers, Mrs. Smith and Mrs. Jones, both with eleven-year-olds. Each teacher selected two of her most deaf (but otherwise 'normal' children) who had better-ear losses between 92 and 104 dB and WISC-R non-verbal IQs ranging from 81 to 121.

The details of procedure and statistical analyses used in these studies have been presented in detail elsewhere (Wood and Wood, 1983, 1984). We will concentrate here on describing and discussing the main results.

Could the teachers change their style at will? Yes. Although, as one might expect, they varied in degree to which they managed to bias their language into one move type or another, all showed marked changes in style along the lines requested.

The teachers changed; did the children? They did. Although the sessions analysed were only of ten minutes' duration, children responded quite differently to them. Were the changes along the lines we had predicted? They were. The more control a teacher exerted over the conversation, the less initiative children displayed and the shorter their responses became. When, at the end of the experimental sessions, teachers returned to their 'normal' style, using a level of questioning midway between low and high control sessions, their children 'followed' them, with lower measures of initiative and loquacity than they had displayed in contribution and phatic sessions. The same pattern of results was found with the six hearing preschoolers too.

The main results of these studies reinforce all the various implications drawn from the analyses of teacher power and its effects in the last chapter. Teachers must accept a large measure of responsibility for the way in which children play their part in conversation with them.

In the remainder of this chapter, we move away from discussions of averages and common patterns to look in more detial at the 'texture' of various sessions. We look in some depth at episodes from interactions high in each move type to seek insights into the way in which each linguistic move influences the structure, coherence, intelligibility and productivity of discourse. We try to highlight the pros and cons of various ways of involving children in discourse and speculate about the structure of productive teacher-child conversations.

Session 1. Enforced Repetitions

In their initial and final sessions, where they adopted their normal styles, neither of the teachers demanded many enforced repetitions. They found the strategy *easy* to adopt: Mrs. Smith increased the proportion of these moves tenfold over her initial, normal session figures; Mrs. Jones managed a sixfold increase.

One important result worth underlining is that these children's mean leangths of turn were no longer (overall) in this session than in normal sessions. Research with young hearing children has produced analogous results (e.g. McNeill, 1966). Attempts to encourage children to imitate utterances that are longer and structurally more complex than those produced as part of their spontaneous language usually fail. Although the teachers did manage, on occasion, to 'build up' a relatively long utterance from children, as in the following example, more often than no children's imitations would include a new word or an added inflexion (for instance, adding an '-ing' to a verb), but, at the same time, some othe r element present in an earlier attempt at the same utterance would 'drop out.' Although we have not used spectrographic analyses or any formal measures of children's voice quality or intelligibility we had no sense that the solicited utterances were any more rhythmic (indeed, if anything, they seemed less so) or more intelligible. Furthermore, we were often unsure, as in the following excerpt, whether or not what the child was asked to repeat was what he had really *meant* to say in the first place.

Mummy is fed up with working—or does she work? (Mrs. Smith)

T. How's your Mummy?
C2. Ah poorly.
T. Mummy's poorly? Can you say 'she's poorly'?
C2. She's poorly -- --- --- --- (gestures and waves round) --- --- headache.
T. She's got a headache.
C2. ?Fed ?up work (?shovelling) ---?heavy ---work.
T. Oh dear, she's fed up with working. Can you say that? She's fed up with working.'
C2. She (then quietly)? fed ?up ?with working.
T. Yes. (to C1) What's the matter with his Mummy?
C1. Fed up of work.
T. Yes, she's fed up with working. Can you say that?
C1. He, he fed up working.
T. Not he . . . *she's* fed up with working.
C1. She's fed up.
C2. (interrupting) Doesn't work!
T. Oh, that's rude. Let him finish.
C1. She = febbe . . . She fed up.
T. She's fed up. . .
C1. (shadows T) She's fed up.
T. With working.
C1. She = febbe with working.

Key: - - -: A work-like utterance.
?word: Our guess at the word.
= word: The sound pattern we can hear.
(gestures): Angle brackets enclose our description of the child's gestures.

We cannot draw any definitive conclusions on the basis of a few tenminute sessions about the extent to which long-term 'language lessons' along these lines might facilitate the development of speech. It could be argued that this strategy—which continually stopped these eleven-year-olds in their tracks—might be of more value down the age scale, where children are only just on the point of putting words together.

For instance, when Margaret Tait tried out this strategy with a pair of three-to four-year-olds, the children gave every sign of enjoying telling a 'naughty' doll to 'Stop it!' and calling it a 'Naughty girl!', offering two word utterances rather than their usual one. Interestingly enough, however, Tait had 'abused' our instructions by making the enforced repetitions part of a game (which, as we said in Chapter 9, is one of the few contexts in which we found teachers using enforced repetitions with hearing preschoolers).

Nonetheless, in view of the fact that child initiative is always very low in such sessions, we would argue that they have no starring part to play in *conversation*, whatever value they might or might not have in more formal 'speech' sessions or games. As we argued in the last chapter, sustained high control tends to exert an effect over the whole 'tenor' of the interaction so that even children's responses to less controlling moves are affected.

Another problem in these sessions was that children sometimes did not recognize the 'force' behind enforced repetitions. In conversation, particularly with young children, a listener might repeat part or all of what the child has just said in a 'phatic' way (e.g. 'I went to town yesterday'—'Oh, you went to town!'). Such moves, we have argued, signal that the message has been received and understood, and children in these sessions sometimes nodded happily in response to an attempted enforced repetition, not realizing that they were expected to improve on what they had just said!

A dangerous nail on the bath (Mrs. Jones)

T. The nail was sticking out?
C1. (nods)
T. Yes, and . . . .
C1. Ow!
T. You stood on it?
C1. (nods)
T. Say 'I stood on the nail.'
C1. Yes.
T. 'I stood on the nail!'
C1. (mouthes in unison with T) I stood = ni.
T. No, 'I stood on the nail.'

C1. (in unison with T) I stood on the = ni.
T. 'On the nail.'
C'. On the ---.
T. Yes, and so you didn't come to school.
C1. Daddy (knocks on edge of desk).
T. Ah!
C1. Daddy, alright.
T. 'Daddy knocked it in. Daddy knocked it in.'
C1. Daddy knocked in.
T. 'Knocked it in.'
C1. Knocked it in.
T. And what did he use?
. . .

(over several turns they establish that a 'hammer' was used, then):

. . .

T. A hammer, right. So Carol's Dad, right? Saw the nail . . . and he thought, 'Ah, that's dangerous.'
C1. (shadows T, mouhes 'nail') . . . ?danger.
T. Your Daddy saw the nail . . . sticking out . . . .
C1. Nail (disagrees, points to self).
T. 'That's dangerous.' He got out his hammer, right?
C1. Daddy what? Me (points to foot). Me cry . . .
T. Yes, Daddy said, 'What's the matter?'
C1. ?Said 'what'. (She starts to add what *she* had said.)
T. 'What's the matter?
C1. Me say ? floor. Where? (seeing it) Ah!
(getting tools) ?Find (i.e. hammer) (hammers nail in).
Right (pats hammered-in nail).
T. Right . . .
C1. Mummy (points to foot) right (puts plaster on). Mummy not better.
T. Daddy said, 'What's the matter?'
C1. Daddy?
T. 'What's the matter?'
C1. ?Daddy alright (knocks 'nail)'.
T. It's alright, is it, now?
C1. Yes.
T. 'It's alright. It's alright.'
C1. Yes . . . .

T. 'It's alright', you say that!
C1. I alright.
T. 'It's alright.'
C1. ?You're alright.
T. Yes. (to C2) What did her Dad say?
C2. (no response)
T. He said, 'It's alright.'
C2. Alright (nodding to C1).

So, whilst children will usually repeat when requested they are sometimes unsure whether or not they *have* been asked to do so. When repetitions remain frequent, children also tend to stop talking and displaying initiative. Indeed, if the cost of trying to say something is confusion and a probable failure to 'get it right,' it seems perfectly understandable that children should want to keep a low conversational profile.

Session 2. Two-Choice Questions

Although the two teachers managed to increase their use of these questions considerably (from 30 to 75 per cent and 9 to 20 per cent) they found these sessions heavy going, as did the children. The children's verbal responses were shorter in this session than in any other. Note, in the following extracts, how children's early loquacity gives way to monosyllabic responses and non-verbal reactions as high control is established and maintained.

Schools and doctors (Mrs. Smith)

T. Are you happy or are you fed up this morning?
C1. I'm fed up.
T. You're fed up this morning!
C1. (nods)
T. You're both fed up. Oh dear, now I'm fed up. Are you fed up because you had to come to school?
C2. I ?hate school, I like Senior school. I like it.
T. You like Senior school. Which school do you like, Senior school or Junior school?
C2. Senior school.
C1. Senior.

T. Senior school. Oh dear ------! Son, do you like Junior School?
C2. No.
T. No. he doesn't like Junior school. Well, you be but fed up!
C2. I like Susie. Hello! Susie——.
T. You like Susie Bates.
C2. Yes.
T. Can you remember Susie Bates?
C1. Yes.
T. Can you remember Anthony Roberts?
C1. Anthony Roberts (nods)

. . .

(and, a few minutes later):

. . .

T. Oh! You went to the doctor yesterday, don't you.
C1. (nods)
T. (to C2) Tom went to the factor's yesterday.
(to C1) Was he a nice incur?
C1. ?Better (puzzled).
T. Was he a nice doctor or a horrible doctor?
C1. Nice.
T. He was a nice doctor. Wast the a man or a lady?
C1. Man.
T. (to C2) is your doctor a man or lady.
C2. Nicholson, lady.
T. A lady?
C2. Yes.
T. Is your doctor a nice lady or a horrible lady?
C2. Lady nice (nodding).
T. A nice lady?
C2. Yes.
T. (to C1) Was she, was he no old man or a -------
C1. --- (probably 'young') man.
T. A young man.
C1. (nods slightly)
T. Mm. And you liked him, did you?
C1. (nods)

As we argued in earlier, when control is him, children tend to give single-word responses or non-verbal reactions (lies in nods and shakes of the head) to two-choice questions. Such responses are legitimate' in that they fulfil the force of the question, but it is the ease with which they can be answered that underlies the difficulty both parties mean knowing whether or not mutual understanding are occurred. Unless chilren are making thematically related contributions of their own or answering more 'informative' questions appropriately they provide no evidence of actually having understood two-choice questions at all. And if the teacher does not *react to* or *build upon* a child's answer then the child, too, is given no basis for determining whether his answer was appropriate or intelligible.

Another problem that emerged in this session we the effect of strings of two-choice questions on the child who was not immediately being questioned. For example, after asking a series of questions of one child, Tom, about whether he liked hospitals and would like to work in one, the teacher turned to the other child, Harry, to ask him what preference Tom had expressed. Harry made no response and showed no signs of having understood any of the preceding discourse. Asked about his own future interests, he 'agreed' on four separate occasions (all single-word or non-verbal responses to two-choice questions) that he would like to work in a hospital. Three minutes later, he said that he would hate to work in a hospital. We doubt that such confusions emerged as a product of any change in Harry's vocational aspirations over the intervening period! He, like other children, answered some questions without really understanding them.

Although two-choice questions might *seem* easy to answer and generate responses that seem intelligible, they are, used in excess, a frequent basis for misunderstanding. This is not to say that the occasional 'Oo, did you enjoy it?' or 'Was he very angry?' might not effective in inviting children to expand on their theme; rather it is the 'abuse' of these moves when they occur in 'strings' that exerts such a stultifying effect on conversation. As Mrs. Smith complained when we discussed the sessons: 'The ball kept coming straight back into my court.' As her session progressed, children became increasingly passive and gave her nothing to work out from. So she found it progressively more difficult to think of things to ask about. Whilst, in a 'contrived' session such as this one, we get an exaggerated and perhaps distorted picture of the way such moves normally function in discourse, the inhibiting effect of these questions on children's initiative (and the teacher-directed course of conversation) are not totally dissimilar to some normal 'bouts' of conversations we have observed in classrooms.

Session 3. Wh-Type Questions

There is an extensive literature on the educational value of Wh- type questions. They are often put forward as important tools for extending children's understanding, encouraging them to reflect and helping them to 'decontextualize' their thinking (see Dillon, 1982, for a critical overview of research in this area). However, as we have already argued, they are also likely, in excess, to inhibit children from playing an active role and taking initiative in conversations (only around 6 per cent receiving elaborated replies). As we had predicted, children's initiative was lower in this high control session than in the lower control ones. However, the effect of frequent Wh-type questions was not quite so stultifying as we had expected; initiative and talkativeness were no lower than they were in the normal sessions. In part, this was because Wh-type questions occasionally led to arguments. Since answers to such questions, when they are given, can be evaluated by listeners, they offer an opportunity for disagreement and debate, as we shall see later. From a teacher's point of view, Wh-type questions, unlike two-choice ones, are unlikely to receive an appropriate response without the child having understood the force of the question. They may thus be an important 'diagnostic' tool for monitoring comprehension. But they are also often difficult for children.

Instances of incomprehension and misunderstanding were higher in this than any other session. In Mrs. Smith's sessions, the frequency of no responses or inappropriate answers from children rose from 8 per cent in the initial 'natural' conversation to 10 per cent in this session. For Mrs. Jones, the comparable figures were 14 to 27 per cent.

In Chapter 9 we reported that teacher power and frequency of repair were highly correlated and suggested that one led to the other. This suggestion was borne out by the results of these experimental sessions. Here, too, sessions high in power were also high in repair which was highest in the Wh-type question sessions (this was the case for the hearing children too). When questions are numerous and difficult, the ensuing misunderstandings and ambiguities in children's responses 'pulled' teachers into repair sequences. As illustrated in the transcript given below, children's failure to understand a question often led the teacher to ask yet more questions in an attempt to reinstate mutual understanding.

Before looking at the transcript, however, we need to consider what it is about some questions that make them so difficult for children. What kinds of questions *do* children answer? There are at least three possible answers to these questions. First, questions may be more or less demanding intellectually. Marion Blank (Blank, Rose and Berlin, 1978), for example, has provided a classification of teacher language in terms of the 'level of cognitive demand' it embodies for young children. This system enables questions (and other request utterances) to be 'scaled' for the degree of difficulty they present. Low level demands include questions on topics such as the names of objects and their attributes—size, shape, colour and so forth. More demanding discourse involves attention to attributes that enable objects to be related, classified, grouped and distinguished. Such questions draw attention to more abstract relationships *between* objects and events—to things that are not directly perceived but stem from linguistic and intellectual structures that serve to organize experience. The most cognitively demanding language in Blank's scheme involves reasoning, speculating, planning and so on. Thus, the level of cognitive demand increases as the topic of discourse becomes less focused on the 'here and now', and moves on to explanations, logical inference and abstract reasoning.

Most of the talk in the experimental conversations, like 'news sessions', concerned events outside the current context and involved questions of different levels of demand. Some questions were concerned with labelling attributes ('What colour is . . . ?') or asked for information about things in context. Others demanded reasons and justifications. Mrs. Smith's session started off with just such a mixture. In examining the transcript note not only the questions that children answer or fail to answer but also the incidence of repair. We also draw attention to what happens after the odd phatic move is allowed to creep in (e.g. 'You like Senior School'), when a child immediately introduces a new element to the conversation.

Schools again and ties

T. How are you?
C1. Alright thank you.
T. You're alright, that's good. Are you fed up?
C1 No (shakes head).
T. (to C1) Let's see, shall we ask him (C2)
'Why are you fed up?' . . . you ask him.
C1. (?to C2) Why are you fed up?
C2. (no response—laughs)
T. (to C2) Why are you fed up? Why are you fed up?
C2. Don't want school.
T. You don't want to come to school. Why?
C2. I like Senior school.
T. You like Senior school.
C2. I like Susie Bates.
T. Pardon?
C2. Susie Bates.
T. Oh, you're always talking about Susie Bates.
(to C1) Do you like Susie Bates?
C1. Yes.
T. Why, why do you like Susie Bates?
C1. ?As ?a friend, friend.
T. You think she's your friend. Well, that's very nice.
C2. Friend.
T. (to C2) Is she your friend?
C2. Yes.
T. Lovely. And do you like school?
C1. No.
T. No. Why?
C1. I like Senior.

T. You like Senior school. Well, I'm very sorry. You don't like Junior school?
C2. (shakes head) No, I like Senior School.
T. (laughs) Well, why don't you like Junior school?
C1. I like Senior . . . Work hard.
C2. ?I ?know Richard, friend, Richard, Richard.
T. You like Richard?
C1. Yes (nods).
C2. Friend, Richard.
T. Yes, well, you'll see Richard again soon. You've got some friends here, haven't you? Why don't you like Junior school?
C1. Too hard.
T. (laughs) It's too hard. You don't work very hard here, not all the time anyway. Do you think when you go to Senior school that will be easy?
C1. No.
T. Or will that be hard?
C1. Easy.
T. Easy, mmm. Who told you it was easy?
C1. Richard.
T. Richard did, did he?
C2. (gestures where tie should be) Senior school green, yellow, green.
T. That's the tie is it?
C2. ?You ?wear shirts (fingers his shirt).
T. Yes. Where's your tie?
C2. --- change, change (fingers sweater).
(still appears to be talking about Senior school).
T. *Where* is your tie this morning? Where is it?
C2. At home, green, yellow, . . . (i.e. still Senior school tie!).
T. Have you got one now?
C2. (nods) Senior.
T. Very nice.
C2. ?With ?my father's money (money counts).
T. Mmm. What colour is Tom's tie?
C2. Green and yellow.
T. No. What colour's Tom's tie?
C2. Brown.
T. Yes, (to C1) Where is his tie? Where is it?

C1. Red.
T. Yes, but where is it?
C1. Pocket.
T. It's in his pocket.
C2. (points) There it is . . . on the desk.
T. (looks) It's on the desk, is it? Why is it on the desk? Why haven't you got it on?
C2. It's red (touches where tie should be).
T. Yes, I didn't say what colour was it . . . .
C2. (tries again to give colour?) ---.
T. I said, 'Why haven't you got it on?' What's the matter with it?
C2. It's over there (points to desk).
T. I know it's on the desk. Why?
C1. (to C2) (questioning gesture) Why?
C2. I ah . . . small.
T. (to C1) You ask him.
C2. I—Small.
T. (to C1) What did he say?
C1. Small.
T. It's too small. It's too small.

There were no obvious relationships between the level of abstraction implicit in a question and the likelihood that children would or would not answer it. Some 'Why?' questions demanding justifications were answered in a sensible and intelligible way when requests for colour names and locations were not. We are not claiming that cognitive demand is not a factor influencing a question's difficulty, but it did not explain most of the comprehension problems children evidenced in these sessions. Put more positively: although, as many people have noted, deaf children find talk about things outside their immediate experience difficult, they are not totally unable to do so. They are not incompetent in recalling and recollecting, reasoning and justifying. The problem lies in the difficulty of *communicating* about such things.

A second potential source of difficulty with questions, especially for deaf children lies in perceptual and linguistic confusions. 'Where', 'what', 'why' and 'when' may be confused because they look similar on the lips. We cannot rule this factor out as an explanation, but did not find many instances where the children definitely confused different Wh-type questions.

A third factor that influences a question's difficulty is subtle and hard to define but important in its influence on understanding and misunderstanding. It revolves around the notion of contingency. We have already cited examples of seemingly simple questions that were misunderstood and more demanding ones that were answered appropriately. The questions that failed to get answers often seemed, so to speak, to 'come out of the blue' and 'cut across the child's conversational bows.' We have not developed a formal description of this feature of discourse but, broadly speaking, what seems to be important is the extent to which a question relates to an ongoing theme and in particular to a contribution or response that a child has already made. If, as in the 'school tie' example, answering a techer's question involves thinking about a different time, place and object than that established in the preceding move, children seem likely to misunderstand. The child has to reorientate several aspects of his thinking following a single move. Where a question arises more directly out of what he says and extends the theme he is exploring, he seems much more likely to understand it. Sudden changes in the 'direction' of talk and a breakdown in shared expectations may thus be an important element in accounting for incomprehension in addition to cognitive or linguistic complexity. We return to a discussion of 'contingency' in questioning in the final section of the chapter.

Another important but, as yet, neglected aspect of the communicative situation is the way in which verbal and non-verbal 'cues' interact in the child's attempt to achieve comprehension. Even when talk is 'decontextualized' chidlren rely on a variety of situational and paralinguistic clues to supplement their understanding. Indeed, the same is ture of communication between hearing people (e.g. McNeill, 1979). Not surprisingly, deaf children often seem very reliant on such information. In the following excerpt, for example, the child misinterprets a relatively simple question from the teacher because her non-verbal cues are at variance with what she is saying.

Wedding dress—or the ring? (Mrs. Smith)

T. What colour does the *lady* wear when she gets married? What colour? (point to ring finger)
C1. White.
T. White, yes.
C2. (points) to ring finger ?No, yellow.
T. Oh Harry!
C1. Gold, gold.
T. Yes, that was the gold ring.
C2. Oh.
T. (points) to ring But I said to Tom, 'What colour does the lady, what colour is the lady's dress?' *What colour*? (indicates dress) When she gets married in church? What colour?
C2. White.

Here the child gets the message that the teacher is asking about colours, but because she touches her ring he assumes that that is what she is asking about. The question itself is not a difficult one structurally and this child answered much more 'demanding' questions within the session. Such problems illustrate the range of cues that children are attending to in their efforts to make sense out of the interaction. There were many failures of mutual understanding on the recordings that sometimes lasted over several minutes of talk. For example, the same child said that his father had worn a black tie to his own wedding and that he himself had attended in a blue suit. He persisted with this story over three and a half minutes of discourse, despite all the arguments from the teacher and the other child (who suggested that he must have been a baby in his mother's tummy!). Eventually the argument ended when the first child capitulated. He had not been there; he'd been sent home! Or had he?

The wedding suit

C2. Blue, blue coat. Blue.
T. You did?
C2. And a white shirt.
T. And a white shirt, when you went to somebody's wedding?
C2. Yes.

T. Who was the lady? What was her name, can you remember?
C2. Mummy.
T. Oh, Mummy. But not when Mummy got married you didn't go to church.
C1. ?Harry a baby. . . . a baby.
C2. Not married, married, yes married
T. Yes, I know she's married.
C1. A baby (points to C2) ?a . . . (rocks a baby).
T. Yes, perhaps when he was a baby, when he was christened, when he was baptized, mmm.
C2. (indicates arm) Mummy ---.
T. Were you a little baby?
C2. No baby.
T. You tell me about it. What happened?
C2. What you say?
T. When you went to church in your blue suit—What for?
C2. Mummy white.
T. Your Mummy had a white dress, did she?
C2. Yes.
T. I think we're a little bit muddled up. When your Mummy was married in chruch . . . (ring finger) your Mummy and Daddy . . . I don't think you were . . .
C2. Mummy Daddy two.
T. Yes, but you weren't there, I know, but you weren't there.
C1. Me married (shaking head).
C2. No, I watch ?on, watch.
T. You were watching?
C2. (nods)
C1. I --- watch . . . .
T. (to C1) No, that's right. You weren't there, were you?
C1. Inside! (points to tummy)
T. That's right, that's right! (laughs)
C2. No! (not what he meant)
(C1 explains situation to C2.)
(C2: 'Ah', and smiles.)
(T, aside; 'They were getting slightly muddled!')
T. (to C1) What does he say? You ask him, you try to sort it out.

C1. He was a baby.
T. (to C2) Yes, you weren't at your Mummy's wedding.
C2. ?Married, Daddy he there me there (still seems to be convinced he was there).
T. Well, you bring me some photographs tomorrow. Have you got some pictures you can show me?
C2. Yeah.
T. Your Mummy and Daddy—
C2. Not me (shaking head).
T. —and you. No, you're not there.
C2. ?No, (shakes head, points to self) before home—finish, go home (being sent away).
T. You went home. I think you're muddled up Harry. Never mind (pats C2's knee), it doesn't matter. What did you have for breakfast this morning?

The question that led to this argument and to subsequent questions designed to check its plausibility or accuracy led to uncertainties that were never fully resolved—another general feature of the Wh-type question sessions. Questions following unanswered questions, seemingly designed to 'get to the bottom of things,' often met this fate. In a more formal teaching situation, where it is important to 'get the answer right,' it may be necessary to pursue inadequate responses to the bitter end. However, if the goal of the session is to encourage conversation and a relatively free exchange of ideas (and if the question is not an important one), it is worth asking whether the uncertainty and ambiguity that often follow on from strings of questions and repair are worth either the effort or the price they demand in terms of lower initiative and shorter responses from children. It might be argued that only by making sure the child 'gets it right' can we provide him with effective 'feedback' about the quality of his efforts and the nature of his communication problems. The difficulty is that when question piles on question, ambiguity on ambiguity, puzzle on puzzle, it is seldom clear what any feedback feeds back to.

Session 4. Personal Contributions

In this session, we asked teachers to try, as far as possible, to avoid questions and concentrate on telling children about their own experiences or commenting on what the children had to offer. As we had expected, children showed more initiative and were more talkative in this session than in either the normal chat sessions or the high control ones. Sometimes children said more in contribution sessions than in the phatic ones; at other times, the pattern was reversed. Some reasons why sessions might vary in effectiveness are explored below.

Although we analysed only ten minutes of each session with each group, the effects of low control were measurable. Initially, however, in both contribution and phatic sessions, teachers and children often suffered a rather uncomfortable period when the children seemed somewhat bemused by the rather unusual behaviour of their teachers. Mrs. Smith started off by trying to comment on C2's answer that he was tired, and then agreed that she too liked to stay in bed and had to travel a long way to school. As the following extracts show, the children were slow to 'take over,' but rather seemed to be waiting for her to 'get on with it,' i.e. to establish the theme or topic of conversation by asking a question. Eventually, however, the 'fear of silence' seemed to gain the upper hand and children began to make contributions of their own, becoming increasingly active and loquacious as the session proceeded.

Hard beginnings

T. (to C2) Oh Harry, you do look fed up. What's the matter?
C2. Tired.
T. Are you tired? (to C1) I think he looks very tired.
C1. (no response)
T. Do you think he looks tired?
C1. No.
T. Do you think he *looks* very tired?
C1. (nods half-heartedly)
T. Look, look at him.
C1. Yes.

C2. I like ?stay ?to home.
T. Pardon?
C2. I --- go home, sleep.
T. Oh dear, I like sleeping as well in the morning. I like to stay in bed.
C2. I --- wake up. (sleeping) Mummy, wake up. Shut up! (?to Mummy)
T. (and C1) (laugh)
C2. --- (pulling at shoulder) Wake up (prods).
T. Yes, I like it in bed.
C2. --- --- ?too late to watch (points).
T. Dear me, poor Harry!
C2. Yes ---.
C1. I ?have dream.
T. (to C1) Did you?
C2. --- ?driver --- (looks at watch) forget . . . car --- see, waiting. ?Here long time, long way house.
T. I know, poor Harry!
C2. -----
T. I come a long way to school in the mornings, in my car.
C2. (no response)
T. I live a long way away.
C1. (no response, yawns, looks at hands)
T. (laughs)
C1. Breakfast? (Does Tom think it's time they talked about it *or is* he asking 'did you have . . . ?')
T. Have breakfast? I had some breakfast this morning. I had some orange juice and . . . brown bread and cheese.
C1. (smiles)
C2. I ah, I like swimming, Senior.

The observation that it *does* take children time to settle in to the role of initiator and controller of conversation illustrates an important, general point. The teacher has to 'hold back' from a normal tempo or rhythm of interaction, leaving longer pauses after her move than she would in normal conversations. There is, in fact, a fair amount of evidence suggesting that teachers generally leave rather short 'silences' between their moves. One study of forty science lessons with hearing children (Swift and Gooding, 1983), for example, revealed that teachers usually gave children just over a second to respond after their questions. Teachers were helped to extend their pauses to three seconds (an electronic buzzer sounded if children had not responded after this time to let the teacher know when to go on). The extended pauses led to longer and more thoughtful responses from children.

Children need more time than teachers normally give them to think about what they are going to say. Perhaps we judge the time they need by the speed of our own thought processes and speech rates. Or it could be that long pauses simply heightens the fear of silence effect. Whatever the origins of the phenomenon we suspect it must be particularly important in relation to deaf children who need even more time both to comprehend what is said to them and to formulate a response. It is obviously difficult to 'manipulate' very basic aspects of one's spontaneous behaviour such as pausing. Furthermore, it takes time for children to understand and/or to accept the fact that they are being offered an active, controlling role if they are not used to it. The hard going experienced by teachers and children in getting the low control sessions off the ground is thus, we argue, symptomatic of the rather unusual demands being made on both.

Mrs. Smith increased the proportion of personal contributions in this session over her initial one from 10 to 44 per cent. After the first, rather awkward minute, outlined above, one child finally asked her a question. 'Breakfast?' Whether he was offering this as a safe, familiar topic of conversation (it had been a focus for questions in previous sessions) or was really interested in finding out how she had broken her fast that morning, we could not tell. However, the teacher treated it as a genuine question and answered it. The child met the answer with a smile and nod, and then the second child took over the floor and changed the subject completely to talk about swimming. The ice was then broken, and the conversation progressed from the cost of swimming to swimming in the sea and being bitten by crabs, to fathers eating crabs and one of the children seeing a 'fish' which may or may not have been the film monster 'Jaws.'

Swimming with Jaws

C1. I like freeze --- cold, cold outside.

C2. (pulls C1's chin round) S'alright, s'alright outside, strong.
T. It's horrible (i.e. swimming) outside, horrible.
C2. I --- brave, --- brave.
T. Horrible, it's much too cold.
C1. Mrs . . . . ?on ?the holiday . . . .
C2. No! I ---.
C1. (interrupts) Mrs. Smith, at ?the holiday --- --- boys, big boys swimming, raining!
T. In the rain?
C1. Yeah.
T. Oh, they're barmy, they're barmy boys.
C2. ?Before . . . long time ago . . . --- --- --- ?bus on ?your ?way holidays, ?shining.
T. Did she? Was it . . .?
C2. ?Goose ?fair, ?dusty ?fair . . .
T. It was sunny, was it? I like, I like swimming in the sunshine. But I don't like the sea.
C1. (shakes head)
T. I like the swimming pool, not the sea.
C1. Jaws! (sounds like 'rough')
T. Yes, it's too rough.
C1. Jaws! (grabbing, roughly)
T. Mm, and it's too rough in the sea.
C2. I like it --- --- ?way.= Eee! (something small) Ah! (pain in foot)
C1. A = boo Mrs. Smith.
T. I don't like crabs.
C2. = Eee = eee (beating them to death!
T. Oh! Do you kill them?
C2. ---?blood dead.
T. Oo . . . how horrible!
C1. Mrs., my father, ?shop holiday ?shop eat it.
T. Crab?
(C2. 'Ah!')
C1. Open (scooping out).
T. They're lovely, they're lovely to eat.
C2. I saw, I saw ?swimming holiday, I saw --- I saw fish, = ages (long, jaws closing, swims).
T. A real one?

C2. (draws J in air)
C1. No! ?not ?real, long, long way . . . Africa.
T. Yes.
C2. (gets C1 by chin) (prints JAWS on shelf)
C1. Jaw.
T. That's a film. Did you see a real one? A real whale?
C2. Yeah (points aghast) --- ?scared swimming, no ?walk =ages.
T. I think I would be frightened swimming where there were whales.
C1. Mrs. Smith, holiday, picture, film, Jaws = hee. ('jaws' open wide) Man inside (points inside mouth).
T. I haven't seen Jaws. I didn't see the film.

Maintaining the role of contributor was not an easy one for the teachers. Indeed, at one point in the interaction the teacher was trying so hard to merely comment on what the children were saying that she 'found herself' saying things that weren't true. When one child mentioned that his sister had been in hospital she said 'I haven't been in hospital,' and then, off camera as it were, complained: 'What am I saying, of course I have. What absolute rubbish. I'm telling fibs just to keep this conversation going. I'm trying so hard not to ask him a question. Oh dear Harry, is she alright now?—I'm sorry, I *have* to ask *that!*'

Clearly, asking questions is a normal part of conversation and can be a way of showing genuine interest in what another person has to say. The 'abnormal' nature of the conversations inspired by our instructions provides some insights into the issue of *when* a question is 'legitimate'. In this session, what the children had to say was almost entirely of their won choosing and, as such, came as a 'surprise' to the teacher. Since she had not dictated what they would talk about, what she heard was often informative. Once the conversation was underway there were many things that the child offered which could have formed a perfectly natural basis for questions. Indeed, we suspect that the points at which the teacher felt most uncomfortable were just those points at which a question occurred to her 'naturally.' Setting out to converse with a child and not asking questions is as unnatural as continually interrogating him (though the latter seems to come far more easily and 'naturally' in schools). Once the child is cast in an active role, by the strategic use of low control moves, any questions that arise are likely to refer to what the child has said or is saying and, hence, will be contingent upon his thinking. Questions asked at such points are likely to be 'invisible,' non-stressful and enabling of further elaboration rather than simply controlling and dictating the course of discourse, as is more often the case.

Mrs. Jones' contribution session proceeded less smoothly. She managed to increase her use of contributions from 27 per cent in her initial session to 35 per cent in this one. Although her children were more forthcoming and verbal in this session than either the normal ones or the high control conversations, they were generally less active both than the children in the other group and than they proved to be in the 'phatic' session. Mrs. Jones asked many more questions than Mrs. Smith in this session and this was reflected in much lower initiative being shown by her group. Another related difference, perhaps attributable to the fact that the second group were less verbally able than the others, was a very different pattern of responses by the two groups to teacher contributions. Once they got started, Mrs. Smith's children almost always took up an opening to make a contribution, responding to the teacher's comments with phatics alone very rarely (2 per cent of all occasions). mrs. Jones' children, however, were far less likely to take up their opportunities—in part because she was exerting more control—and simply acknowledged what the teacher said a good deal of the time (23 per cent phatics). Here we find the 'classic' problem of cause and effect. Because children are initially unwilling to take up an opening to speak and simply give a phatic response, the teacher is more likely to 'fill the gap' with a question. In so doing, she *decreases* the probability that children will take up later openings to contribute. This, in turn, leads her to be more likely to question. Thus, the downward spiral of increasing control begins and expands.

A major difference in the two sessions, in consequence, was the amount of 'warm up' time children needed to take initiative. Mrs. Jones started out the conversation with a question, which was answered, but ensuing contributions were met with nods from children and few contributions. Eventually, after several minutes of hard going, a dramatic change in the 'tenor' of the interaction occurred. She picked up on a child's comment about the kind of toaster he had at home, to say that she herself did not own one, but had to use a grill to toast bread and 'many times it gets burnt and I have to throw it away'. The children finally got 'with her' and took over control. One child observed 'black . . . black' with a fair degree of mime. Then both children talked about sandwich-makers, and went on to other domestic chores like cleaning out bedrooms. The teacher took up the cleaning theme to talk about clearing out desk drawers at school. This topic extended for some time, and one child, en route, produced conversational turns 17 and 23 words long (early in the session, her average had been 5.8).

Once conversation was initiated, the teacher was able to steer and elaborate on the topic without excessive questioning. Children occasionally picked up on her contributions and pursued them, asking questions or reacting to them in some other way. Though one cannot always be confident that children understand contributions (they can be ignored legitimately or not responded to because they were not heard or understood) these responses showed that, some of the time at least, children did both understand and were prepared to respond to what the teacher contributed. These were the beginnings, then, of a more equal and (certainly for us as observers) more interesting 'shared construction' of stories which both the teacher and children created. Helping children to converse in this way is not easy, but can bear fruit. Although we would not recommend that teachers try to avoid questions all the time (more later) it might be a useful rule of thumb to start out with the *intention* not to question children. One will fail, since questions will come 'naturally', but, in so doing, one might well avoid the 'dydactic traps' that talking to deaf children usually open up.

Session 5: Phatics

In this session, we asked teachers to sit back and, as far as possible, say nothing substantive. They were simply to acknowledge what children said— 'Yes' or 'really!', 'Ah-ha' and so on—or make vague comments like 'Good gracious!' or 'That's nice'. We asked them to avoid all questions as far as they could, including 'tag' utterances like 'Oh, did you?', since children sometimes react to these as 'genuine' two-choice questions.

Here, as in the contribution sessions, the opening sequences were somewhat tense and heavy going. The teacher's silence ultimately forced children to 'take over,' but it took a minute or so to establish the fact that it was to be 'their' conversation. But, once children began to converse, the effect was dramatic, particularly on the second, less 'verbal' group of children. In every other session their MLT was less than 2 words; here it rose to 4.1 words per turn. One girl produced turns 17, 16, 25 and 50 words long. She went into considerable detail about an episode in which, somewhat reminiscent of Poor Orphan Annie, she had been forced out into wet and cold streets to help her older sister, Alison, to deliver newspapers.

Delivering newspapers

C1. Mummy, Mummy (shaking ?chips. Tea finish. ?Alison -- - writing)? Alison ?poorly, poor. --- ! (shaking head) Me, ?before (poorly). Me ?make finish (i.e. the 'beautiful' paper creation she has already mentioned) me --- paper (taking it somewhere?), --- ?newspaper (opens newspaper). Alison 'Help me.' (She thinks about it) (I) ?Help ?Mummy; Mummy 'Alright, leave it.' (She goes off to do it) ---? (?asking where they go), searches for right house, comparing ?numbers on papers with house numbers) Ah! (as finds right one and posts it. Is given another, asks) There? (points) That in. (pushes it in. She looks around for next and posts it). ?Alison (hands out things). ?Heavy heavy bag over shoulder Heavy, heavy (trudges along with it) ---(hands over something) --- (gives something) --- (reads ?address and gives) (me) ?don't ?know, ?don't ?know house, me (hands out) --- me post. Me home, home. Cold, cold, wet, wet (pulls 'wet' hair). ?Dry, finish. ?Eat dinner, --- ?finish watch (TV). ?Lots ?Daddy --- car hand to head—?police ?play, finish, (me) bed. ?All (i.e. that's all folks!).

One striking feature of children's responses to the low control sessions, and of this child's performance in particular, was that once they began to tell stories, they become not only verbally but also physically active. They would sometimes stand up, mime and gesture fluently. Indeed, we were led to wonder if the freedom of movement engendered in these sessions might not be one reason why teachers usually exert so much control. It is more difficult to 'manage' active children, and the mime and gesture they produced might well be anathema to a teacher who is looking for 'speech.' Our own view is that, whilst techers do have to maintain order and discipline in order to ensure the smooth running of group discussion, children can only be encouraged to communicate freely, readily and productively if they are allowed to do so, as far as practicable, in their own way. Any attempt to make them stop their physical activity is likely to depress their desire to communicate. As we argued earlier, various aspects of linguistic competence arew facilitated by attempts to tell 'stories.' If a child is only encouraged to make short communicative responses within a tightly controlled framework established by the teacher, then he has little opportunity to discover how to *construct* such frameworks for himself. Lacking these skills, he will have little facility in organizing his thoughts and experiences in such a way that they can be communicated to others, either *en face* or in print.

It was often difficult to follow what children were communicating in this session. In questioning sessions, the framework supplied by the teacher makes even short and often poorly articulated vocalizations by the child interpretable most of the time. But the child's role is minimal. In the contribution session, the teacher was able to help direct and even clarify aspects of what children were saying to ensure some degree of coherence in the discourse. In the phatic session, where teachers played a minimal role, the children's offerings were often difficult to decipher not only because they used a good deal of gesture and mime but also because they would leap from topic to topic without establishing any intelligible connections between them. It was as if theey were painting a series of pictures rather than relating stories. This lack of coherence in their organization of discourse also, we feel, explains why teachers usually exert so much control. But if a child is never given an *opportunity* to try to produce a coherent story, how is he ever to learn what this involves? It is unlikely that repeated and extended 'phatic' sessions would provide him with enough guidance and feedback ever to discover how to make himself worth listening to. At some point, contributions, questions and requests for clarification are called for. The issue is how we integrate low and high control moves into a pattern which enables children to contribute and elaborate but also to discover how to take their listener's needs into account. How do we balance control and initiative with children who are very difficult to converse with?

CONVERSATION: INITIATIVE VERSUS CONTROL

By encouraging teachers to change the way in which they talk to children, we have been able to show that the effects of numerous teacher questions and frequent repair go hand in hand and inhibit children from playing an active, productive part in conversation. When teachers question less, become more receptive to what children have to say and talk more about their own views, ideas and so forth, children reciprocate by making more frequent and longer contributions to the discourse. They are more likely to elaborate on their answrs to teacher questions when these are relatively infrequent and they become generally more involved in the interaction.

However, at the other extreme, we found that exposure to a 'laissez-faire' style was equally unsatisfying, though in different ways to high control sessions. When the teachers abdicated their role as managers and orchestrators of interaction, children became more active and loquacious but were also often incomprehensible. Too much control stifles the child, but too little robs the teacher of any opportunities to help the child discover how to make himself understood. How is it possible to steer a productive 'middle course' between the extremes of over-control and self-defeating attempts to repair children's understanding on the one hand and an approach that provides no opportunities for teaching on the other?

The first point to make is that there is no 'rule book' or 'script' that can be written to dictate how one achieves productive conversations. We have emphasized the 'contingent' nature of effective teaching which demands an opportunistic and responsive attitude towards a child's ongoing activities and utterances. When children tell us interesting and surprising things, then, by definition, we are not able to *anticipate* their offerings. Indeed, we do not *want* to anticipate them. The essence of conversation is the transmission and sharing of *new* ideas. If the child's role is not to be predetermined by teacher questions, then the teacher will have to react as the moment dictates and, since we cannot anticipate what that moment will bring forth, we cannot write down any scripts.

However, whilst there are no such scripts to guide the achievement of productive conversations, we can highlight ways in which teaching styles are often self-defeating and explore possible tactics for helping to avoid the pitfalls that classroom conversationalists often fall into.

Obviously, we would recommend that, in general, teachers ask fewer questions than they usually do and that they give children more time to think and communicate after they have addressed them. They should also become more attentive, accepting and responsive to what children have to say. However, any slackening of control should not imply that teachers will never ask questions to extend, develop or in some other way raise children's awareness. Nor should it imply that the teacher will not be giving the child clear signals about the clarity, coherence or accessibility of what he is saying. Given that we can encourage talk from children, which, we have argued, we can, two specific issues arise. When is a question likely to facilitate and extend the child's understanding without depressing his desire to communicate? When and how should repair occur?

EFFECTIVE QUESTIONS

In an extensive and detailed (but not easily availbale) study of teacher questions and children's responses to them, Robinson and Rackstraw (1975) draw attention to several features of the uses and abuses of questions. Generally speaking, attempts to encourage children to entertain a line of thought or to engender curiosity about a topic of discourse by starting an interaction through questions are usually unsuccessful. Even when (hearing) children respond to such opening questions, their replies are likely to be inappropriate or irrelevant. They seem to respond more to 'please the teacher' and to assume that all of her questions have a single 'right' answer. Rarely do they seem to think about the import or implications of questions.

When, however, questions arise *after* a shared 'realm of discourse' (our term) or verbal 'text' has been established, questions which relate to it are more likely to meet with appropriate and thoughtful responses from chidlren (Prosser, 1974). Indeed, we suspect that this is one of the main reasons why children are more likely to produce relatively long and elaborated answers to teacher questions in low control sessions. Sessions in which both teachers and children have made a variety of contributions are more likely to provide such a realm of discourse for questions to arise out of and refer to.

The implications of our results and the study of questioning with hearing children are that teachers are more likely to receive considered answers to their questions if they first 'set the scene' to establish a background against which these can be interpreted. There are many different tactics which might achieve such a state of affairs. For example, a teacher might begin a conversation by telling a 'story', describing a scene, speculating about the future, or recalling a past shared experience. Put another way, narrative should precede inquiry. Alternatively, children might be encouraged to introduce and develop their *own* themes. This can be achieved through 'chairing' moves like 'You tell us about your weekend.' Although such moves determine who will talk, they do not necessarily exert control over what is *said*.

Establishing a shared realm of discourse before asking questions is not easy, as we saw in the contribution sessions. It is likely to take time, will require patience and all concerned may need to tolerate the 'fear of silence.' However, we found that within a few minutes of conversation, children usually began to take the lead. Similarly, Lees (1981) discovered that after a few weeks of offering frequent contributions to children she found it very difficult to return to her 'traditional' style which involved more questioning and repair because the children were reluctant to *let* her do so. they were likely to 'ignore' her attempts to control them. They interrupted her, went beyond the force of her questions and so on. We can only speculate about any longer-term effects of such an approach, but we suspect that they would be significant. Once any new 'rules' of the conversational game have been estbalished and children realize that their options in talk are relatively open, we believe they will begin to 'expect' to paly a more active and egalitarian role in talking to teachers and that this will improve both their confidence and competence as communicators.

Once a topic has been introduced and developed, then, we believe, questions are more likely to be comprehensible to children, particularly when they are given time to think and respond. Answers to two-choice questions may well be elaborated upon if they build on an extant topic and are not too numerous. Similarly, more demanding Wh-type questions, such as those encountered in our experimental sessions, may lead to argument, discussion and genuinely informative responses from children if they relate in some sensible way to an established line of thought. Furthermore, if, following a child's response to a question, the teacher either makes a contribution that develops or extends the theme or simply acknowledges what the child has just said, then she gives the child an opportunity to think further and, if he has anything left to say, to make additional comments.

In general, then, a productive conversation will be characterized, to use a nautical metaphor, by an 'ebb and flow' of control. Questions following narrative may help to explore and extend a child's thinking. Question following question in an unbroken sequence of teacher control are counter-productive and inhibit children's initiative, but, embedded within lower control moves, they lead children into new lines of thought and greater understanding of the topic at hand. Thus, we suggest that questions should be used more sparingly and selectively to extent, develop and explore themes and topics which are first established through teacher or child narrative.

REPAIR—WHEN AND HOW?

Children must dicover 'how to mean.' They not only have to learn how to make intelligible sounds and acquire the 'rules' of syntax, but, to be meaningful, they also have to discover how to work out the needs of a listener, monitor his understanding, diagnose the nature of any misunderstandings and find ways of reestablishing mutual comprehension. The study of these aspects of children's developing linguistic competence have been neglected until recently, most attention having been paid to the acquisition of 'syntactic' rules (see Romaine, 1984). However, evidence is beginning to emerge about everyday experiences that may underlie the development of these wider aspects of communicative competence in hearing children. One series of studies in particular is important to our discussions of repair and its place in productive discourse. For example, Robinson (1976) observed what parents did in talking to their preschool hearing children when their child said something unintelligible or ambiguous. One common reapir strategy (as in schools for the deaf) was to ask children questions designed to clear up uncertainty or to check an interpretation of what they said (e.g. 'Do you mean . . .?'). Another, less common approach was to respond to children's utterances with a repairing contribution of the form 'I don't understand what you mean' or 'I don't know whether you mean *x* or *y*.'

Children whose parents repaired through contributions were more knowledgeable about how communications between *other* people break down. They were better than others, for example, at detecting when misunderstandings arose because a speaker gave an inadequate 'message' or because his listener had not understood adequate ones. They knew who to 'blame' for a breakdown in mutual understanding. In a follow-up study, Robinson and Robinson (1982) showed that preschool hearing children who were exposed to interactions in which their inadequate utterances were repaired through contributions learned how to interpret communication breakdown whereas those exposed to a questioning style of repair did not.

The implications of these observations and experiments for repair with deaf children are relatively easy to summarize but, we suspect, are rather more difficult to put into practice. Basically, attempts to repair children should take place in the 'declarative' rather than the 'interrogative' voice. In other words, teachers should draw children's attention to breakdowns in comprehension *not* by *asking* what they said or meant (e.g.

'What did you say?', 'What do you mean?') nor by *guessing* with two-choice questions such as 'Do you mean yesterday or tomórrow?', 'Did you go with Mummy or Daddy?'. Rather, they should be as explicit as possible in *telling* children about the source of their own uncertainty. If a child's offering is totally incomprehensible, then a general, repairing contribution such as 'I don't know what you mean' or 'I didn't understand that' may be all that is possible (but read on). However, if the child's message is simply *ambiguous* and permits more than one interpretation, then the teacher should be as explicit as possible about her state of uncertainty: 'I don't know whether you mean you went with Mummy or with Daddy.' In other words, repairing Wh-type moves should give way to general statements of incomprehension, and two-choice repairing questions should be replaced by contributions which specify the possible interpretations of what a child has said.

In response to the 'how' of repair, then, we suggest the use of contributions rather than questions. These are preferable in three ways. They do not increase teacher power and, hence, are less likely to inhibit children from active responses. Second, they give the child a chance to *understand* another person's stage of mind in response to what they have tried to say. Finally, in our view, they mark the fact hat any breakdown in communication is the *shared* responsibility of both the speaker and the listener. As we see in the transcripts below, for example, when teacher repair is achieved mainly through contributions, children begin to 'reciprocate' by trying to help the teacher understand what they mean. Thus, they are not only encouraged to be active partners in conversation but are also provided with opportunities to develop skill and confidence in helping other people to understand them.

What about the 'when' of repair? In general, we suggest that teachers need to tolerate greater levels of uncertainty than many of them (in our studies) currently do in conversations with deaf children. In practice, this will mean that a teacher will not repair each and every ambiguous or unintelligible move from children. If and when a child learns how to 'stay on topic' and to signal the fact that he is changing topics (which some of the children in our study were starting to do), then, by letting the child take a few more moves in conversation, the teacher may get further insights into what he means. Then, if and when the 'penny drops' a checking phatic move like 'Oh, I see, you mean . . .' can provide the child with an opportunity to see if the teacher has indeed understood the message. Another approach, which is even more demanding, is for the teacher to interpret what she *thinks* a child has said and respond appropriately. For instance, if she formulates a contribution that only makes sense if the child actually *meant* what she thought he had tried to say, then the child is given information which might help him to check her understanding.

If such 'rules' of conversation were to become a *familiar* part of classroom interactions, we are reasonably sure that deaf children would begin to appreciate them and start to reciprocate by paying more attention to what the teacher says and by helping her to understand them.

We turn now to three transcripts. In the first, a teacher responds to a child's utterance that is intelligible but employs descriptive phrases (round and round, sit down) for which a name (musical bumps) exists. She responds with a move that involves 'invisible' repair through phatics ('Oh yes, musical bumps'). The child is five years old and very deaf (102 dB). He is managing, however, to monitor the teacher's utterances and take elements from them.

T. Did you go out to play?
C. (pause) Not out play (shakes head). ?I --- the music.
T. You played with the music!
C. --- --- ?games.
T. You played games!
C. Yeah.
T. What sort of games did you play?
C. Um?
T. What sort of games did you play?
C. Round and round, sit down.
T. Oh yes, musical bumps.
C. =Mu, musical bumps.
T. (nods) That's right. Any more games?
C. --- --- ?did that (poses).
T. Musical statues.
C. Statues.

The next, more extensive examples, show two very different styles of repair. The first involves repairing *questions* and the second more repairing *contributions*. Note how, in the latter, children react to the generally low control of the teacher by actively trying to make her understand. They do *not* let her explicit statements of uncertainty and lack of understanding go by.

Whose birthday was it?

T. No. (to C6) Graham, whose brithday was it?
C6. Graham, he.
T. Whose birthday?
C6. Graham.
T: No. Ah, yes, it was Graham's birthday. But what about Tom? (C5) Was it Tom's Mummy or Daddy?
C6. (no response)
T. (after pause) Don't know. Right Tom, you come here. I want you to tell them whose birthday it was, whose birthday.
C5. Daddy's, Daddy's.
T. Tell them all.
C5. My Daddy's.
T. 'My Daddy's birthday'.
C5. My Daddy's birthday.
T. Good lad. Wose birthday?
C6. Daddy, your Daddy.
(C1. Card, was a nice card) (?question)
T. (to C6) Your Daddy's birthday?
C6. No. Tom's.
T. Tom . . . .
C6. Daddy, Daddy, Tom's Daddy . . . .
T. Tom's Daddy's . . . .
C6. Birthday.
T. Birthday. Whose birthday was it?
C1. Send a birthday card (points to C5).
T. Your Daddy's birthday?
C1. Card, card.
T. Who? Whose birthday?
C1. Daddy.
T. Your Daddy?
C1. No, Tom's.

T. Tom's birthday?
C1. Yes.
T. No. Wasn't Tom's birthday.
(C2 to C1: 'No!')
C4. Tom's Daddy's birthday.
T. (to C2) Terry!
C2. Mummy birthday.
T. Mummy's birthday?
C2. (nods)
T. No.
C2. No! Me!
T. Your birthday?
C2. ---
T. No. We're talking about Tom.
C4. Tom.
C1. Daddy.
T. Just a minute, Pam (C1).
C4. Tom Daddy's birthday.
T. 'Tom's Daddy's birthday.'
C4. Tom's Daddy's birthday.
T. Good boy. Right

Star Wars—Cars and mammoths together?!

T. Er. David! David! I don't understand that bit. David, I don't understand this bit. Waht are you hitting your cheek for? What do you mean?
C3. ?A ?mammoth elephant.
T. An elephant? Elephant?
C3. No, no, er, different kind of horns. (tusks)
T. A different kind of helmet.
C2. No! No! (picks up book)
C3. Yes! (points to C2's book)
C1. A thing --- horns --- elephant.
C2. Look, look! (shows book)
T. What's this, let's have a look. (goes over to look at book)
C2. Mammoth. (points to book)
T. Oh! A mammoth. A different kind of elephant. An old-fashioned kind of elephant with big tusks.
C3. I see one ---.
T. Oh. Where did you see that?

C3. I see in a picture.
T. In a picture, yes.
C3. --- ---, --- two.
C2. Tell them about --- --- story.
C3. Er . . . R2, R2 went hide in a cave (gestures ???) ---. (NB. Rs-D2 was one of the robots in *Star Wars.*)
C2. R2 --- ?find ?a ?cave, ?go (round and round) and a little man hit him, that man fell down, a man with a bread . . . man with a beard.
T. A man with a beard, yes.
C3. --- ---, --- see him.
T. He saw the mammoth in the cave.
C3. And sit in car, no wheels, no ?road.
T. You don't have cars and mammoths together.
C3. No! No, --- wheels ?float car.
T. There were mammoths long before there were cars.
C3. No, two man, two man ---.
T. You're getting it all mixed up, all mixed up David. (David gets up and goes to blackboard.)
C2. No! No!
T. There were mammoths a long time before there were any --- ---.
C2. --- --- --- story.
T. Funny story!
C2. They ?only ?lived in the story then ?the ?cameraman --- see. Then --- ---, ---.
T. And what, was he dreaming about the film or something?
C2. No, --- --- cameraman on film.
T. It was a made-up film.
C2. No. (Gets up and joins David at blackboard—they draw mammoth and hovercraft.)

CONCLUSIONS

The children who took part in this study were eleven years of age. Shortly after taking part they left the junior shcool to move on to a senior school where, in the normal course of events, they would be exposed to more 'formal' educatior and to lessons in which teachers try to transmit information and knowledge. Some of the problems they face in communicating with their teachers have been illustrated in this and the preceding chapter. If they find formal instruction difficult, and if their progress through the curriculum turns out to be much slower than that of hearing children, we should not, perhaps be surprised. Similarly, given the problems they face in trying to provide 'narrative' accounts of their own experiences and ideas, it is also unsurprising that they are unlikely to be able to write or read very well (even if they had no other problems in this direction).

Whilst changes in teaching styles towards lower control of conversation resulted in longer, more animated and interesting contributions from children, they also revealed the tremendous difficulties children face in trying to present a coherent, intelligible narrative. Although we do not know how often deaf children are given opportunities in the classroom to tell stories or narrate accounts of their experiences, such chances, in our experience, are very rare. Even when teachers do attempt to do so, the characteristic 'register' of the classroom, the question-answer exchange, effectively inhibits children from trying to produce coherent, lengthy accounts.

When we consider the enormous problems facing both children and teachers in trying to lay the foundations of receptive and expressive linguistic competence in conversation, we can, perhaps, understand why so many years of experience in school result in what seem like 'depressing' outcomes. Some will conclude, no doubt, that the communication problems facing children that we have been illustrating are an inevitable and largely inescapable consequence of severe or profound deafness. We are not so sure. We believe that the child's problems are often exacerbated by styles of teacher control. Possibly, if the 'balance of control' in interactions can be adjusted, so that low rather than high control becomes more typical of children's experiences in discourse, then their powers as conversational partners and, eventually, as narrators will improve. Any such improvement, however, will demand not simply a laissez-faire policy from teachers but an approach that achieves contingent control of interactions and the strategic use of repair and feedback. We have illustrated the great skill that would be needed to achieve this state of affairs.

It is obviously not going to be easy to find or train teachers to whom contingent control of interactions will become 'second nature.' We have gone only a short way in trying to understand the complexities of discoruse with deaf children and made a very few preliminary suggestions about how improvements might be sought. We suggest that teachers and schools—whatever methods of communication they are using—can measure the efficacy and value of their attempts to facilitate the development of their children's linguistic competence by examining and analysing their own techniques for *conversing* with them.

11

Teaching Reading to Deaf

THIS is our gloomiest chapter. How marvellous it would be to be able to write a treatise outlining an approach to teaching reading to deaf children that would guarantee them reading levels at least on a par with hearing eleven-year-olds when they leave school. Sadly, we are not able to write such a treatise. Rather, we have to be content with an attempt to gain greater understanding of why, despite years of effort by teachers to teach them how to read, the vast majority of severely and profoundly deaf children leave school essentially incapable of doing so. First, we will look at attempts to assess deaf children's reading ability and ask what various tests have to tell us about what they do and do not know about written English. We move on to outline some of the explanations that have been put forward for deaf children's poor levels of literacy and explore their educational implications. We take a brief look at attempts to teach children how to read and get some ideas about where all the time goes and why so much effort in teaching reading usually bears so little fruit. Finally, we consider some of the relationships between language and literacy.

Why do the majority of deaf children leave their classrooms illiterate? This is a vast and complex question. Although many years of study have gone into the investigation of reading in both deaf and hearing people, the many processes involved in skilled reading and the relationship between these processes are still not fully (or even largely) understood. When we add our uncertainties about the nature linguistic competence in deaf children to our ignorance about the precise nature of reading processes we are confronted with a problem of quite staggering complexity.

We would be prepared to demand a Nobel Prize for anyone who could provide a compelling solution to this problem. However, since we have not come across a suitable candidate, we will have to be content with an exploration of some potential contributing causes to deaf children's problems in trying to read.

> It is clear—and not an over-statement—that we do not know how to teach deaf, or even partially-hearing children to read (Conrad, 1979).

This bold, challenging and pessimistic statement was based on a review of the now-extensive research literature on the reading achievements of deaf children and Conrad's own findings from a large-scale survey of deaf and partially hearing children about to leave English and Welsh schools in the mid-1970s. As Conrad and others (e.g. Quigley and Kretschmer, 1982) point out, studies in many parts of the world over a number of years, involving children from very different educational backgrounds, have yielded consistent results. Since Conrad's investigations also included a study of the relationships between literacy and several other aspects of linguistic competence, we will concentrate on his findings here.

Conrad's fifteen-to sixteen-year-old sample included 468 deaf and partially hearing children who were tested using the Brimer Wide-span Reading Test (Brimer, 1972). In this test the child reads a cue sentence and selects one word from this sentence to fill in a gap in another. For example:

Pack the eggs in the box.	Hens lay . . . .
Brush up the leaves and burn them.	When logs . . . , smoke rises.

The 468 children achieved an average reading age of nine years on this test. Conrad not only tested reading but also measured lip-reading skills and speech intelligibility; he administered tests of 'internal speech' designed to show how far they read using a phonemically based approach (i.e. 'translating' printed symbols into speech sounds), and collected teacher assessments of oral language levels. He also measured non-verbal intelligence and obtained better-ear hearing losses. Broadly speaking, he found that these measures were interrelated. Children displaying more 'internal speech' (we discuss this more fully later) were more likely to read and lip-read relatively well, to speak more intelligibly and be rated higher on language ability by their teachers. All these measures correlated with degree of hearing loss and, less powerfully, with non-verbal intelligence. Thus children with losses in excess of 85 dB in this study were unlikely to evidence internal speech and produced mean reading ages of about eight years. However, those children with losses greater than 85dB who *did* evidence 'internal speech' also read relatively well, suggesting that the capacity to read and memorize words in terms of their sounds, rather than degree of deafness *as such,* was what differentiated good and poor deaf readers.

The pattern of associations between these measures implies that children without internal speech read using a visually based strategy in which the orthographic 'shapes' of printed words are associated 'directly' with meaning (e.g. Hung, Tzeng and Warren, 1981). In other words, they do not access the meaning of what they read by first converting the visual symbols into speech sounds, but rely instead on memorized associations between printed word shapes and the things to which they refer.

WHAT DO TESTS OF READING TEST?

In a series of studies (Webster, Wood and Griffiths, 1981; Wood, Griffiths and Webster, 1981; Beggs and Breslaw, 1983) we have compared the scoring patterns of deaf and hearing children with nominally similar reading ages on three tests of reading. One was the Southgate Sentence Completion Reading Test (Southgate, 1962). In performing this test, the reader is required to complete a sentence with a word drawn from a set of five alternatives. For example:

> Ducks can . . . .
> pond / swim / water / farm / sing
>
> I drink . . . .
> cake / hens / milk / picture / man
>
> Birds are covered with . . . .
> trees / skirts / sky / nests / feathers

We gave the Southgate test to sixty deaf children (with a mean hearing loss of 87 dB and mean age of eleven) who achieved a mean reading age of seven years nine months. They were matched with sixty hearing children who achieved similar mean scores on the test. We found that deaf children attempted far more of the test items than hearing children did. In scoring the Southgate and other tests, when a child gets a string of wrong answers, no further items are analysed since to do so would increase the number of correct scores by 'chance', thus artificially inflating the reading age estimate. In this study, however, deaf children usually got enough right answers scattered throughout the test to keep scoring. Indeed, many of them reached the end of the test in the allotted time span. The test starts with easy items and gets progressively more difficult. The hearing children tended to do those items that were consistent with their reading age, try one or two more beyond this 'ceiling' and then give up. The deaf children, however, did not; they tended to persevere to the end. Thus, they made more errors in achieving their reading ages than the hearing children.

THE ANALYSIS OF ERRORS

The analysis of errors is a most revealing process and one of the most useful things one can do with the results of formal tests. An examination of children's errors often reveals patterns that can be used to obtain some insights into what they know and how they interpret the test itself. We also use error analysis, when we explore deaf and hearing children's mathematical abilities. When we examined the errors of deaf and hearing children on the Southgate test, we found some marked and informative differences. The test is designed to offer children a number of plausible bases for error. Some of the 'distractor' words look rather like the right answer (e.g. A pig has a curly . . . . tall/tail/stale/tell/stile), some sound rather like it (e.g. A sheep's babies are called . . . . lame/calves/look/lambs/lamps) and others mean similar things (e.g. The alphabet has twenty-six . . . words/figures/letters/laces/books). These distractors work because children are likely to confuse words that look the same, sound the same or mean similar things when their knowledge of written language is tenuous. This limited understanding is revealed by their choice of plausible distractors.

When we examined the errors made by hearing children we found, as we would expect, a relatively even distribution across the distractors. Put another way, knowing what mistakes one hearing child with a reading age of nine made on a given item does not generate any good predictions about the errors made by other hearing children of the same reading age.

This was not the case with the deaf children. In fact, when we looked at their performance on all items we found that, by and large, they made the *same* errors. This implies that they were adopting a systematic strategy for handling the test but not one that was very sensitive to the orthographic or grapheme—phoneme cues that mislead hearing children. Below we list some examples of these common errors (popular answers in capitals).

> Birds are covered with . . . .
> trees/skirts/sky/NESTS/feathers
>
> Careless driving leads to . . . .
> happiness/CARS/tractors/accidents/improvements
>
> Rich men can afford to live in . . . .
> luscious/poverty/luxurious/luxury/WEALTHY
>
> Ducks can . . . .
> POND/swim/water/farm/sing

These examples suggest that deaf children are capitalizing on word associations. In fact, we need attribute to the deaf reader no more than a sight vocabulary for isolated words and a sense of the real-world associations between those words to get such a score. We are not saying, however, that this is all that they do have (read on). Although word association does not help explain errors on all tests, on the Southgate it is consistent both with many errors and some rather sophisticated-looking correct answers to later items, where the right answer happens to be the only highly associated word in the list of possibilities. For example:

> There was a bridge over the . . . .
> rain/running/RIVER/rest/ruler
>
> I drink . . . .
> cake/hens/MILK/picture/man
>
> A dog's babies are called . . . .
> chickens/papers/PUPPIES/calves/potatoes

These results, we argue, lead to the conclusion that the reading ages given by the Southgate test for hearing-impaired children are not simply reflecting delayed reading development. Most hearing-impaired children are doing something quite different from hearing children to gain their reading score.

Although some tests, such as Brimer's (see below), do not permit extensive use of a word association strategy, others do. A recent analysis of reading tests completed by a large sample of deaf and hearing children in the United States found similar 'test-taking strategies' being used by deaf children to those identified in our research (Wolk and Schildroth).

On the Brimer Wide-span Test (Brimer, 1972), used by Conrad, we found many errors which were more 'inscrutable' than those made on the Southgate test. Here we used a technique for classifying errors designed to estimate the degree of linguistic sophistication involved (see Webster, Wood and Griffiths, 1981, for details). Basically, hearing-impaired children made more 'non-linguistic' errors than their hearing controls (again, of similar nominal reading ages). On some items, for example, they inserted into the test sentence a word from the cure sentence that occupied the same spatial position (e.g. the fifth word in each sentence). On the basis of our examination of these and other analyses we concluded that the reading tests we have used do not measure the same things in deaf and hearing children.

If one accepts this conclusion, then we must reconsider the status of the 'reading plateau' found in many studies of deaf children's reading and the various implications that may be drawn from it. Furthermore, if deaf children are using special, non-syntactically based strategies on reading tests, does it follow that they are *not* developing a productive grammar for spoken and/or written English at all? We shall now turn to a consideration of the first of these two questions. The second question provides the focus for the next chapter.

ASPECTS OF SYNTACTIC COMPETENCE IN DEAF CHILDREN

The most comprehensive attempt (that we know of) to look at *how* deaf children interpret different aspects of written English, rather than concentrating simply on their scores and the errors they make on hearing-referenced reading tests, is a series of detailed studies by Quigley and his colleagues from Illinois in the United States. Their research culminated in a 'Test of Syntactic Abilities' (or TAS) which, as the authors explicitly point out, is not a test of reading in the normal sense but investigates how children handle a wide range of syntactic devices in print. Like all research, it has its limitations; the main constraint on this work (which is acknowledged by its authors) is that it looks mainly at children's performance with 'isolated' written sentences and does not examine the factors involved in reading extended text. However, notwithstanding this limitation, the test provides some valuable insights into children's levels of performance and developmental progress on a range of features of written language.

For example, one technique they used to explore deaf children's knowledge of various complex syntactic structures was to present a series of pairs of simple sentences such as 'I saw the man. The man hit the dog' and then to ask children to judge whether more complex constructions, such as 'I saw the man who the man hit the dog,' represent an acceptable combination of the simple ones. If the child judges that it is not, then he is asked to write a correct version. Another strategy was to provide children with a number of candidate complex sentences and ask them to choose the one that looked correct.

One important feature of the test which grew out of these studies is that the 'distractor' sentences it uses are derived from empirical studies of deaf children. Thus, the test gives valuable information not only about what deaf children cannot read and the syntactic structures they find most difficult, but also provides insights into how they think acceptable written English is structured. Since the various different distractors also embody a developmental sequence, it is possible to chart progress in children even before they get correct answers. In short, the error patterns are revealing.

It is not our aim here to go into detail about the items in the test, nor the developmental sequences it suggests. Rather, we wish to address a number of general features of the research that serve both to address the 'ceiling of reading achievement' issue and to give some insights into the grammatical knowledge of deaf children. The research involved deaf children aged from ten to eighteen years of age and a smaller age range of hearing controls. In relation to almost every aspect of syntax tested, the deaf children showed consistent if very slow progress throughout the age range tested. Although, by eighteen, their performance was still rather poor in comparison to ten-year-old hearing children, there was no evidence that the process of learning to read actually stopped at any specific age, which implies that any improvements in techniques for teaching reading might be useful over a wide age range.

More important, perhaps, are the insights that the test gives into what children think the structure of English (at least as written) is like. We want to draw attention to two general features of the children's scoring patterns. These, we suggest, reveal aspects of deaf children's performance that are not specific to particular features of grammar (e.g. auxiliary verb systems, pronominalization, determiners and so on) but have the status of general 'rules.' First, is the 'subject-verb-object' rule (or S-V-O). Many constructions in English, particularly in the speech addressed to young children and encountered by them in early reading books, are consistent with this syntactic rule (although some linguists prefer to use the 'semantic' terms 'Agent-Action-Patient'). If a child assumes that the elements in the surface structure (the physical arrangement of sounds in speech and graphemes in print) are always organized such that the first noun encountered is the subject (or agent) of the sentence, followed by a verb (action) and then the object (patient), he or she will have few problems in understanding the meaning of structurally simple sentences such as 'Fred is eating ice-cream.' Similarly, if simple sentences are conjoined with no 'deletions' of subjects or objects as in 'Mary likes ice-creme and Peter likes cakes,' then the child (who can read the main words) following the S-V-O rule will have no difficulty understanding what is meant.

However, English is not nearly as simple as this. There are no foolproof, simple or direct relationships between semantic and syntactic features of meaning. In passive constructions, for example, such as 'Mary was hit by John,' the 'deep' subject (agent) is not Mary but John. The relationships between word order and 'deep' underlying meanings are not simple nor limited to a single set of 'mapping' rules between meaning and expression or, more technically, between semantic relations and grammatical roles (e.g. Brown, 1973, p. 149ff; Wanner and Gleitman, 1982, p. 29ff). Similarly, when we come to look at complex and compound sentences we find that subjects are often deleted as in 'Mary fed the dog and went out.' Here the deleted subject of the verb 'went' has to be 'retrieved' from the first clause. In sentences such as these, presented in isolation at least, young hearing children (aged up to eight or nine) and deaf children (as late as eighteen years) seem to work on what has been called the 'Minimum Distance Principle' (Chomsky, 1969). They tend to choose a noun in the sentence that is closest to the verb with a deleted subject. Thus, the errors produced by deaf children in Quigley's test are all consistent with either S-V-O or MDP.

The boy was helped by the girl.	(boy helps girl)
The boy who kissed the girl ran away.	(girl runs away)
The opening of the door surprised the cat.	(door surprised cat)

Before going on to consider the implications of these findings, let us outline some caveats about using such evidence to talk about children's general linguistic abilities. First, we have to bear in mind the fact that the data come from studies of reading rather than speaking or speech comprehension. As we will argue more fully, written text is not simply speech written down. The written word involves features that are not present in spoken discourse, and *vice versa*. So, we have to be cautious when making any general statements about linguistic competence on the basis of tests of reading. In speech, for example, there are often pragmatic cues arising from situational factors, non-verbal and paralinguistic information, as well as from the structure of discourse, that supplement meaning and may help children to understand (or ignore) syntactic structures. In print, robbed of such cues, children may fail. Furthermore, there are syntactic structures in print that are rarely found in speech (for instance, 'Harry's leaving surprised the girl').

A second caveat is that the origins and processes involved in the development of S-V-O and MDP strategies by hearing children are still the subject of debate (Bowerman, 1979; Romaine, 1984). Uncertainties about the factors that lead hearing children to understand complex structures in the way they do make it difficult to predict how and why deaf children show similar patterns. We explore this question more fully, when we consider environmental factors that might limit children's development of complex linguistic structures. A third, and final, caveat is that statistical generalizations based on large numbers of subjects do not tell us very much about the processes that go on inside an individual child's mind as he reads. However, bearing these reservations in mind, let us explore some possible implications, both theoretical and educational, of these findings.

The first point we want to underline is that the statistical patterns found in the analyses of language comprehension of hearing and (older) deaf children are similar in some important respects. Despite the problems of drawing inferences about the abilities of individual children from group data, the fact remains that such data generate common *patterns* that have to be explained and which suggest some parallels in the development of deaf and hearing children.

If one accepts the argument that deaf children make use of rules like S-V-O and MDP, then it follows that these children possess a generative, if limited, linguistic system. Further evidence of this fact is presented in the next chapter. If this is true, how is it implicated in reading?

BARRIERS TO LITERACY

The problems faced by poor (hearing) readers and the development of reading schemes designed to help them overcome their problems have been the subject of a great deal of research and theory. Contemporary debates between different theorists and between teachers with different views on reading are heated and, in relation to the concept of dyslexia in particular, have reached temperatures usually reserved for arguments about the education of deaf children. Having braved the fires of one debate we have no intention of entering that relating to 'poor' readers (see Bryant and Bradley, 1985; Underwood, 1979). However, since there are some similar issues involved in discussions of deaf and poor (hearing) readers that have been explored in studies of the latter, it is worth attempting a brief overview of such work.

Theories of reading and explanations for the problems of poor readers traditionally fall into two camps. One concentrates on the 'basics' of reading, namely the nature of 'grapheme-phoneme correspondence (GPC) rules.' These rules specify how the sound system of speech relates to the graphemic elements of writing (and involve many complex irregularities in English). Adovcates of this approach provide so-called 'bottom-up' explanations of the reading process. They argue that the first stages of learning to read and the principal source of problems for poor readers is achieving mastery of such rules. Good readers, the argument proceeds, have 'automated' GPC rules that enable them to read text quickly and without any conscious effort at 'decoding' words into sound. The poor reader and beginning reader do not possess this automated system for 'encoding' print. Rather, if they do not immediately recognize the shape of a written word, they have to deliberately sound out each element of it and 'build up' a spoken version of it. This, a slow and laborious process, limits not only how fast they can read but the number of words that they can 'hold in mind' long enough to relate them and achieve comprehension. Thus, the poor reader is not only slow but also understands less of what he reads than a better reader because the effort of working out each word takes up the time and mental capacity that the good reader uses for achieving comprehension of sequences of words and text.

The opposing view is that GPC rules are less central both to the reading process and the explanation of poor readers' problems. Advocates of this view point out that good readers 'interact' with what they read. They do not read each word in a text, as studies of eye movements in reading illustrate. Indeed, since skilled readers may read at 200 to 300 words per minute it is clear that they do not read every word. Rather, they tend to look selectively at specific words or structures in text (although no one has yet managed to explain why they look at what they do look at nor what they do with it!). The skilled reader, the argument proceeds, formulates and tests hypotheses about what the text means, exploiting knowledge not only of GPC rules but grammar, general knowledge, and so on. Poor readers, the argument concludes, do not make use of these higher level resources (hence, the term 'top-down' explanations of reading problems). They limit their attention by looking at each word in turn, rather than trying to interact intelligently with the text.

Conrad's research into 'internal speech' may be used to provide a 'bottom-up' explanation for the reading levels of the deaf. The deaf reader, like the poor (hearing) one, does not possess automated GPC rules. Indeed, unlike the hearing reader, very deaf children may have no *basis* for developing such rules because they lack the phonemic knowledge to map graphemic information onto (although Dodd and Hermelin, 1977, argue that this is not the case). Such a child, from a 'bottom-up' perspective, *cannot* become a good reader. But how did Conrad find out that such deaf readers lacked 'internal speech?'

If hearing people are given a list of words to read which sound similar (e.g. blue, zoo, true, etc.) they find it more difficult to memorize them than they do a list of words which sound different (but are otherwise similar in length, familiarity, etc., e.g. home, farm, bare). The explanation for this phenomenon, which is reflected in other aspects of learning, is that similar things are more likely to cause mental 'interference' and, hence, are more difficult to memorize. It is found a list of similarly *sounding* words no more difficult to memorize than a dissimilar list. From this, Conrad concludes that when these deaf children read words they do not convert them into 'internal speech.' If they did convert what they read into sounds, then they would have shown the interference effect (which less deaf children who read better tended to do).

This evidence, in the hands of a 'bottom-up' theorist, would mean that such children cannot become good readers; they lack the 'basics' out of which reading grows. If one accepts this view, then only by developing a child's auditory awareness and auditory memory could he ever be expected to improve his reading. If this proves impossible, he will not improve.

Conrad's test, however, only used lists of isolated words. The evidence we reviewed in the last section shows that deaf readers possess and use some knowledge of the *structure* of written language and can read some sentences at least. For a radical 'top-down' theorist, this would imply that the child might be able to read well but only within the limits of his 'higher-order knowledge.' Put another way, perhaps deaf children do not have a specific *reading* problem at all but can read anything that they possess the requisite linguistic knowledge of. What limits their reading is an impoverished understanding of the structures of *language.* If so, any improvements in their understanding of English (with or without phonemic awareness) could lead to improved standards of reading. Furthermore, if the child does not invent or is not taught strategies for *interacting* with text, but learns or is taught that reading involves a word-by-word approach, then he may lack effective 'top-down' skills which, if developed, might also improve reading comprehension.

These issues are not resolved and cannot be resolved here. We will give our *opinions* later. However, a more recent theory of reading development and reading problems attempts to integrate 'bottom-up' and 'top-down' approaches in an account that, in company with our study of deaf children's reading lessons presented in the next section, puts reading problems into a somewhat new light and may suggest new strategies for approaching the teaching of reading. Briefly, Stanovich and

West (1979) have provided evidence for a model of the reading process based on the general idea the poor readers, who, they argue, lack automated GPC rules, try to enrich the information they have to work with when they read by making *more* use of 'top-down' information than good readers do. Thus, poor readers rely more on cues and clues derived from their general knowledge and knowledge of language to 'fill in' gaps left by poor reading. Because this strategy is prone on error, takes longer and demands a good deal of conscious effort, the poor reader reads slowly and understands less of what he reads than the good reader.

Deaf children, we shall argue, are in an analogous situation but are doubly handicapped as readers. They, too, as we shall see, use information from the immediate context and their general knowledge to supplement what they read. But they also have available fewer linguistic resources (e.g. less knowledge of grammatical aspects of language and word meanigs) than the poor hearing reader does. So, we suggest, the deaf reader is likely to put his or her intelligence to work in using paralinguistic, non-verbal and contextual cues to help understand what is being 'read.' If this process turns out to be slow, laborious and error prone, we should not be too surprised.

TEACHING READING TO DEAF CHILDREN

There are a bewildering number of different 'schemes' for teaching reading. Some are specially written for groups like deaf children; many are designed to teach any child. So far as we are aware, however, few attempts have been made to look systematically at *how* children are *actually* taught to read in the classroom. Nor, to our knowledge, are there any well-designed evaluations demonstrating the effectiveness of any reading scheme being used with deaf children. The field abounds in opinion but is noticeably lacking in evidence.

We have undertaken one small-scale but detailed study of reading lessons with deaf children aged between six and ten years. The aim of this research was to provide some insights into the experience of deaf and hearing children being taught to read (Howarth *et al.*, 1981). We do not claim, of course, that such a study is representative of all teaching practice, but we will argue that the processes and problems we observe are likely to be common ones for many deaf children and their teachers.

While we do not intend to go into details of statistical analysis here, we need to say a little about the procedure used. We wanted to compare the experiences of deaf and hearing children being taught to read. But one problem facing us was who should we compare with whom? Chronological age is not, as we know, a suitable basis for comparing the linguistic abilities or literary skills of deaf and hearing children. We also rejected the use of standard reading tests since any estimates of reading ages were likely to suffer from the difficulties outlined above.

It is often said, and has been demonstrated by Quigley and his colleagues, that the relationships between language abilities and the demands of reading are quite different for deaf and hearing children. The deaf child is likely to be exposed in print to both vocabulary and syntax that are not part of his existing linguistic competence. Indeed, Quigley *et al.* (1978) have argued that it is through reading that deaf children may first be exposed to many aspects of language. Whilst the structures encountered by young hearing readers, by and large, will have been present in their speech for some time (though, as we have said, reading is likely to introduce new structures and to make rather different uses of existing ones) this will not be true for most deaf children.

In sum, the relationship between the reader and what he is reading is likely to be fundamentally and quantitatively different for deaf and hearing children. We wanted a research strategy that would enable us to test this hypothesis.

Eventually, Patricia Howarth invented a simple but ingenious technique for matching children—one that, we feel, gives insights into the very different demands placed on hearing and deaf children when they are being taught to read. She filmed deaf children (from a number of schools) being taught to read in the normal course of classroom activities, recording a lesson that would have taken place had she not been there. Then she hunted around local primary schools for hearing children, to discover schools that were using the same reading books as those in the deaf sample. Having matched schools in this way, she waited until a teacher came to teach the same pages of the same book used with one of the deaf children. Thus, children were matched in terms of what they were being asked to read in the normal course of schooling.

The videotaped reading lessons were transcribed and several features were analysed. First, we determined how often reading 'stopped' and who initiated the stop. Did the teacher stop the child or did he stop spontaneously? Second, we looked at the reasons for stopping. How did the teacher react to and interpret each breakdown in reading? Third, we examined the children's reading rates. Together, these analyses suggested that both the experience of reading and the structure of the reading lesson were quite different for hearing and deaf children.

On average, deaf children both stopped reading spontaneously and were stopped more often by their teachers than the hearing children were. Furthermore, many more stops with hearing children included an element of praise from the teacher. There were also clear differences in the reasons for stopping. Teachers of hearing children usually interpreted stops as signalling a breakdown in a child's knowledge of grapheme-phoneme correspondence rules. In other words, they seemed to assume both that the children already knew the words and syntactic structures within the text, and that they were able to articulate the speech sounds appropriately. They simply could not *read* very well, having yet to develop adequate 'word attack' skills.

In contrast, although deaf children were also stopped because teachers decided they did not know these rules, they were more likely to be stopped because they did not *pronounce* a word properly (even though, at times, it seemed the child knew the word he was stopped on). The most marked difference, however, was that teachers of the deaf stopped their children much more often in order to teach the *meanings* of words. They also interpreted many of the child's own stops as evidence that he had met a word he did not know. In consequence, deaf children were stopped not only more frequently but for a greater *variety* of reasons than the hearing readers. Teachers of the deaf interpreted their children as having a greater range of difficulties and therefore pursued more complex and varied goals than the teachers of hearing did with their children. Thus, for most deaf children, the experience of reading and the structure of the reading lesson were quite different from that of hearing children reading the same pages of a book.

The third feature of the reading lessons we analysed—reading rate—was also revealing. In order to get a rough measure of reading fluency, we counted the number of words read between stops and divided this by the time taken to read them. In addition to differences between deaf and hearing children we found some marked differences between deaf children from different schools. Children from one school for the deaf were reading much more fluently and faster than other children.

If, for the moment, we ignore children from the 'successful' deaf school, the reading rates for the remaining deaf children were around twenty words per minute. For the hearing children, reading the same material, the average was sixty-four words per minute.

Experimental studies have shown that when we are exposed to speech rates of less than forty words per minute our comprehension starts to break down. It therefore appears highly unlikely that a deaf child with poor expressive and spoken language can make much sense out of text read at half this rate.

For a deaf child whose knowledge of language was well below that demanded in the text, reading lessons became a language lesson and speech-training exercise. The overall result was a slow, disjointed lesson punctuated by long periods of questioning, story telling and demonstration as the teacher attempted not only to get the child to read but also to learn language. We were left in considerable doubt about how such a lesson could leave the child with a sense of any 'story' or even of phrases and sentences in reading. What exactly, we wondered, does the deaf child think reading *is*?

Clearly, the behaviour of the teachers in this situation is an understandable response to a child with underdeveloped language, poor articulation and, perhaps, with little understanding of what 'stories' are all about. But, is the child 'ready' to read?

Returning now to the issue of 'top-down' processing and the gap between the demands of the text and the level of ability of the child, we can put forward some more specific hypotheses about why reading lessons are so difficult and, arguably, often counter-productive for both teacher and child. First, because deaf children read so slowly, stop so frequently, and, like young hearing children, tend to 'bark at print,' it is unlikely that they are exploiting any knowledge they might have about speech rhythm, intonation or stress. Even if they have enough low frequency hearing to hear and understand such cues to linguistic structure, they are unlikely to be producing or hearing them in lessons typified by long stops and slow, deliberate ariticulation. Furthermore, teachers never actually *read* to a child whilst he looked at print. Whereas, with a young hearing child, we can read to them, 'mapping' our fingers onto words read whilst he looks on, there was none of this with deaf children. The problem of divided attention discussed in chapter 8 emerges to further exacerbate the child's reading problems and the teacher's difficulties in teaching him. If the teacher wants to get the child to listen to a word or lip-read it, then she attracts his attention to her before doing so, presumably on the basis of the not unreasonable assumption that he will not hear the sounds well enough nor understand what she says without the help of lip-reading and other paralinguistic cues to meaning. This means that the child now has to *remember* the word, phrase or whatever and go back to the text in order to relate it to the written form. Thus, the process of reading for the child is disrupted by the problem of divided attention and limited by his intelligence and powers of memory.

Next comes the question of the gap between what he is trying to read and his likely level of linguistic ability. On our recordings, deaf children usually stopped reading, presumably because they could not read a word, did not recognize it, did not know it, could not pronounce it or could not understand its connection with other words (grammar). If they stopped on a noun or verb, teachers would usually try to define the word or remind them of it if they thought the children knew it. In the following examples, we illustrate some of the ploys used by teachers either to teach or prompt the child to recall a word.

C. (reads) The waves will take it on the rocks.
T. (interrupts) What are they? (pointing to the word 'waves')
C. Waves (waves 'goodbye').
T. Waves, yes, not that kind of wave. What wave . . .? Can you show me the wave?
C. (Child picks up a bookmark and starts to wave it.)
T. No, not that kind of wave.

C. (Undulating, 'sea waves').
T. Those waves. Yes.

Even more difficulty was encountered with 'function' words such as demonstratives and pronouns. For example, consider what happened a little later in the 'wave' session.

T. The waves will take it. (Points to boat and to rocks in picture. Looks questioningly at the child.) . . . It? What's 'it'?
C. It.
T. What's it?
C. It.
T. What will they take? What's 'it'?
C. (Child points to a rock and squeals.)
T. No, not the rock. They're the rocks, look (pointing to 'rock' in text). Can they get it on the rocks? Can they get what? . . . It's the boat.
C. The boat.

In this we will illustrate the complex 'pluri-functional' nature of many so-called function words. Pronouns, for example, serve more than one purpose in language. They take their meaning from the role they play in grammar and cannot be defined 'ostensibly' as can some nouns, verbs and adjectives. The child's problem in *reading* and *understanding* such words often lies not in his inability to *recognize* the word but in an inadequate knowledge of its function and the grammatical structures within which it is embedded.

Research by Quigley and his colleagues has illustrated the problems that deaf readers face with many aspects of written syntax. They have also shown that the gap between deaf children's comprehension of syntactic structures and the demands of texts written to teach children how to read is so wide that it presents enormous if not insuperable demands on the deaf reader (Quigley and Kretschmer, 1982). In our study, too, children were often expected to read text containing grammatical structures that were not a part of their linguistic knowledge. If the deaf child has a potential to read, we suggest that the sorts of reading lessons we have just considered are hardly likely to achieve it.

We have already mentioned that seven children from one school (average hearing loss 92 dB) were much more successful than the other deaf children. They were reading at an average seventy-seven words per minute and, in some cases, were articulating at a faster rate than their (younger) hearing matches. One deaf child, for example, was reading at 142 words per minute. The fastest hearing child read at 130. There were stops for reflection on linguistic meanings but usually of a quite different order to those considered above, as the following excerpt from a transcript illustrates. The child involved in the interaction below is ten years of age, has a hearing loss of 108 dB and a non-verbal IQ on the WISC-R of 129. She was one of the deafest but also one of the most intelligent children in the sample. She read at an average of almost eighty-eight words per minute from a text with an estimated reading age level of ten years.

C. (reading) . . . sitting on the edge of the rocks, waiting for the dragon to finish his forty winks (stops reading, laughs and looks at the teacher).
T. What are forty winks?
C. (Pupil laughs again and blinks her eyes rapidly) Meaning nap.
T. No, oh no, it doesn't mean it literally that he goes one (blinking . . .) two, three.
C. (Giggles.)
T. It doesn't mean it literally.
C. (Shakes head.)
T. If you don't mean something literally, like *catching* a cold . . . .
C. Oh, I see. It's an idiom.
T. Yes, he's not literally going to have forty winks.
C. (Giggles and starts to read again.)

Although we have no objective measures to determine how far these children *understood* what they read, their rate of articulation (much of which was intelligible) together with their responses to teacher questions and the occasional outbreak of mirth at funny bits persuaded us that they were understanding what they read.

It would obviously be unwise to try to make any general pronouncements about the 'causes' of success from such a small sample. However, in other studies of children drawn from this same school we found evidence that their linguistic abilities (and mathematical competence) were significantly better than those of children of similar age, sex, hearing loss and (in some studies) non-verbal intelligence but drawn from other schools. In addition to using and maintaining the most appropriate hearing aids available for each child, this school also places a great deal of emphasis on how language is *used* with children.

In relation to their reading, one factor that we believe is implicated in their success is that the school leaves formal reading lessons to a relatively late stage (this varies according to the child's linguistic development but is often around eight years or so) on the grounds that reading should only begin when the child's language meets the demands of text. They reject the notion that reading can or should be used to *teach* language. Rather, before this, every child experiences regular, intensive concentration on conversation and a great deal of emphasis on listening to story telling. Our evidence cannot be offered as conclusive support for this view, but the success of these children does show that severe or profound hearing loss is *not* an inevitable barrier to reading. We suspect that the quality of teaching contributed something to their success.

WHY CAN'T MOST DEAF CHILDREN READ?

Deaf children, taking a reading test, are likely to adopt special and often non-linguistic or non-syntactically based reading strategies. Where the demands of the test, or a reading text, are well beyond the child's levels of linguistic competence it seems inevitable that this must be the case. Deaf children are bound to put their intelligence to work to seek solutions to such demands, using their knowledge of the world and their pragmatic knowledge of language (e.g. word associations) in attempts to use general contextual cues to overcome their limited linguistic resources.

When we looked at reading lessons we found analogous and complementary features in the teaching and learning process. Often the child's attention was concentrated on the meanings and 'sounds' associated with words isolated from their syntactic and story context. Furthermore, the process often took place at such a slow pace that it seems inconceivable that children could be discovering much, if anything about the structural properties of text or language. Indeed, when, in another study, we examined the eye movements of deaf children reading and compared them with those of hearing children with similar reading age scores. Beggs, Breslaw and Wilkinson, 1982), we found that the deaf (but not the hearing) children were reading using a word-by-word strategy, their eyes sighting on each word in turn. The eyes of their hearing 'matches' ranged more widely and less predictably over the text, bypassing words or word sequences, as happens in more skilled reading. One deaf child in this study not only displayed word-word fixations in reading but actually read from left to right on one line and then dropped his eyes to the word at the right-hand side of the line below and proceeded to read that line *backwards!*

Our analyses of reading assessment and teaching of reading must surely show that for a group of deaf children, who we have no reason to believe are atypical, the experience, purpose and significance of reading were often fundamentally different in kind from that of hearing children. But these studies focused on linguistic structures that were often too far in advance of children's knowledge of language to make productive reading possible. Indeed, if there is any weight in the hypothesis explored in chapter 3, that effective teaching and learning demands that a child is confronted with *manageable* and *intelligible* problems, then we must conclude that the activity of reading for the deaf child in many of the lessons we have observed is not only unlikely to be successful but may be counterproductive. Constant failure in the face of insuperable difficulty destroys the learner.

Conrad's research, in company with several more recent studies (e.g. Leybaert, Alegria and Fonck, 1983; Quigley and Paul, 1984), shows that deaf children read well to the extent that they display a knowledge of the phonemic structure of language. Children lacking such knowledge rely on visual features of text and, within the limits of known methods for teaching reading, there seems to be no way in which such children can achieve literacy. Rather, in reading lessons and tests of reading they must supplement their limited abilities to read by using their general knowledge and intelligence to develop strategies that guarantee only a limited degree of success. Similarly, when faced with complex grammatical structures, they display strategies for trying to understand what is on the page, often leading quite systematically to misunderstanding. Teachers, faced with trying to teach reading to children with these difficulties, often respond by converting what are designed to be reading lessons into sessions on language and speech. In so doing, we suggest they are likely to help children 'learn' those special but limited strategies that they adopt to try to make sense of what they read.

More optimistically, the fact that some children were relatively fluent in reading lessons despite hearing losses in excess of 85 dB (the average was 92 dB) questions any absolute statements about the theoretical impossibility of deaf children learning to read. It may be that these children have something 'special.' Conrad found only five 'special' children in his group with losses over 85 dB whose reading ages were commensurate with their chronological ages. They evidenced good internal speech. However, beyond congratulating the child, his teachers and parents, Conrad was unable to give any insights into 'how' these children achieved their special status. We need to explore the possibility that this arises out of experience and education. This also means that the focus of research into reading must change from a concentration on tests and large-scale issues to detailed studies of different processes of instruction and evaluations of their effectiveness.

WHAT ABOUT TEACHERS OF READING?

Although our research into reading has been largely descriptive and was not designed to test any particular theory of if and how reading can be taught, we do have some practical suggestions that might help to improve the practice of teaching reading to deaf children.

First, we suggest that teachers of the deaf use their reading lessons more 'diagnostically.' By recording lessons (an audiorecording should suffice) it should be possible to estimate a child's reading rate and fluency. The number and purposes of any stops in reading can also be diagnosed. If the number of stops for 'teaching' language and articulation are in excess of those for *reading per se*, then it is a clear signal that the text is too difficult or that the child is not ready for formal reading lessons. Similarly, if the child's rate of articulation drops below forty words or so per minute, it is unlikely that he understands much of what is being read. If the teacher is having to recourse continually to models, drawings or interactions with a child, designed to give him more information to help understand a word or phrase, then the teacher might ask whether they are, in fact, helping to *create* problems for the child by building up or even teaching those inappropriate reading strategies that many children display.

Given the problems that many deaf children face in speech *articulation*, the possibilities offered by more frequent use of 'silent reading' might be explored. This might also direct teachers' (and perhaps children's) attention away from the meanings of 'words' to the comprehension of *text* as advocated by Ewoldt (1981).

More radically, we suggest that more attention should be paid to conversation and story telling as foundations for literacy, for reasons explored in this book.

There is quite clearly no known 'answer' to the reading problems of deaf children. Whether our own findings simply shed more gloom onto an already depressing scene or help to reinforce attempts at new approaches to teaching deaf children how to make sense of reading remains to be seen. The issue of 'internal speech' and phonemic awareness as 'inevitable' constraints on the potential for literacy in deaf children is still an open one. Conrad (1981), for example, has recently discussed possible strategies for teaching reading that are not based on a knowledge of GPC rules. As yet, however, his speculations, like those of all of us in this complex area, only provide promissory notes and, perhaps, the motivation to try to find some new approaches to the teaching of reading.

READING, WRITING, TALKING AND LISTENING

In the last section, we used the results of tests of reading involving large groups of children to gain some insights into the deaf child's understanding of grammatical structure. However, as we admitted, using such evidence to make statements about what is going on in a particular child's mind when he reads or communicates is hazardous. Now, however, we begin to explore the linguistic abilities of severely and profoundly deaf children in more depth in order to test some of our ideas about linguistic competence.

The obvious strategy for exploring what a particular child knows about and does with language is to study that child in depth. Using this approach, for example, Ivimey (1976) was able to show that the one very deaf child he studied did develop a productive linguistic system, although it displayed a number of unusual characteristics in comparison with what we know about hearing children's language. Hearing children, however, also display very marked individual differences in how they develop and use language (e.g. Bowerman, 1982). Tests of language, based on group averages which overlook such individual differences, may present a misleading picture of a 'normal child', one who does not, in fact, exist, except in numerical form! On the other hand, case studies may tempt us into false overgeneralizations if we assume that the study of one child necessarily tells us much about any other.

We need both types of research. When the outcomes of case studies can be integrated with the general picture derived from larger-scale ones, they reinforce each other's conclusions. Since this ideal state of affairs has not yet been achieved in studies of hearing children's linguistic development, we should not be too surprised to find that it is far from being achieved with the deaf, who are rarer, more difficult to study and present so many other challenges when we try to interpret what they know.

In this study, we steer something of a 'middle course' between these two approaches. We look in some detail at several aspects of fifty severely and profoundly deaf children's (mean hearing loss 93 dB, average age ten years eight months) experience and use of language but achieve nothing like sufficient depth to enable us to say in any detail what each child's 'theory' of language is, although we will test ideas about aspects of such theories. However, our main motivation in undertaking this work was to explore the relationships between children's receptive and expressive abilities with spoken and written English.

There are many different opinions about and attitudes towards the nature of linguistic competence in the deaf. In the last chapter we saw, for example, that their reading abilities can be conceptualized as a rag-bag of special 'tricks' involving little more than a limited sight vocabulary, some knowledge of word associations derived from everyday experience and certain special strategies for meeting the demands of tests. On the other hand, we also cited evidence favouring the view that deaf children possess a limited but productive understanding of linguistic strcutre. However, it might be argued that very deaf children, such as those we are studying, only possesss knowledge of a few stereotypical or 'baked' sentence forms (Van Uden, 1970) which they have learned by rote memory. The hallmark of linguistic competence is a remarkable degree of 'generativity' and creativity (Chomsky, 1980). Young hearing children produce spontaneously a vast number of 'original' utterances that they have never heard. They use linguistic 'rules' to create novel acts of speech. Are deaf children also 'generative' in their language, as we argued in this book, or are they simply using rigid and well-learned 'formulae' for producing and understanding the written word?

Another related issue concerns the relationship between talk and text for children with hearing losses greater than 85 dB. Conrad, recall, produced evidence indicating both that internal speech was important for reading and that most children with losses greater than 85 dB did not possess that competence. Does this mean that *reading* processes in such children, being visually based, show no connection with their powers of speech or their receptive ability in understanding speech? This question, amongst other things, is what our study of fifty deaf children was designed to answer.

The investigation includes observations of children's performance in classroom conversations and their scores on a reading test. We also asked each child who took part to play a communication game with one of his peers (communicating both through verbal and written messages). We videorecorded the interactions and developed a system for scoring children's utterances for degree of syntactic accuracy. Non-verbal IQs, teacher ratings and audiograms were also collected.

For each child, then, we had a number of indicators of his receptive and expressive language. We outline each of these indicators and explore the relationships between them below. For fuller details see Griffiths (1983). We have used several of these measures of linguistic performance in previous studies, but with different groups of children, so were not able to explore the relationships between them. This investigation also provided an opportunity to test the robustness of some of our previous findings. Could we repeat our previous results with another set of children and teachers?

PERFORMANCE IN THE CLASSROOM

By filming each child in normal classroom conversation sessions we were able to check our previous results of the relationships between teacher moves and child responses and those between teacher power and child initiative and loquacity. Would we find the same pattern of relationships? We did. In fact, the results of this investigation were almost identical to those found in the initial analyses.

More important for our present purposes, however, was the study of individual children. The main measure we obtained from the classroom sessions was each child's average length of turn, but we also used a number of more specific and, we hoped, revealing measures. How often did the child respond to his teacher's questions with appropriate answers? How lengthy were these? Did he take up options to speak after a teacher made a contribution or phatic or did he simply respond non-verbally with a nod or whatever?

THE COMMUNICATION GAME

In a previous investigation we had adapted a widely used technique from the study of hearing children's communicative competence. In this task, two children sit or stand facing each other across a table. Interposed between them is a screen which hides two sets of materials. In the situation used here, that material consisted of two identical books containing a series of pictures which depict the same set of characters in somewhat similar settings. Thus it was possible for a child to confuse one picture with others if a description given to him was incomplete or ambiguous. The children could see each other but not their partner's picture book. One child was asked to describe a given picture to his peer who then had to try to select the target picture from his copy of the book.

The interactions were videotaped for subsequent transcription and analysis. In previous studies using this technique, we compared deaf and hearing children's performances and found that when deaf children recognized and could identify the important elements of the task, their performance was comparable to hearing children's. We found, for example, no evidence that deaf children were any more 'egocentric' in providing appropriate messages than similarly aged hearing peers. In this earlier study (Breslaw *et al.*, 1981) we were interested in the children's degree of success in getting messages across to each other. We the found not only similarities and differences between deaf and hearing communicators but also some very marked differences between the performances of deaf children from different schools. Although they were matched for age, sex, hearing loss and non-verbal intelligence (and suffered no known additional handicap) the children from one school performed much better than their comparison groups (note that the successful children were drawn from the same school that produced relatively fluent readers described in chapter 11).

Such marked differences in performance prompted us to look in more detail at the language used by the children and led us to develop a measure of 'syntactic accuracy' of verbal communication; this was employed in the present study of fifty children. Even without a formal system of measurement it was clear to us that the deaf children who produced good scores on this task were also producing more grammatically well-formed utterances. But how might we produce a more formal measure of accuracy?

As anyone who has listened to very deaf children will testify, transcribing their language and 'glossing' what they say to give an account of what they are trying to *mean* is no simple affair. The situation we used confers two advantages over the use of 'spontaneous' utterances. First, knowing the material being described we have some sense of what the child is talking about. Second, if that child gets his message across successfully, then we could be reasonably confident that it contained the minimal units of information needed to make a selection. However, even with these constraints to guide us we were not confident in our ability to provide a good measure of syntactic accuracy. When we transcribed the interactions, we also coded any gestures that could help to interpret and augment what the children said.

How could we derive a numerical assessment from such utterances? Basically, what we did was to compare each (communicatively successful) utterance from every child with an 'idealized' version of it. This 'idealization' involved keeping as far as possible to the actual words and word order used by the child. We would *add 'missing' elements* such as pronouns, auxiliary verbs, tense endings and determiners where, we felt, these would normally be uttered in a well-formed version of what the child had said. We also *deleted* any 'incorrect' elements such as an irrelevant tense ending or an 'extra,' redundant pronoun. Third, we *substituted* for wrong elements the correct ones (e.g. if a child used a pronoun that did not agree in number or case with the noun it referred to). Fourth, we *relocated* words where necessary. When we had completed this 'idealization' process we simply counted the number of elements in the original version and the number of additions, deletions, substitutions and relocations we had made. The 'accuracy' score was derived from these.

We accept that this is a rather crude procedure. Conversely, if we *did* find some reasonable relationships between this attempt to assess linguistic competence and the others, it seemed reasonable to accept it as a crude but useful technique. In the event, as we shall see, it did show some interpetable connections with other aspects of linguistic competence.

We used the same idealization and calculation techniques to assess the accuracy of *written* messages derived for each child from the same task setting. These, of coruse, were somewhat easier to score since we did not have problems of speech intelligibility and non-verbal, gestural communication to deal with.

READING TEST ASSESSMENT

Given our scepticism about the use of hearing-referenced tests of reading with the deaf, it may seem surprising that we elected to employ one in this study. However, as we have already said, we do not suggest that reading tests measure *nothing* linguistic with deaf children; rather, they are likely to tap *different* processes in deaf and hearing readers. Indeed, this study was designed, in part, to see if reading test performances by deaf children *do* relate to other measures of their linguistic abilities.

The test we decided to use, the Edinburgh Reading Test (Stage 1, 1977) was chosen because it fulfilled a number of criteria. First, the test designers offer it as a test that teachers can use *diagnostically*. It includes a number of sub-scales concerned with vocabulary, syntax, comprehension and sequencing ability to provide a 'profile' for each child. The items within each sub-scale were also designed to test specific aspects of each area of reading. Second, the test designers had not only recently standardized the test on a hearing sample but had also kept detailed records of *error patterns* which we could use to make comparisons with those of our sample.

Each child was tested individually by the same member of the research team to help maintain consistency of administration.

RELATIONSHIPS BETWEEN MEASURES

Children who produced the longest turns in the classroom gained higher scores on the reading test. They also produced the most syntactically well-formed written messages. Those children who *wrote* relatively well-formed messages were also likely to show relatively accurate *spoken* messages.

From this pattern of relationships, we suggest, it is reasonable to conclude that this group of very deaf but otherwise 'normal' children possess different levels of generative linguistic competence. This competence includes the creation of written and spoken messages, listening and talking in class, and reading. There were also some more detailed and specific relationships that strengthened and enriched this interpretation.

When we looked in more depth at the relationships between classroom language and the other indicators, we found that the strongest relationships involved the length of children's responses to a teacher's *Wh-type* questions, and, to a lesser extent, responses to her *contributions*. Responses to phatics and two-choice questions were much less 'predictive' of reading and syntax. We suggest that this finding is consistent with the view of that the various measures are 'genuinely' linguistic in nature. Answering a teacher's Wh-type questions appropriately with relatively wordy responses demands competence in *both* receptive and expressive language. As we saw already in this book, answering such Wh-type questions is demanding and, in consequence, we would expect longer, more appropriate answers from the linguistically more able child.

The fact that responses to *contributions* were also predictive of other aspects of linguistic functioning supports another observation made in chapter 9. Generally speaking, children who gave long, appropriate answers to Wh-type questions also gave long responses to teacher contributions. This is consistent with our observation that the verbally more able children were 'understanding' their teachers' contributions and making relatively long comments in return (rather than simply nodding or making a phatic move). This, of course, is a speculative *interpretation* of the findings but one that is consistent with other features of our observations.

Responses to two-choice questions are usually terse and easy' (but recall the two-choice question sessions in chapter 10). Perhpas this is why they do not discriminate between the relatively competent and less competent children. Similarly, as we said in chapter 10, even verbally less able children can be encouraged to give long responses to phatic moves, but they also tended to become incoherent and difficult to understand when they did so. Perhaps this is why phatics, unlike Wh-type questions and contributions, do not help to sort out the relatively more able children.

However, it might still be argued that some other factor, such as intelligence, explains why some children do relatively well in different 'test' contexts. To see if this might be the case we examined the relationships between our linguistic measures and intelligence (amongst other things).

LINGUISTIC COMPETENCE AND INTELLIGENCE

As part of the investigation, we noted every child's age, sex, hearing loss and non-verbal intelligence score on Raven's Progressive Matrices (Raven, 1958). One can ask, for example, if children who are relatively less deaf with high scores on the intelligence test fare better on our linguistic measures than those who are deafer and scored well on the IQ test. We found no evidence that intelligence or hearing loss contributed to success on the linguistic measures.

On first sight, this might seem counter-intuitive and at variance with the results of other studies. However, the reason is almost certainly due to the very different composition of our group compared with those in other studies such as Conrad's (1979), which involved a larger and more heterogeneous sample than ours. Conrad, for instance, tested children whose levels of hearing loss varied considerably. It would have been surprising if he had not found, for example, that partially hearing children did not read better, on average, than the profoundly deaf ones. Our group of children were all severely or profoundly deaf, and so were far more similar as a group. Conrad did find a relationship between measures of linguistic ability and non-verbal intelligence, however. But he too found that intelligence was *less* influential in its effects on the performances of very deaf children, such as those involved in our study.

We conclude, then, that neither differences in levels of measured intelligence nor differences in hearing loss acconted for variations in children's performance. Rather, the different measures, we suggest, were tapping variations in levels of *linguistic* competence.

BOYS AND GIRLS

We also investigated the effects of gender on our language measures. Although we found somewhat higher overall scores from the deaf girls, this was not statistically significant. However, we did discover a pattern in the scores that is consistent with our argument that the various tests measure linguistic competence.

As we have already said, the Edinburgh Test includes four different sub-scales (syntax, comprehension, sequencing ability and vocabulary). We found that girls who were relatively good on one sub-scale were also likely to do relatively well on others and on the other measures of linguistic competence. A similar pattern was found for the boys but the correlations between measures (though still significant) were significantly weaker than those for the girls.

Work with both hearing and deaf children (e.g. Norden, 1975) has produced similar findings. Bascically, a given measure of *linguistic* ability in girls tends to be predictive of a *range* of other abilities. Such relationships are usually less marked in boys. The 'greater variability of the male' is characteristic of hearing children (Hutt, 1972). A similar finding in our deaf sample suggests that we were tapping differences that are linguistic in nature.

As part of the study, we asked teachers to rate their children's levels of verbal proficiency and general ability. Were the teachers' assessments of children's intellectual and linguistic competence consistent with our measures? They were. As Conrad also found, teachers' assessments of children's linguistic abilities correlate relatively well with scores on more formal tests. The fact that teachers agreed with our findings, particularly on assessments of verbal competence, suggests that both their perceptions and our tests are reasonably sensitive indicators of linguistic competence.

More interesting, however, was the pattern of relationships between teacher assessments, measures of children's competence and teacher's *behaviour* in the classroom.

We found that teachers were significantly more likely to *control and repair* children whom they perceived, and we measured, as being less competent linguistically. This strengthens and extends the observations made in chapter 9. Children who are presumably less easy to understand and who find understanding more difficult are the *most* likely to encounter styles of teacher interaction that inhibit their active involvement in conversation. Such teaching styles, as we argued in chapters 9 and 10, do not make the less able child's task in communication *easier*. Rather, an increase in teacher control and repair exacerbates his problems and is likely to depress his desire to communicate.

These results suggest that simply by listening to a *teacher's* utterances towards a child, one gets a reasonably good picture of his likely competence. If that child is continually subjected to high control and a good deal of repair, then he is *unlikely* to be verbally competent. Nor is he likely to be gaining much from the experience.

We are thus brought back to our notion of the 'spiral of control and repair,' along with some new insights into why our classroom measures correlate so well with other indicators of verbal competence. Because teachers are controlling and repairing the less able child, we know, from the work outlined in chapters 9 and10, that the child is going to remain low in initiative and say little. Thus, the teacher, so to speak, 'emphasizes' individual differences in children's classroom performance by greater control and repair of the less able child, depressing his initiative and loquacity. Connections between children's classroom performance and our other test scores are *strengthened* by teaching styles.

THE EDINBURGH READING TEST AND MDP

In last chapter, we outlined our hypotheses about aspects of deaf children's grammatical knowledge of English. These, however, were formulated on the basis of other people's data and such *post hoc* analyses are always questionable. Only when one makes and tests predictions *before* seeing the evidence can one be confident that any hypothesis has been tested. These provide an opportunity to see if children follow the Minimum Distance Principle outlined in the last chapter. We made predictions about children's answers by applying the MDP to each item and found that the majority of the group always gave the answer we expected. Sometimes, these produced a correct response. For example, one item is 'Janet kissed Philip, who ran away.' The reader then has to answer the question 'Did Janet run away? . . . yes/no.' Almost 80 per cent of the children circled the 'no.' The MDP would lead to the interpretation 'Philip ran away' and, thus, gives a 'correct' response. However, on another item: 'The policeman who chased Fred was angry,' only 36 per cent gave the answer 'policeman,' since the MDP would lead to the interpretation that 'Fred was angry.'

The fact that children's errors on this and many other items were predictable, illustrates both that they 'interact' with text in the way we expected and also that the test can be used diagnostically to gain some ideas about the strategies a child is using in reading.

SUMMARY AND IMPLICATIONS

Casual observation of deaf children in various language situations might lead one to believe that their linguistic competence was a selection of 'special tricks' (like those strategies used in reading tests) learnt to enable them to cope with the specific demands placed upon them at school. However, we have identified four measures of linguistic competence that show a high degree of intercorrelation. This led us to conclude that very deaf children *do* display a generative linguistic competence, albeit one limited in scope.

Having established that these measures are sensitive to differences in linguistic ability, we can consider the possibility of developing them into assessment tools. The Warnock Report (DES, 1978) on the education of children with special needs in England and Wales, and the ensuring Act of Parliament in 1981, made similar recommendations to those incorporated in legislation in other Western countries. It recommended that all children with special needs, including deaf children, should be educated in ordinary schools as far as possible. It is therefore becoming increasingly important for educational psychologists and the peripatetic teachers involved in specialist back-up services for deaf children to have access to reliable and valid tests of progress and achievement. These tests will be necessary not only to establish which children are likely to benefit by being educated in ordinary schools but also to monitor their progress once they get there.

Our work on the value of hearing-referenced reading tests with deaf children has pointed to several problems in interpreting the scores of deaf children. One possible route to improved assessment would be to undertake the development of a battery of assessment tools (based on measures like those used in this study and also those outlines in our discussions of the stages of pre-verbal development in chapter 8) that have been specifically designed for, and could be standardized on, deaf children. Using such techniques, it should be possible to monitor the progress of children in their examination *context* with some reasonably 'direct' measures of communicative competence.

Since the several indicators of linguistic performance we have provided suggest a generative linguistic system, it may well be a useful exercise not only to use these measures for the purposes outlined above but also to identify exceptions to the rule and look more closely at children who do *not* follow the usual pattern. It is possible, for example, that a child who offers relatively long turns in conversation with his teacher (especially after teacher Wh-type questions and personal contributions) but who performs poorly on reading tests may have specific reading problems. There is no reason to suppose that such reading problems are any less rare amongst deaf than hearing children. The difficulty is to separate any specific reading problems from the effects of deafness itself. What we do once we have identified any such children is, of course, another matter! However, knowing who they are might be the first step in helping to improve their situation (particularly if their receptive and expressive language levels are relatively good).

A further issue concerns the extent to which teaching techniques and educational philosophy influence children's linguistic competence. We have provided some evidence of 'school effects' in this and other chapters and studies in the United States have also identified such effects (e.g. Quigley and Paul, 1984). Conrad has shown that intelligence and hearing loss are two determinants of linguistic abilities in the deaf. However, our data include the existence of other determinants which may be associated with home, school and/or teaching techniques. These demand further attention in research into the nature and origins of individual differences and their relationships to social, educational and demographic factors. We also need to establish whether helping teachers to avoid unprofitable strategies in conversation will lead to long-term changes in children's conversational and grammatical abilities. Would such improvements lead to progress in reading and writing?

This leads us to consider the role of teaching style and teacher judgements of child ability. Conrad has shown that hearing loss and IQ are the variables that correlate most highly with reading. We have shown that these variables are also associated with a child's experience in the classroom. Children with less hearing and lower IQ scores are likely to be judged (and measured) as less verbally competent. These are the children who usually meet with most repair and control. This underlines our earlier suspicions that such children are more likely to meet with secondary consequences of their handicap. Our intervention studies have shown that such a relationship is not inevitable; teachers can change their style and children change their responses accordingly. Again, an exploration of the effects on children of long-term exposure to more contingent and enabling styles should help to determine the extent to which children's problems are 'made,' or an inevitable consequence of their handicap.

We have established connections between various measures of speech and literacy Conrad used different measures and also found connections between these aspects of deaf children's linguistic competence, whilst the work of Dodd and Hermelin (1977) raises the possibility that lip-reading may form a basis for reading. Their hypothesis could provide an explanation for the relationships between the measures of spoken and written language of very deaf children found in this study. Another possibility is that the relationships between speech and text for such children may be mediated by vocal articulation. If a child's speech, even if it is largely unintelligible, is based on *systematic* patterns of articulation, then it is conceivable that when such a child reads he does so by recognizing words in terms of the vocal movements he has to make in pronouncing them. Thus vocal articulation (which some afford an important place in theories of reading, e.g. Baddeley, 1979) also provides a potential explanation for connections between talk and text in our group of children.

Whilst we cannot yet provide a compelling theoretical explanation for the data from this study, the fact remains that connections between the receptive and expressive speech abilities and reading and writing competence exist in very deaf primary school children. This conclusion implies that the development of spoken language influences reading and writing; that exposure to print facilitates the development of receptive and expressive speech—or both! What we cannot do, as yet, is to say how and why such connections originate and develop in a particular child. However, as we have said, we suspect that educational management and classroom experiences in discourse play a central role in influencing the child's abilities.

Finally, our studies revealed some interesting sex differences. Generally speaking, although there were no significant differences in overall levels of achievement by boys and girls, the girls' scores on each test tended to be more closely related to each other than was the case for boys. We will not be drawn here into arguments about *why* this should be the case (see Springer and Deutsch, 1981 for a short but succinct review of the question of neural organization in deaf and hearing people). Whether one subscribes to the view that such sex differneces are attributable to biologically determined differences in the structure of the male and female brain and/or to the different social and linguistic experiences of boys and girls, it seems to be the case that the same influences act upon deaf children too. This could, then, be cited as one line of evidence favouring the view that linguistic development in deaf and hearing people displays some important similarities.

The final conclusion, though, is that however we eventually explain how very deaf children develop linguistic competence in spoken and written language and why their competence is often limited in characteristic ways, the findings of our research indicate strongly that there *is* such a competence to *be* explained.

12

From Childhood to Adolescence

Influence of visual handicap on personal development

UNPREDICTABILITY with inconsistent attitudes towards parents and teachers can be a well-known characteristic of adolescents as they attempt to adjust to change and search for identity, but idealistic and generous aspects of behaviour can be strongly evident at this stage of personal development too. Those who teach and counsel visually handicapped adolescents must be moved to consider whether lack of sight or defective sight is likely to be a source of additional stress and anxiety at this sensitive time.

Certainly it might be expected that doubts about personal acceptability and attractiveness and apprehension that the presence of visual handicap may limit career and marriage prospects would be experienced. Lowenfeld (1971) considers that the stages of adolescence through which the young person normally passes in growing up are likely to be encountered in the same sequence in the case of visually handicapped adolescents. However, the self-concept that he has developed by adolescence will be a crucial factor, governing the way in which such a young person tries to come to terms with new or newly perceived problems and opportunities in personal and working life.

A study of personality differences between blind and sighted children by Zahran (1965) reviews the literature which is divided between those who contend that blindness leads to compensatory behaviour which may be accompanied by introversion and even maladjustment, and those who find that the process of adjustment in blind persons is not significantly different from that of the sighted with regard to basic personality variables. Using matched groups of blind and sighted chidlren tested with the Williams Intelligence Test for Children with Defective Vision, the researcher also constructed a Blind Children's Structured Interview, a Sentence Completion Test and a Semantic Differential. He also used the Junior Maudsley Personality Inventory. The results of most of the tests showed a statistically non-significant difference in favour of the sighted, which, on balance, lends some support to the second point of view.

But Meighan (1971) on examining the self-concept of the visually handicapped adolescent reveals a fragility in this aspect of the personality in many of these young people evident to their teachers as either timidity or over-compensation. His study evidenced that on the Tenessee Self-Concept Scale the scores of the majority of the visually handicapped showed a distinctly negative direction with doubts about work achievement and implications of anxiety and unhappiness; identity scores were low revealing the tendency for these young people to see themselves as impoverished in terms of their physical self and in their behaviour although, perhaps remarkably, their levels of self-criticism approximated to the norm in the majority of cases.

A striking fact emerging from this study is that the scores of the visually handicapped had an almost universally recognizable pattern cutting across differences in sex and with little difference between demographic groups. The common factor of visual disability seemed to be the one that affected the scores profoundly to the extent of showing up profiles of striking similarity. The discussion which is a sequel to the enquiry, concludes than an attempt to resolve the tendency of fixing a negative identity should be considered as a major development hazard in the case of the visually handicapped adolescent. In view of the crucial role of the self-concept in all areas of striving this is indeed a vital matter of concern.

That lack of self-confidence about social competence, personal appearance and adjustment to blindness increases towards adolescence is shown in Miller's (1970) study in which Hardy's anxiety scale for the blind was used with 50 blind young people at a residential school, giving further point to the need these young people have for specialized training and an understanding of their needs in a social situation. The period of adolescence itself is late to begin such training; techniques and counselling to forearm the young person against the challenges and uncertainties that he will encounter as he faces adult life in a world designed primarily for those who see, should be introduced during his school years.

Self-concept in the years at school

The roots of his self-confidence or lack of it may well go deep into the feelings that the adolescent has had about his acceptance or rejection during the first school years. This in its turn can be dependent upon the relationship which he has been able to make with people whom he considers 'special,' possibly reflecting in his own person the attitude of his parents towards his school and his teachers.

As he grows up his general confidence may be enhanced if he is able to develop basic skills at an age that is reasonably approximate to that of his seeing peers. Timely and effective training without over-stress can be helpful in enabling him to master day-to-day skills, such as those involving mealtimes, travelling and dressing and looking after himself in a way that will tend to minimize embarrassing situations which could otherwise be resented by the adolescent who is especially sensitive about the impression he makes on others. Indeed throughout his childhood and adolescence he may be vulnerable to the evident reaction of sighted people to his handicap.

The child who is obviously and evidently blind may have to bear with comments or even exclamations about this fact from seeing adults whom he encounters casually, whilst the child who is poorly sighted may have his difficulties ascribed to causes unrelated to his vision. It would hardly be surprising, therefore, for the visually handicapped adolescent to shrink from being noticed because of his handicap, although he is likely to be in a stronger position of tolerance if he has felt valued for himself and has experienced success; enthusiasm and interest in commonly accepted activities—swimming, stamp collecting, piano playing or singing can provide him with a talking point to share and a recognizable reason to increase his self-esteem.

In his primary school years the visually handicapped child will need both structured and unstructured situations in which to learn as much as possible about the people and the environment that surround him, through exploring, investigating and conversing; it must not be assumed that he will spontaneously be driven by curiosity to do so. Active play may need to be initiated, but through it he can be helped to externalize some of his inner conflicts. He needs the chance to destroy and build, to act out hate and love, and to test out his relationships with others. As he grows up his self-regard may risk being affected by the differences that he can become aware of between himself and his fully sighted friends and acquaintances, more especially if this is a subject of remark by onlookers. He may become aware that some things that they cna do easily he cannot seem to do at all, such as recognizing distant objects or people, and there will be some things he can only do imperfectly or in an adapted way, such as playing football or reading. Resentment of these facts is possible but genuine success in its own right, such as the ability to read braille well or in having a good memory for the sports results can help him to be well regarded. His sense of security can be fostered by a stable framework of dependable events and reactions from adults, including steadiness and lack of dismay in the face of frustrations. These qualities he may need to draw on from his teacher upon whose reserves of emotional stability and tolerance he can depend.

Confidence is likely to have been helped if during his school years the visually defective pupil has had enough time to complete his tasks and secure his objectives, so that by the time he reaches adolescence, he has behind him repeated experiences of achievement; a childhood history littered with unfinished tasks and unachieved goals can undermine this.

When he progresses from primary to secondary school, the educationally blind or partially sighted child may, like his sighted peers, have a complete change of educational envrionment. This can be stimulating, and offer him the challenge of a larger community, bringing a fresh start that can flower into a greater maturity in social adjustment as a result of contact with older pupils. The opportunity for greater personal independence in a community should be afforded to him. In the case of some residential schools for the blind or the partially sighted a secondary school may take a large regional or even a national catchment of pupils, and thus be situated further from the pupil's home than his regional primary school with subsequently longer periods of separation from parents and family. Increasing attention is being given to providing opportunities to go home at week-ends from secondary schools in this category, and when distance makes this prohibitive, several long week-ends a term are usually organized. Some schools for blind and partially sighted children are described as 'all-age' and this means that the pupil can be in the same school from infancy to adolescence. Should this be the case it is important that situations are offered in which the pupil of secondary age has distinct reasons for feeling more adult and independent than in his primary years. He cannot make the transition from childhood to adolescence in one step, and needs the chance increasingly to make his own decisions, decide for himself what to eat, what to wear, what to do, what new pursuits to follow and what new responsibilities to undertake. One problem that can exist in an all-age school (and there are many for the blind) is that the early impressions that a child makes in his first year at school can cling to him and remain a talking point even after his growing personality has outstripped his initial reputation. It takes tolerance and understanding to give him the equivalent of a fresh start with the chance to take step away from dependence on the adults who have often given him affectionate support in his early school years.

The visually handicapped adolescent who is over-dependent on adult approval may have had insufficient opportunities for independence, even at the level of making decisions about small matters, although his need to do this is increasingly well-understood in schools. Conversely inappropriate reactions of belligerence can be evident if he has had to struggle with adults for the chance to express his personality in his own way and to develop growing levels of personal autonomy. Either of these manifestations on an alternation of both can be expected as he tries to come to terms with himself as a young adult, perhaps with physical maturity at variance with emotional maturity. Cutsforth 1951 claims that there is a need for aggression and defiance in the blind youngster if he is to achieve and attain self-respect as the person he truly is, rather than conforming to the ideas of the sighted about what a blind young person should be like.

Development of communication and self-expression

It can be an asset for the young blind or partially sighted person if during his years of growing-up he has become meaningfully articulate; his inability to receive clearly, or perhaps at all, signals through non-verbal communication which the fully sighted would appreciate through glances, gestures and facial expressions, can make him seem insensitive to the appropriateness of the expression of his ideas and feelings in a particular context. He may give an impression of embarrassing shyness or brashly aggressive egocentricity that makes him particularly in need of the ability to distinguish, discriminate and formulate experience through language. Some difficulties in communication at least will be minimized if powers of verbal communication have been strengthened, developed and sharpened during his school years. Pride of place is frequently given in schools and colleges of further education for the visually handicapped to providing opportunities for self-expression through discussion of current affairs, through debates and in public speaking. This potentially valuable area can unfortunately all too easily become a time-filler consisting of desultory chat or undirected monologues by those who have developed the habit of indulging in this pastime.

Indeed talking at too great a lengt without pause for response can be a particular hazard for the young person whose blindness or severe visual limitation renders him unaware of warning signs of irritation or boredom from his listeners. Realizing the need for interaction in conversation demands a maturity and awareness that may not be easy to achieve.

Problems of this kind are referred to by Langford (1968) in describing his experience as a blind student at university. Some of the subtleties of inter-personal communication posed difficulties. For instance, when a sighted companion does not make the effort to speak, the blind student can pass by him in ignorant solitude, since in initiating conversation the onus is almost invariably on the sighted. This is a particularly awakward situation for those possessing a little sight, especially if they pretend to see more than is actually the case since normally sighted people expect to be recognized and greeted. Accumulated experience in inter-personal situations involving both the visually handicapped and the fully sighted before reaching adolescence is highly desirable in order to lessen the chances of embarrassment and inappropriate responses to situations.

Personal relationships and sex education

The basis of guidance and counselling for adolescents who are visually handicapped should, in essence, be comparable to that offered to young people generally, without an over-protective concern which could stunt their own developing powers of decision and responsibility. But in order to make responsible decisions these young blind and partially sighted people may need particular help, and may need to have information presented to them in a specialized way. This is certainly the case with regard to sex education, and it is essential that visually handicapped pupils should have full and appropriately presented facts as well as opportunities for discussion and questioning before they reach adolescence. Lest the provision of this area of education should be considered to usurp the role of the parent, who would ideally give such guidance, it is relevant to note that Langdon's Survey (1970b) sounded out the views both of parents and former pupils of schools for the blind. The majority of parents were firmly in favour of sex education being provided in school, whilst former pupils reported that although many of them had received what they considered to be adequate sex education by the time they reached the stage of further education, information could well have been given earlier and few had been alerted to the genetic aspects of their visual disabilities.

There are considerable difficulties to be faced and overcome in providing sex education for pupils who see poorly and especially for those who are totally and congenitally blind. The support and interest of the staff in the school as a whole with regard to education in matters relating to sex and family life is essential, since such a course will entail far more than simply a necessary provision of factual information as a classroom subject to pupils who are about 12 or 13 years of age.

The young blind or partially sighted child, like any other child, will need to have his questions about sex and reproduction, as about any other matter, answered in the language and at a level that he can understand. His questions are likely to show more ignorance of situations than if he could see, but the readiness with which he asks them is likely to depend for him, as for the sighted child, on the confidence and good relationship that exists between the child and the teacher. Through infant and primary stages of school increasingly detailed information can be presented to the pupil in this area of education within the framework of his increasing understanding. A child with enough vision to do so can be helped by illustrated books, but the child who is born blind will be in particular need of time spent in individual as well as in group discussion and explanation. The normal secondary school curriculum is likely to include biological facts, and films, whilst diagrams and models will be used. The time-honoured practice of keeping and looking after pets and their litters is of educative value here, too. But the child growing up must be helped to understand sexual impulses in himself. The presentation of factual information is not enough. Personal and social expectations, family, cultural and religious allegiances need sensitive and full consideration. Negative and prohibitive attitudes relating to sexual matters were sometimes encountered in schools for the blind in past years. An examination of day-to-day records and regulations can sometimes show a preoccupation with keeping boys and girls apart. The underlying fear may have been that the blind would marry the blind and in the relative absence of genetic counselling, an over-riding consideration seems to have been the apprehension that visual disabilities would be perpetuated or increased. Speculation as to whether such restriction made the visually handicapped youngsters of thirty years or more ago prone to guilt and ignorance must remain academic questions, but such rigidity seems unlikely to have contributed to their personal happiness. Today, most of the schools for the blind and the partially sighted are like most ordinary schools, co-educational, and visually handicapped youngsters who attend non-specialized schools will in the majority of cases be in a co-educational environment. Attempts to explore and find out about the human body including sexual experience will occur, whether they are permitted or not. But the young person, used to making his discoveries by touch, must understand that the tactile exploration of another person can be emotionally arousing. The responsibility of involving another person in an intense relationship needs to be understood. the presentation of graphic material and models as a means of imparting information will probably clarify the facts and processes only. Davis (1962) lays stress on the need for the communication of information about sex and family life to be accurate, adequate and with a content and expression at a level commensurate with the pupil's social maturity and his language level.

13

Special Education

EDUCATION would be pointless if the skills learned at school failed to generalize in other situations, such as play. The generalizations of experiences which occur when children apply their skills in their free play are particularly important because they occur when children are acting without constraints and following their own inclinations, so that whatever they achieve is the result of their own efforts. Free play is as important for the development of a handicapped child as it is for the development of other children, and obstacles to free play are as significant for general development as obstacles which interfere with learning processes.

The essence of free play is that it is maintained by its own momentum—that it develops without interference or assistance. Handicapped children need to be helped in their free play when their activities are blocked by an obstacle caused by the handicap, just as they need special teaching to overcome obstacles when these bring learning to a halt. At school, under supervision, there are always adults available to guide, encourage and help the activities of handicapped children. The result is that they also tend to expect help to arrive even when they are left to manage alone, and wait for assistance when their actions are blocked by an obstacle rather than try to find a way round the problem unaided. Handicapped children who have adopted attitudes of this kind need to change them in order to develop in their free play.

Many of the exercises set out in the preceding chapters took the form of playing with infants and children, but even if the result is that children play with their parents, they do so in a special way in order to develop their skills and to gain new experiences. When parents are teaching their child, they direct his activities so that he practises particular skills, or they arrange the conditions in which he is playing so that he will gain the experiences he needs for his development. Under these conditions a child may have freedom to select his response to a particular demand, but he cannot be said to be able to play freely; the aims of the exercise and the way in which he can respond to it have been planned by his parent, and the child can only decide to use one of a few alternative responses. In a sense it is a paradox to discuss free play along with teaching plans, which must be directive by their very nature. If the effects of a handicap did not interfere with free play to such an extent that some children are condemned to the television screen whenever they are left unattended, there would be no need to plan their activities or to arrange special conditions which will enable them to play.

There may be no completely satisfactory solution to the paradox, but a reasonable compromise can be achieved by close co-operation between home and school. If the handicapped child can be taught at school how to manage the skills which he can use in his free play at home, without having to rely on help, and if the teacher can show the parents what kinds of conditions should be set up so that the child can be independent in his activities, then a measure of free play can take place. The difference between deciding what a child should do next and leaving him free to engage in an activity of his own choice is that when he is free to choose for himself, he gains experiences about success or failure which he cannot get in any other way.

To teach children how to play as part of their normal school programme is no new idea. All schools have games lessons and teach gymnastics and arts and crafts. Even if the lessons are formal and follow a systematic programme, they all train skills which the children can develop as they please out of school hours; indeed this is often why such subjects are taught. The reason for using school time to prepare handicapped children for their free play elsewhere is that they do not have the same opportunities for learning how to apply their skills as other children. In the normal course of development, young children 'help' their parents when they are active around the house or in the garden, and their parents show them what to do at the same time. Handicapped children have far fewer opportunities for engaging in a joint activities with their parents, though it would be possible for many of them to do so.

To make plans for training handicapped children for free play might seem to be a nonsense from the start, because if the children need to be trained to play, their paly is only free to develop within the confines of the plan. To some extent this is true. Nevertheless, without preparation the handicapped children who should be trained in this respect would not be able to play freely at all. As in the case of other teaching plans, the end effects cannot be expected from the beginnings. If the result of training is that the children gradually reach a stage when they can develop their own forms of free play, then the aims of the plans will be fulfilled in time.

There are significant differences between plans for preparing handicapped children for free play and teaching plans which are concerned with general development, and particularly with the development of their skills. A child may well be able to do something; it does not follow that he wants to do it. His ability to carry out and understand what is required in the classroom is decisive for learning, and not whether he enjoys or dislikes the lesson. Provided that he can understand what is being taught, he can profit from the experience. Later, when his general understanding has developed sufficiently, he may be pleased that he persevered and that he has reached a high level of all-round ability. What happens in free play is different. Free play exists when children are without constraints, when they can decide what they do and how they do it, without pressure to succeed. If they fail, so much the worse, but they can go on to do something else if that gives them more pleasure. Any child who chooses voluntarily to read a textbook during his break at school would be considered to be odd and worrying by his teachers. Play is important for children, and the break between lessons is the time when children should play.

The reason why children should play when they are free to do so was indicated at the beginning of this chapter: children experiment during free play and apply what they have learnt to their own experiences. What they learn from their free play is how to organize their behaviour, and how to bring their various skills to bear on each other.

Free play draws on skills which are full mastered and established. This is as true for handicapped children as for others; the reasons for this were discussed earlier, namely, that a child cannot be sure if he will be able to manage an activity if he is uncertain about the skill he will be using; and as the aim of free play is pleasure, uncertainties of this kind are avoided. Preparing handicapped children for free play therefore does not mean developing or training new skills. Ideally the children should become able to apply all the skills they have mastered in different ways and for purposes which were not practised when the skills were taught, and which might not have occurred to the child or to his teacher at that time. Preparation for free play is, in great measure, a preparation for the new application of a skill in situations which have not been explored before by using that skill.

The preparation for free play should enable children to combine two or more skills together for purposes which cannot be attained by the application of only one of them. This happens when a child, who can roll a toy car down a slope so that it runs into a garage and who can put together Lego pieces, builds his own garage first from the Lego pieces and then places it in position so that the cars can roll into it. There are numerous opportunities for joining skills together for complex operations which would elude a child but which can be suggested to him by his teacher. When playing in the classroom has covered a number of combinations of skills in this way, it becomes likely that some of the combinations will find their way into the free play of the child; if not, he needs further preparation.

Planning to combine skills together for complex actions is usually called 'lateral thinking' and does not generally develop spontaneously in mentally handicpaped children, who tend to resist attempts to change their responses. Physically handicapped children are much more ready to combine skills with each other, but they are often prevented from doing so because of their problems of motor control when they change from one action to another. The kinds of opportunities they have for combining skills together are dictated by the conditions in which they play, rather than by their ability to plan what they might do. Nevertheless, until they have experienced that various skills can be combined with each other, they remain ignorant about the possible effects which could be produced.

A physically handicapped child might be able to strike a cymbal or a xylophone at a set rhythm and he might be able to vary the pitch, without realizing that both can be varied together, until he has been shown how this is done. Socially handicapped children who have a good command of skills may be surprised by what they can achieve if a particular effect has not been experienced before: the fact that they can cause pleasure to another person without inconvenience to themselves could be surprising, just because no one has ever expressed pleasure about their activities. When they happen to create an effect of this kind, they may well try to repeat the experience.

A programme for training handicapped children for free play should be able to set out the skills which they can manage with success, and plan to give them experiences about the results of combining various skills with each other to achieve effects which are interesting and which will lead on to further developments.

Free play continues most successfully when children are flexible in their approach and when they can adapt their responses to the outcome of their actions. Handicapped children are less flexible in their behaviour than other children, because their capacity for adapting their actions to unexpected events is limited by the same obstacles which generally block their learning to make a new response. They can learn, however, that there are alternative directions in which their play might develop, by trying out a number of different variations one at a time; and they can be shown how to deal with commonly occurring mishaps which would otherwise bering their activities to a half. It is essential that the teacher should keep parents informed about how he is preparing their child for free play, and to let them know what the child enjoys doing at school and what he finds boring. He will have to rely on his own motives for his free play, and there is no point in setting up arrangements which appeal to the parents if they do not appeal to their child. Motives for playing are stimulated when the child is trying to bring about a particular effect, and even more so when an unexpected success is achieved by a combination of skills which had not been attempted previously.

Obstacles to the development of free play

Children use only fully established skills for their free play and gain new experiences when they apply them in a novel way. They combine and re-combine well-established skills, and they can achieve effects which would be impossible otherwise. Obstacles to the development of free play exist when the effects of a handicap are such that the child cannot combine his skills in any new ways, and only uses them according to the pattern which he has been taught. In theory there should be no such obstacles, because the skills used in free play are already well established, and therefore there should be no reason why they cannot be applied together. The conditions for the development of free play are different from those which apply to learning, because learning takes place when the child acquires a new skills, while free play is a matter of putting into operation skills which the child has mastered so that any obstacles to learning have already been overcome. The motives for learning, as set out in earlier chapter, are the result of having new experiences which the child can only achieve when he changes his existing mode of response, while the motives for playing are to find out what happens when a skill is used in a special way, and to produce effects which can be created by a skilled action. The efforts which had to be made in order to learn the skill are no longer required when an established skill is put into operation, and this is one of the pleasures of free play.

A handicapped child who has had no previous experience of free play cannot be expected to develop motives for doing so. It is therefore, important to give him opportunities for free play from an early age so that he will develop motives to engage in free play when the opportunity arises. The conditions are that he should be in a familiar setting and have toys which have become familiar through frequent use. Lack of familiarity of either the setting or the toys is as much of an obstacle to free play as it is for learning. Other obstacles are due to problems of choice and decision: when a child cannot choose what he wants to do because there are too many alternatives. Attention to the number of alternatives for playing is an important part of the preparation for a child's free play.

Different forms of free play

In order to prepare a handicapped child for free play, a scheme of reference can be set out so that the successive developments of play can be kept in mind. The following lists refer to the normal development of solitary and social play separately. Some of the activities are beyond the capacities of handicapped children, but suitable adaptations can often be devised for individual children so that they can gain at least some of the experiences created by a particular form of play. Careful training for social play can have far-reaching effects if a handicapped child can learn to anticipate how a game is likely to develop, and to adapt his responses to fit in with the plans of the other children. When a group of children see that a handicapped child who is playing with them does not rapidly feel lost, and that they do not need to interrupt what they are doing to help him to keep up with the game, they are much more likely to welcome him into their group and to give him the occasional extra impulse which he needs in order to carry on.

The plan for the first list, about solitary play, follows the general notion that development possess from gross motor skills to fine motor skills and to symbolic representation, but the development of play only follows such a pattern in very broad outlines. It might be true to say that the incorporation of new elements into free play runs along these lines, but as the development of free play takes place when existing skills are combined with each other to achieve increasingly complex results, skills from all stages of development are included in the process. Any attempts to keep skills separate would be counterproductive; the list is only for reference and convenience. Whenever possible, gross motor skills and fine motor skills should be joined to each other, and play should be given a symbolic content, in order to gain the most varied experiences from playing. Separate lists are made up for solitary play and for social play because the conditions for the two forms of free play are different. A child who is playing alone relies on effects which he produces for himself to stimulate his play; he is not distracted by other children and he does not have to adapt his actions to their interests. Social free play, with other children, must take account of both of these conditions, and these should be given due attention when preparing a child for social playing.

Solitary free play

In the early stages some parental presence is important, if only to support, encourage and admire what the child is doing.

Gross motor skills

1. Movements of the whole body. At home: riding in cars, propelling himself on a trolley, pushing around in a box, rocking on a horse or in a chair. Out of doors: swings, slides, roundabouts, climbing-frames, riding on a three-wheeler and then on a bicycle.
2. Differentiated skills: roller skating, skateboards, scooter.
3. Differentiated movements of the limbs. Legs: walking on stilts, jumping on a pogo stick, Arms: swing-a-ball, deck quoits, jockari. Trunk: hoola-hoop; dancing. Whole body: hopscotch, riding, various forms of gymnastics.

Play involving toys and object relationships

1. Manipulations: moving cars, trains, etc. around on the floor.
2. Constructions: building with bricks, Lego etc.; then, toy soldiers and castles, dolls and dolls' houses; then, simple model-making.
3. Adapted actions: posting-boxes, jigsaw puzzles, building-kits.
4. Sensori-motor skills: sand and water play; modelling and painting; using simple musical instruments,

xylophone, recorder, tin whistle; knitting, sewing; woodwork, model-building.

5. Fantasy: dressing-up, playhouses and fantasy situations in the house and in the garden.
6. Play with animals: cats, dogs, rabbits, etc.

Social play (as distinct from organized games)

The successive stages of social play are parallel play—when children paly in each other's company—co-operative play—when they each make individual contributions to a joint activity—and group play—when contributions are made by groups of children acting together, and when each group has its own special plan of actions. As in the case of solitary play, more highly organized interactions are developed in the course of time, but they do not replace simpler forms of play; games organized along simple lines continue to occupy children at a stage when they can also play in a more complex manner.

Parallel play

Any of the activities which go into the play of young children can take place when they are playing in each other's company. It is stimulating for a child to be able to observe how other children play; they copy each other and extend their own activities at the same time. Children interact whenever one child wants to have toys which are being used by another child, and their interactions stimulate their language development.

Co-operative play

Early forms of co-operative play begin when children are using the same toy(s) together, and then their co-operation consists in taking turns to use the same toy, rather than to make individual contributions to a common end, for instance when they take turns to use a slide or a swing.

Group play

1. Simple groups: races, hide-and-seek, catch, 'he'.
2. Complex groups: cops and robbers, Cowboys and Indians.

3. Fantasy games: with differentiated roles, such as mothers and fathers or doctors and nurses; or with differentiated functions, to build a camp or to prepare for a picnic.
4. Games with rules: in which children are able to anticipate what their colleagues will do because there are rules to be followed: taking turns, as in marbles, conkers, hopscotch, and in simple and complex ball games; and games with formal rules, for instance in draughts, card games and other table games.
5. Symbolic play: acting, charades, forfeits and other guessing games.

Plans for training handicapped children for free play

Plans for training handicapped children for free play need to be based on knowledge of their existing skills, because these must be sufficiently developed for the kinds of play envisaged; the special characteristic of training is to give experiences of what happens when skills are combined. Also skills from different stages of development should be combined with each other: elements of gross motor and fine motor skills, together with different kinds of symbolic expression. When the child is being trained for free play, he should have opportunities to choose what he wants to do, by selecting from a number of equally instructive alternatives, and he should be shown how to overcome obstacles which could bring him to a half when he is left to himself.

All the forms of play listed as gross motor play can be trained at the appropriate stage of development. Play with objects and object relationships requires more planning to ensure that a variety of applications is experienced in each case. Some activities can be introduced in the manner of nursery education, when children are given suggestions and shown, for instance, how to roll cars into a garage, how to construct buildings with Lego or how to use a construction kit. They can be given instructions which bring out the potential uses of their toys. The most careful planning, however, is needed for social play, and this requires much longer periods of preparation so that the children learn to anticipate activities and do not merely wait and copy what the others are doing.

At the stage of development when a child begins to take part in co-operative play, he should be put into situations in which he has to delay decisions about his own actions until he has observed what someone else has done. At a simple level this might take the form of constructing something together with other children, when each child takes it in turn to add a brick to a building or to place a piece for a mosaic on the floor. Even such simple rules can create problems which must be overcome so that social play can develop.

Sequential individual contributions are one aspect of group work which can be trained. Co-operative acts performed by two or more children together are performed at a more advanced stage of social play. Children might collaborate, for instance, when two children hold open a bag, while another child fills it with toys; or two children might be needed to carry a bench or to move a table. They have to adapt their movements to each other during such an attempt and to keep on doing so until the task is completed; for the previous example, regarding a construction, each of the contributions followed a rule, but decisions took place one at a time without calling for continuous adaptations.

A further stage in social play is the ability to anticipate a coming event. In playing fathers and mothers, a house might be needed: covering a table with a blanket, pinning the blanket and arranging the folds; furniture is needed and the roles are characterized by dressing up. The whole preparation might be too difficult for a handicapped child without preparation, but the separate steps can be taught one at a time: the roles can be practised, the clothes selected, and so a total scene is built up for later use in free play. There are many classroom situations which can be exploited for training children to anticipate a coming event, for instance when materials need to be set out for an exercise.

A more difficult problem is posed by skills like catching a ball or kicking it. Usually this goes wrong because the child goes on looking at the person who threw or kicked the ball, instead of transferring his attention to the ball. There are two ways for preparing a child for playing with a ball. One is to teach him to attend to the direction of a moving toy by rolling a car or a trolley along a pathway on the floor so that the child can anticipate where it will run, taking up his stance in anticipation and be ready to receive it when it arrives. The other is to slow down the rate of movement, for instance by using a balloon, and patting and catching it.

Handicapped children are sometimes surprisingly heedless of the mood of others around them. This is particularly true for socially handicapped children, but it also applies to other handicapped children. They may be capable of interpreting signs of pleasure, irritation or anger when their attention is drawn to the signs, and yet for all practical purposes behave as though such signs did not exist. Training a handicapped child to observe and respond to the changing moods of other people is best done by using mimed actions. It is another aspect of social interactions which can be trained, and the training is valuable for the development of social play.

All preparations for free play must be child centred. The child should be able to develop his own plans, consistent with his own experience and endowed with meaning corresponding to his current stage of development. All constraints and modifications, as well as all kinds of encouragement, must be adapted to the interests of the child. Plans which are imposed on a child make him obedient at best. They teach him to respond to adult approval or disapproval, but cannot ensure that he understands the reasons for the attitudes. When a child is free from observation, he is also free from control. Children who have not been encouraged to develop in their free play, or to follow their own behest in the presence of their parents, tend to be at a loss when left to their own devices because they lack standards of reference to guide their own activities.

A parallel can be drawn between the combinations of skills which take place during free play and the way in which children refer to previous learning and their past experiences when they develop the ability to think and reason. When the effects of previous experiences can be recalled by a child who comes across some problems which he wants to solve, he does not need to go through the laborious process of experimenting and trying out actual ways of dealing with it; he can work out the possible actions he might try, and guess what their effects would be, by referring to his recollections. A child who can make use of his past experiences can guess what plan of action would be right and how he should adapt the elements of the plan in order to solve his problem. While he is thinking and planning how to solve his problem, there is no risk of failure, which can only happen when he turns his thoughts into actions. In his free play, a child can bring any of his previously acquired skills into action, and he can apply them as the wishes. He does not have to achieve a particular goal, and there is no limit to the number of ways in which he can combine his skills, just as he is free to refer to any past experience which comes to mind when he works out how to solve a problem at a later stage of development.

Children need to be taught many skills in order to master their environment; they learn how to master their skills when they play, and especially during free play. Until a skill is fully established, the child has to rely on help from his parent or teacher to complement actions which he cannot manage fully on his own, and he remains dependent in this way throughout childhood. Skills can only be used confidently when they have been fully established; and while a skill is being learnt, the child will only bring it into action when he knows that there is help available to bridge those parts which are yet unsure. Children learn how to get help and when to ask for it while they are being taught.

What they learn in their free play is different: there is no one whom they can ask, and so they must choose and decide independently. Their ability to do so depends on their memory for actions which had been successful in the past, and on their capacity for bringing that memory to bear on their present course of actions. A good memory, however, can only help a child who has the ability to select the relevant aspects of his previous experiences which he should use. When children cannot judge the significance of an action, because the circumstances which call for that action are strange, they are unable to adapt past experiences to their present plans of actions. When that is the case, their activities cannot develop; they remain set pieces and the child resists any invitation to try out a new combination of skills.

Handicapped children are often in situations of this kind. Their past experiences might seem to be adequate for deciding what to do next, but uncertainty about any action which has not yet been completely mastered makes it impossible for them to choose that action and to combine it with their other skills. Only memories about past experiences which were independent and successful can be adapted for use in free play. Children can be taught to have experiences of this kind. They can learn to avoid accidents and how to deal with them when they do happen, for instance what to do if a tower of bricks is knocked down or how to go on with a jigsaw puzzle if the wrong piece has ben selected. What matters is that the child should correct his own mistakes as and when he makes them. When he can do so, he can play successfully, but he needs to be able to decide about his own observations.

For free play, the results of an action are less important than whether the child is interested in the effects which he is producing. Children prepare in their free play for independent thought and action. It represents that aspect of learning which releases the child from the control of his masters.

The argument presented in the foregoing chapters is that any handicap has secondary consequences which increase the effect of the handicap on the development of the child, and that in many cases these secondary effects could be avoided. Three handicaps are considered: mental, physical and social, as well as the conditions of learning for autistic, blind and deaf children. Each kind of handicap presents its own management problems, and often potential abilities are overlooked in the attempt to meet the immediate needs of handicapped children and to avoid frustrations. This attitude is questioned, and a plea is made to pitch the demands made upon the child to his best level of ability, rather than to make the most convenient arrangement for the moment.

A distinction is drawn between the learning process of handicapped and normally developing children. Handicapped children have characteristic gaps in their experience, which result in a corresponding fragmentation of learning. All children experience such gaps from time to time, but the gaps do not persist in the course of normal development because there are enough subsequent experiences to unite any existing fragments into a whole.

Index